Teacher induction

Developing Teacher Education

Series Editors: Hazel Hagger and Donald McIntyre

The focus of this series is on teacher education, with particular reference to the problems that research has revealed in established approaches to teacher education, to solutions which have been offered to these problems, and to elucidation of the underlying processes of teachers' learning on which effective solutions must depend. While different countries have inherited different systems of teacher education, and are therefore faced with different problems, all countries are faced with the same dilemmas of helping beginning and serving teachers to teach as well as possible within their existing schools while at the same time mobilizing their critical and creative thinking so that they can contribute to the development of better schools for the future. Authors in this series explore such opportunities and challenges and seek to understand and explain how the processes of professional learning and of facilitating that learning can best be understood.

Published and forthcoming titles:

Les Tickle: *Teacher Induction: The Way Ahead*
John Furlong, Len Barton, Sheila Miles, Caroline Whiting and Geoff Whitty:
    Teacher Education in Transition
Hazel Hagger and Donald McIntyre: *Learning about Teaching from Teachers*
Donald McIntyre: *Learning to Teach*

Teacher induction
The way ahead

Les Tickle

Open University Press
Buckingham · Philadelphia

Open University Press
Celtic Court
22 Ballmoor
Buckingham
MK18 1XW

e-mail: enquiries@openup.co.uk
world wide web: http://www.openup.co.uk

and
325 Chestnut Street
Philadelphia, PA 19106, USA

First Published 2000

A catalogue record of this book is available from the British Library

ISBN   0 335 20178 4 (pb)   0 335 20179 2 (hb)

Library of Congress Cataloging-in-Publication Data
Tickle, Les.
    Teacher induction : the way ahead / Les Tickle.
        p.   cm. – (Developing teacher education)
    Includes bibliographical references and index.
    ISBN 0-335-20179-2. – ISBN 0-335-20178-4 (pbk.)
    1. Teacher orientation.   2. First year teachers–Training of.
3. Teachers–In-service training.   I. Title.   II. Series.
LB1729.T53   2000
371.1–dc21   99-41466
                                                              CIP

Typeset by Graphicraft Limited, Hong Kong
Printed in Great Britain by Biddles Ltd, Guildford and King's Lynn

To my parents, who, at the beginning of the twentieth century were badly and sadly let down by schooling.

To some of my teachers, who in mid-century taught me how to overcome being let down by the education system.

To Anna and her teachers, who recently made the most of it.

To teachers who are entering the profession, who will need to lead their communities in imagining what education might be in the future.

Contents

Series editor's preface

Over the past decade teacher education has attracted considerable attention. In England and Wales, new conceptions of where, how, by whom, and for what teachers should be trained have brought about a dramatic transformation of initial teacher education. Government intervention in this first phase of professional preparation, enhancing both the role of school-based teacher educators, and its own control over the process, was recently extended to the next phase of professional development with the (re)introduction of a statutory induction period, and regulations providing for both the support and assessment of teachers in their first year. The 1998 Green Paper proposals for a new 'performance threshold', along with the introduction of the Advanced Skills Teacher grade and a fast track scheme for serving as well as trainee teachers, make it clear that the continuing professional development of established practitioners is also undergoing significant change, stimulated by new initiatives intended both to support and direct the process.

For all those concerned with teacher education, these changes represent valuable opportunities. The new commitment to professional development that they imply, the demand for high standards that they entail, and the engagement of schools on a much wider scale than ever before, prompt us to question traditional assumptions and practices. Recognizing the central function of schools as places of teaching and learning – for the adults working within them as well as their pupils – they offer the prospect of real improvement across all phases of teachers' professional education.

For this prospect to be realized, however, it is essential that the new practices and the assumptions which underpin them are subjected to serious critical scrutiny. The books in this series are all intended to help those involved in teacher education take just this kind of critical perspective. Based on research evidence they explore the ways in which teachers and those working with them can most effectively and realistically bring about high quality professional development, setting out and defending what they consider to be valuable, with careful regard for what is actually possible. Les Tickle is extremely well placed to do this in relation to induction. His own understanding of professional development is rooted in long experience as a teacher educator, concerned particularly with induction but also involved in innovative programmes to support the learning of teachers beyond the first year in practice. His insights are informed not only by his own research work, but by extensive and authoritative reviews of the literature. They are further illuminated by international collaboration and a rich dialogue with colleagues abroad.

It is obviously a particularly opportune moment to be asking what the way ahead for teacher induction should be. Schools, with a new confidence and expertise in teacher education, gained from their involvement as full partners in initial training, are now being required to pay serious attention to the continuing professional development of newly qualified teachers. In the context of these new statutory requirements, Tickle's warm support for policies that pay serious attention to the induction process is suffused with concern for a more humanist perspective – a perspective that risks being lost in a narrow focus on management issues.

Central to the induction process, Tickle argues, is a dynamic and creative individual. Whilst that individual has much to learn, he or she also has a great deal to offer. An exclusive focus on externally defined competencies yet to be acquired, is not only likely to be counter-productive in its neglect of the learner's role in the active creation of professional knowledge. It also risks wasting the resources each individual brings to the complex, demanding and evolving practice of teaching. Recognition of the professional commitment, creative potential and intellectual capabilities of new entrants will not only help to establish the foundation for their own continued professional learning, but also harness valuable resources in the ongoing transformation of education.

This book is not a simple instruction manual. Although it has many valuable practical suggestions for those involved in implementing the new induction arrangements, it is also a call for serious reflection on the nature of professional education. It is a book for anyone interested in debate about the kind of teaching profession we want and how we attract and retain true professionals within it. The questions it raises and the insights it offers are of profound importance to all those concerned that the welcome provided for new teachers will equip them not merely to function effectively within existing educational systems, but to question, challenge and renew them.

Dr Hazel R. Hagger

Preface

When I was asked by Hazel Hagger and Donald McIntyre to contribute this book to the Open University Press Series *Developing Teacher Education* I did not hesitate to accept. At the time (the mid-1990s) I saw it as an opportunity to extend my work in support of the localized induction of newly qualified teachers, at the same time as taking my research interest in their lives and learning into new areas. By new areas I had – and continue to have – in mind an extension to the study of the complex, detailed, day-to-day, interactive experiences of young professionals, coming to terms with their chosen careers, and learning in the process. That perspective, primarily, reflects my humanistic interests in education as a potentially empowering activity, as well as my criticisms of schooling as an oft-times debilitating system which has within it the capacity to perpetuate educational deprivation, for both pupils and teachers. The tension between these two notions has autobiographical origins, as well as observational ones.

As happens sometimes in the sweep of history, my intentions were ambushed by events of global as well as more parochial dimensions. While my concerns to understand the scope and pursuit of individual agency in the self-construction of the new teacher as a 'learning professional' remain, national policy for teacher induction in England has twisted and turned rather dramatically in the period since I agreed to this project. In line with the general buffeting of the profession and its members, from pre-service to pre-retirement, those events in policy were part of both the confusion of a previous Conservative government, and the 'Education. Education. Education' sloganism of its New Labour substitute from 1997.

During the late 1990s we have witnessed in education maybe more than ever before that, just as parish boundaries are permeable and parishioners reactive to wider events, so are national boundaries and governments when it comes to education policy. Among those wider events has been a surge of activity in many countries to improve teaching standards; to find the secrets of teacher effectiveness; to promote the quality of schooling. This is not, I hasten to say, a collaborative international venture among policy makers. Quite the opposite – it is driven by economic competition, aimed at getting or maintaining national prosperity and the economic upper hand which is supposed to derive from the education of our citizens.

Curiously (and for me fortunately) while academic and professional communities have been driven crazily in the direction of school standards by national policy bodies within our own countries, we seem to have been encouraged to engage willingly and openly in forms of 'educational espionage' with representatives from other nations. Researchers and educational practitioners are pressed, for funding reasons as well as intellectual ones, to adopt international perspectives in the pursuit of the betterment of educational understanding and education practice. This is not new, but with regard to teacher development and school quality it has taken a recent surge, teacher induction included. So, since accepting the invitation to create this book, I have found myself in the US, Australia, Israel, South Korea, Namibia, Ireland, Hong Kong, Slovenia . . . giving and gaining ideas on teacher induction and teaching quality with people from these and many other places.

The events and opportunities have combined to widen the perspective I have adopted here in ways which place the complex experiences of the lives and learning of newly qualified professionals in a much bigger picture. The details of some of those individual experiences were published in 1994 in my book *The Induction of New Teachers* (Cassell). There are other studies which enabled that book, and this, to represent those experiences in ways which I believe will have resonance and meaning for individual new teachers about to enter the profession. By presenting the broader picture in this new work I hope I will help them and their supporting colleagues, worldwide, to imagine the scope and scale of what they can bring to education and humanity, and the size of their newfound professional responsibilities. In some places, including the policy making corridors of England, there appears to be a serious lack of imagination, as teachers are regarded like some teachers regard their pupils – blamed, shamed, and treated with indignity. The challenge to change this point of view, to recreate the way ahead for professional induction, belongs to the educational communities of the world, led by new teachers themselves. Yet there is a distinctive problem with the collective point of view and the fact that the blame and shame mentality is perpetrated upon the induction process in an individualistic way. It is the individual new teacher who is assessed, held accountable, has a contract renewed (or not), feels inadequate and/or guilty, is driven by personal ambition, and so on. In the face of a culture of individualism I have knowingly tried to incorporate the personal responsibilities of the new teacher into a picture of the collective responsibilities which surround her or him.

Acknowledgements

While writing this book I was invited to be a visiting research fellow in the School of Teacher Education at the Bathurst campus of Charles Sturt University, Australia. The opportunity to work with and learn from its dedicated staff was made possible by Professor Bob Meyenn and Dr David McKinnon, who also encouraged contact with staff of the New South Wales Department of Education and Training. New perspectives which developed during this period have been extended through teacher educators in Hong Kong, North America, Britain, and mainland Europe, too many to name individually, but whose work ensures that it is possible to remain expansive rather than parochial in outlook on the question of teacher induction. I am equally indebted to my colleagues and the teachers with whom I regularly work at the University of East Anglia, Norwich, for helping me to maintain a grounding in school life, while encouraging my curiosity and educational hope.

1 Understanding teacher induction

The bridge of desire

There is a widely held view that a continuum, or bridge, is necessary in the professional development of teachers, linking initial training, entry into full-time teaching, and subsequent longer-term learning. The central span of that bridge is usually referred to as the period of induction – the first year of employment as a teacher. However, although I will to some extent follow this analogy, I will also argue that the bridge might not be a helpful metaphor. It presumes too much about the need for, or the possibility of achieving, a safe and smooth crossing from studentship, through novicehood, into experience, expertise and excellence as a teacher. I will urge that we should not think of induction simply as if novices are to be socialized into some well formulated and accepted practices which exist on the other side. That idea is partly applicable in areas of education with demonstrable success, but it is especially misleading given that there appear to be many unresolved problems within the education service. These include the difficulty of defining 'good teaching' or effectiveness (Hamacheck 1999), which is connected with the more fundamental difficulty of agreeing what schools are for, what curriculum should be followed, and what forms of education are most appropriate for a new age (Barber 1997; Elliott 1998). In short, it is not clear what this bridge is supposed to lead to, or that we should regard those on the other side of it as having secured clear conceptions of education's future and the most desirable professional practices. It is also likely that issues as yet unforeseen will emerge within the career span of new entrants to teaching, setting challenges for which the professional landscape of today's, and tomorrow's, practices will need to be exchanged for novel and imaginative educational visions. So I will make the case that this image of professional growth and development is not entirely appropriate, given the problematic and changing nature, and dynamic contexts, of professional practice which induction might help teachers to enter.

Instead, I will present the view that the factually accurate but conceptually limiting terms 'beginning teachers' or NQTs (newly qualified teachers) are symptomatic of a tendency to think solely in terms of the deficiencies of novices compared to so-called master practitioners. This tendency leads to missed opportunities to capitalize on the creative potential and professional commitments of graduate entrants to the education service. I want to suggest, therefore, that we should see new teachers as an enviable resource of intellectual capability, able to significantly help to transform education and to meet its unforeseen challenges. If that image is adopted, then we can see induction as a process in which the capital already vested in new entrants by the time they become teachers can be extended by way of systematic and sensitive provision for their further professional development, in accord with the need for transformative and dynamic dispositions towards educating which they will need to share with more seasoned colleagues.

Induction can be seen as an educational opportunity which previous generations in the service have failed to grasp. In that sense, it is itself one of education's many unresolved problems. There is certainly plenty of evidence that throughout the twentieth century, despite persistent (but spasmodic) attention, satisfactory opportunities for new teachers to utilize their expertise, and provision for their professional development in the first year of teaching, have remained very elusive (Hall 1982; Doyle 1985; Griffin 1985). This is surprising given that the experience of induction has been a recurrent and common theme in the profession (McNair Report 1944; Ryan 1970; James Report 1972; Bolam 1973; Evans 1978; Earley 1992; GTC 1992). It has also been the focus of numerous reports by government agencies in Britain confirming that it is a subject of interest in the central administration. Yet these very reports show it to be underdeveloped at all levels in the system (DES 1968; 1976; 1982; 1988a; 1990; 1992b; 1992c; Ofsted 1993; DfEE 1997; TTA 1998a).

In the face of research evidence and seeming failure in policy implementation, the debate has intensified about what is expected from teachers in general and hence from teacher induction and new teachers. The intensification has been on a global scale. New forms of school-based teacher preparation have been attempted, and the expectations relating to further professional development have increased, as reforms require older teachers to engage with new issues and adopt new practices – to cope with what Smyth and Shacklock (1998: 21) describe as the 'daily exposure to educational aerosol words'. Notions of continuing learning by teachers are now widely espoused. The global intensification of expectations has presented a new surprise. At the end of the second Christian millennium education authorities across the world, from Switzerland to Thailand, Australia to Canada, the United Kingdom to China, the United States of America to Japan, have discovered that they have not adequately identified and articulated what it is that they expect teachers to know and be able to do, or to be and to become. In an exaggerated way, and in a lighthearted context within a conference in Israel, I suggested recently that the constant renewals of education policy were intended to ensure that teachers should never know who they are supposed to be tomorrow! It is difficult enough to discover what they are supposed to do today. The sudden surge in the search for professional standards, joined by governments, academics, professional associations, and administrators, demonstrates a considerable gap in the conceptualizations of teaching and teaching knowledge. In a frenzy of activity, the Organization of Economic Cooperation and Development (OECD 1994) surveyed work on the definitions of quality teaching in 11 countries; administrators in Ontario scanned the Internet to discover what was happening in Norway and elsewhere (Marrin 1999); ministerial staff in New South Wales searched other parts of the Australian Federation (NSWDET 1998a); the USA established a National Board for Professional Teaching Standards (NBPTS 1989); and the Teacher Training Agency in England created its own national Career Entry Profile (TTA 1997). These events are mirrored across nations.

So the surprise is twofold. There is uncertainty about what should be done in the way of support programmes to maximize the further professional development of new teachers; and there is uncertainty about where and in what precisely to invest in their lives and work, or what returns the investors expect from those in whom they entrust education's future. In that context it should not be surprising if teachers, especially those who are new to the profession or aspire to join it, find themselves unclear or even confused about how they are to become best equipped to serve their pupils. It is within that context that this book provides arguments for a reconceptualization of induction, makes the case for further investment in opportunities for the professional development of new teachers across the world, and presents principles and practical proposals for induction provision. The ideas and proposals result partly from studies of policy and partly from practical projects which have attempted to reconcile the needs of new teachers as learners with their potential as qualified, professional, full-time educators. I have given detailed consideration to scholarship on the nature of teachers' professional knowledge and learning on the grounds that the messiness of professional expertise and its acquisition needs to be understood, rather than ignored in simplistic portrayals of teaching. That search for understanding is set within the broader landscape of social change which is affecting teachers and their work.

As a result of research and practice in supporting new teachers' learning, I am convinced that professional induction raises such complex issues that simple solutions should not be anticipated. Nor, for that matter, should we expect to easily understand the phenomenon in the first place. In fact recent years have shown up the complexities of both initial teacher education and continuing professional development, as these have been subject to political and economic buffeting, and the topic of academic research and scholarly debate (see other books in this series). Precisely because induction comes between the two it combines these complexities, and adds other factors associated with the rapid adjustments required for a life in schools. So, while providing principles and practical proposals in the book, I have also tried to maintain a view which acknowledges that induction is problematic, conceptually as well as practically. In that respect, the book represents aspects of induction 'as it is', maintaining a sense of realism by portraying the experiences of teachers, as well as representing that messiness of policy and research. Alongside the realism, which also sees the education services in western developed nations as seriously flawed and in need of change, the proposals are nevertheless tinged with an idealism which sees new teachers as major contributors to the educational experiences of pupils, and as a potential force for change – in their own induction and in the services they provide to pupils and their communities. It proposes ways to move forward, towards a professional conceptualization of induction, as part of educational practices based on learning institutions and communities of enquiry.

That induction is an unsolved problem can easily be detected from recent policies relating to teachers' professional development. There are many acknowledgements that initial training for teaching (where it exists) is not on its own an adequate form of preparation for the education service. In England that was reasserted succinctly in 1997 in a way which also recognized that initial training plus induction were not enough:

> every teacher should have structured support during the first year of full-time teaching. This should build on their initial training, where strengths and development needs will have been identified, and set the pace and direction of future professional development.
>
> (DfEE 1997: para. 14)

The ministerial case made here adds to a long list of implied promises which have been recorded at least since 1925 (see Tickle 1994: 1–2). Indeed, the assertion 'We shall therefore introduce an induction year for newly qualified teachers to consolidate their skills' (DfEE 1997: para. 14) belies the fact that an induction period has existed for several generations of teachers, in England and many other countries with developed systems of formal schooling. Restatements of unfulfilled promises provide some of the evidence that solutions have not yet been found to the long-identified need to provide effective continuation of learning in the first year of full time teaching and beyond. Such desires acknowledge that learning by experience, in isolation, after appointment to a teaching post, is both undesirable and unacceptable.

During 75 years of recorded evidence the desire to extend learning through induction support programmes has not subsided. But consistent failure on a systematic scale to find better arrangements than simply casting people into practice in the hope that practice will make them perfect has left provision mainly to chance, or to the insight of enthusiastic individuals in some schools and some local education authorities. Small bridges of desire have been built and rebuilt in the landscape of education by the imagination and skill of those individuals. So the primary question which still needs putting to people at all points of responsibility in relation to the employment and education of new teachers is: what are the best ideas about teachers' learning that can be brought to the first period of in-service experience? The second questions is: how can teacher education at this career stage be designed, constructed and utilized to best advantage?

Those are not new questions. They were asked in significant ways during the emergence of teacher education in the nineteenth century and by many others later (Rich 1933; McNair Report 1944; James Report 1972; Bolam 1973; Dent 1977; Tickle 1994). However, they remain unanswered in any satisfactory way and are central to the broader questions that this book considers. It does so based on a search for a better appreciation of the nature of the problem than was available when I began to consider similar questions in the late 1980s. At that point research on what and how teachers learn from their classroom experience at this particular career phase was an emergent rather than established field of study. It remains so today. That means that these are research questions – questions that can be shared by all those concerned with induction – which in turn means adopting a research disposition towards the matter, rather than expecting immediate recipes for solving its problems. The way ahead is, in that sense, a communal and ex-ploratory one, but it is one in which the development of understanding and a range of immediate actions can be achieved.

What clearly remains in the surge of accountability measures is the ten-sion between teachers needing to learn more and become better at what they do, while being expected to perform to the highest standards possible. This inherent contradiction can be confronted very simply. As Agne (1999) puts it, we are all perfectly imperfect. If there is a reasonable tendency to think that new teachers are less perfect than others, McLean (1999: 56) provides a worthwhile message when she acknowledges the different know-ledge bases which are held by beginning teachers and teacher educators:

> conceptualizing those differences as deficits in the beginning teacher is now considered useless at best, and at worst, as perpetuating the powerlessness of beginning teachers in the process of their own profes-sional development . . . [all] parties [in education] are engaged in work characterized by conflicts between personal commitments and public demands; trying to enact change within the problematic entrenchment of institutional culture, [all] are experiencing personal uncertainties and professional dilemmas.

For both new and experienced teachers, where there is room for learning and improvement in practical performance, there is obviously a deficit in one sense, but deficits are open spaces for learning, a precondition of educa-tion and a foundation for optimism to flourish, and for the celebration of becoming better educated. That depends on the perceived level of deficiency of course, and the capacity to carry out responsibilities towards others in an ethical profession. Where newly qualified teachers are concerned, I have presumed that recommendations for provisional certification are an assurance that proficiency has been achieved to a level deemed appropriate for taking up those responsibilities, as a substantial foundation for further learning. Yet that presumption is set within the trap of accepting that the prevailing definitions of proficiency are sound.

I do not accept that, and will show that definitions of good teaching are socially contended, and socially constructed. I will therefore be arguing that it is not only a few individual new teachers who might be deemed to be deficient, and hence fail their induction period or leave the profession voluntarily. It is also, I will contend, that the currently dominant conceptions of teacher and of curriculum are unsatisfactory. So the focus of attention will range around the lives and qualities of new teachers and the events of communal and global change within which they seek to establish themselves as professionals. This is a complex set of relationships that has been portrayed in different forms linking individual identities, personal agency, and social structures. Smyth and Shacklock (1998: 5) portray the 'accommodation' as a contrast between compliance with and dependence upon managers, and active contributions to educational processes:

> Whereas, in the first case, teachers are inducted into and inculcated with an externally defined agenda, in the latter, they actively question the circumstances making them the way they are, and in the process construct an alternative agenda that is more informed by the internal workings of teaching, learning, curriculum and pedagogy.

There are numerous case-study reports of survivalism as a feature of the experiences of inductees, advice on how to survive, and descriptions of attempts to establish programmes of support. These perspectives underrepresent the positive aspects of induction: having a job, the exhilaration in working with children and young adults, carrying major ethical and educational responsibilities for large numbers of people, regenerating enthusiasm in the profession, learning new skills at a rapid pace, and so on. Reports of the experiences of young teachers certainly serve to confirm that the year of entry into full-time teaching is a challenge that faces the newly qualified, their colleagues, school managers, teacher educators, inspectorates, professional associations, and ministries. It remains a collective professional issue, or as I would prefer it, an opportunity for the taking. The reasons why induction remains a persistent problem, and why the provision of a satisfactory professional development curriculum for it remains elusive, are several.

Difficult crossing

First, induction is in the most simple sense a process of becoming a teacher in a system of mass schooling, which is increasingly buffeted by structural economic, technological, political, and social changes, resulting commonly in contradictory pressures and increased role expectations. Exposure to scrutiny of performance in traditional practices in which some people are deemed to have failed, or in new measures which have yet to be tried and tested, leaves new teachers vulnerable in their work.

Second, from these tensions arises a central paradox faced by new professionals – of being inducted into old practices, traditions, and circumstances, in which behaviours are prescribed and performances assessed, while expecting and being expected to participate as reformers in search of solutions to endemic educational problems.

Third, such problems are both deep and widespread, and attention to them has a tendency to cloud the successes and celebrations which professional educators might themselves claim. They include curriculum disaffection among students; truancy; overloaded and fragmented use of curriculum time; social disadvantages of significant sections of the community; irrelevant and redundant curriculum goals and content; the educational and social divisiveness of assessment and qualifications; financial disinvestment in education; shortage of vision among policy makers; injustices related to race, gender, and social class; difficulties in defining effective teaching and improving teaching quality; the need to maintain educational idealism and morale in the face of the allocation of blame on teachers; keeping pace with communications technology; overcoming bad management; coping with poor forms of teacher education; handling the spoil-heaps of educational research; the failure sometimes to recognize that education involves discord, argumentation, and curiosity; and so on.

Fourth, from the perspective of new teachers, induction is a local and personal problem of school-based acculturation and assessment of performance, combined with the infusion of new blood capable of bringing about change. That is, it means being assimilated into the existing conditions and milieux of schools, which might clash with their identities, ideals and ambitions as members of the new graduate force in education. At their best, energized with desires for educational advancement and social imagination, while faced with the intellectual poverty of schooling, this is inevitably a period of negotiation and adjustment.

Fifth, from a quite different angle, of induction as planned provision for supporting further investment in the learning of new teachers, there is the logistical difficulty of tracking tens of thousands of newly qualified graduates as they move from different pre-service programmes into diverse locations of employment. In England alone in the 1990s, many thousands of new entrants in a year moved from a hundred or more initial teacher education institutions to jobs in many different types of schools, scattered among diverse local education authorities. It is estimated that two million new teachers will enter the profession in the USA between 1998 and 2008. China (excluding Hong Kong and Taiwan) has over 700,000 schools, 200 million students, and over 10 million teachers (Lo 1999). As Lo (1999: 8) aptly puts it:

given its gigantic size and the huge number of stakeholders involved, the school system in the Chinese Mainland can only be understood in terms of diversity and disparity. Getting students into school and making sure they stay there is a Herculean task. Similarly, recruiting people with appropriate qualifications to teach and helping them to develop a career in teaching present a tremendous challenge.

In order to achieve some kind of continuity of curriculum experience or some common provision of support, this situation would require many links. If the goal of those responsible for induction is to provide coordinated and systematic support to ensure progression in learning for newly qualified teachers, logistics provide a major problem.

Sixth, these logistics are compounded by frequent fluctuations in the supply of and demand for the intellectual capital of our graduate population and qualified teachers. Recruitment and retention rates, in times of both over- and undersupply, affect levels of interest in and attitudes towards what needs to be done for new teachers' learning. This is also affected when teachers are regarded as a social commodity in the labour market, and when the main concern of employers is the assessment of minimum levels of competence.

Seventh, for employers, school managers, and teacher colleagues who do take a serious interest, the local problem is one of knowing the detail of an individual new teacher's knowledge, experience, capabilities, and fit for a particular job. Thereafter the task for the individual new teacher and his or her professional tutor is to know what major contributions can already be made to a department or school, and what knowledge, experience and capabilities need to be developed.

Eighth, those who provide support are not just professional tutors and managers in schools. The task also falls to people in local education authorities, higher education, and policy making and funding bodies. At the systems level, the existence of disparate players creates its own problems – a sort of systemic anarchy in which these discrete agencies each works on its own interpretations of its role, based on their own conceptions of the needs of new teachers, and within their own funding possibilities and restrictions.

Ninth, it is also complex because the contexts of individual teachers' work, the range of responsibilities they hold, and their own educational backgrounds and personal dispositions, are very varied. Recent attempts to achieve common standards among teachers could be interpreted as calls for standardization, which is both inherently anti-educational and practically impossible to achieve. Perhaps we should celebrate that, inevitably, there will remain a need to take account of individuality, diversity and difference among new teachers.

Finally, the identification of teaching standards that is happening across the globe is evidence of the most endemic problem of induction. There has been a failure to comprehensively identify the nature of professional knowledge, of what new teachers should know and be able to do, or what kinds of persons they should be or be willing to become. A failure to manage the changes in responsibilities that teachers have, in such a way that new entrants can reasonably make sense of what they must learn and do, has added to that problem. Both identifying and managing teaching standards are essential in working out what it is that teachers are to be inducted in to, and how it is to be achieved. The Teacher Training Agency's work illustrates the problem of both the difficulty in agreeing on standards, and the implied regression to minimum standardization in aspects of knowledge and classroom instruction:

> The standards set out in this document replace the more general 'competences' set out in DfE Circulars 9/92 and 14/93 and DfEE Teacher Training Circular Letter 1/96 (DfE 1992b; 1993; DfEE 1996). The standards apply to all trainees seeking Qualified Teacher Status (QTS) and who are to be assessed for QTS from May 1998. Successful completion by a trainee of a course or programme of ITT (Initial Teacher Training), including employment-based provision, must require them to achieve *all* the QTS standards, and courses must involve the assessment of all trainees against *all the standards specified for the award of Qualified Teacher Status* ... The standards have been written to be specific, explicit and assessable, and are designed to provide a clear basis for the reliable and consistent award of Qualified Teacher Status, regardless of the training route or type of training leading to QTS.
>
> (TTA 1997: 1)

As I have already indicated, this is by no means the only example of the attempts to make explicit what the nature of professional knowledge is, and what new teachers might reasonably be expected to do. A survey by the New South Wales Department of Education and Training of similar work in many countries, much of which focuses on the beginning teacher as the key point for establishing what constitutes satisfactory standards in teaching, shows clearly that this is an international quandary (NSWDET 1998a).

These conceptual difficulties and logistical problems suggest that any programme of learning may well be, in part at least, in the hands of the individual teacher to define in the absence of support. Indeed, even the Career Entry Profile (TTA 1997; 1999a) which claims to identify essential competencies, presumes procedures for its use in which it is the inductee who will carry a record of their experience and capabilities forward, in the hope of continuity and systematic extension of learning. It certainly seems likely that she or he will be the one with the fullest sense of what has been achieved, the greatest capacity for determining learning needs, and possibly the best placed to decide how to meet them. However, identifying individual new teachers as the locus of professional development decisions is an insufficient answer, especially if the criteria are constrained by a narrow definition of professional skills. Successful individual profiling would presume that each teacher has:

- knowledge of professional practice in its fullest sense;
- the capability to assess needs and anticipate future responsibilities;
- awareness of opportunities for supporting professional learning and improving practice;
- the skills, time and resources to negotiate access to those opportunities.

It is almost certainly more realistic to recognize that appreciation of existing expertise and capability, as well as professional development needs and opportunities, will be greater if it is a shared venture, a matter for discussion and negotiation between new teachers and supportive colleagues, managers, and in-service educators. It is also important to assume that this will be a chancy and dynamic process, in which expertise might not be acknowledged, goals may shift, outcomes may be unpredictable or inconsistent, and chances for learning might not occur at the most fortuitous times. These are not the characteristics for which systematic induction of a programmed kind, towards standardization, easily allows. What's more, the environments of induction both reflect and imply an inevitability about the intensity, uncertainty, and individuality of the first year of experience in particular, as a reflection of the volatile nature of events in professional practice in general.

To maintain a sense of the inevitable uncertainties of those environments does not mean abandoning inductees to the turmoil of the storm. That is how it appears in the survivalist reports of new teachers' lives (and more recently in all teachers' lives), but it does not need to be like that. Rather, for new teachers themselves and their supportive colleagues, anticipating the conditions can be done in a way that can help to manage both the circumstances and the experiences of teaching and learning to teach. By circumstances I mean all dimensions of it: the personal and domestic; classroom, school and locality; the profession; and the broader context of education within its own space of social, economic and political conditions.

Since the experience of circumstances is individualized, one might very helpfully ask:

- what are the possible circumstances in which a new teacher can find him or herself?
- what are the possible states of mind and learning that she or he might experience?

Awareness of those questions provides a powerful stimulus to look for evidence; to understand what the actual circumstances are; to define what are ideal circumstances and states of mind; and to manage events and professional actions in such a way as to meet those ideals as far as it is possible. They are questions that can be asked by all contributors to induction experience, including new teachers themselves. In short, they imply and even demand that a research stance should be adopted, collectively, by all those involved.

Abandoning continuity

So is it reasonable to think of the shift from pre-service training to the induction period and beyond as a continuum, when it is likely that the demands of a new teaching job and the knowledge and capabilities it requires will at best bear only partial relationship to the experiences gained for qualified teacher status? We should not, I believe, simply assume that continuity is achievable in some smooth, transitional sense, regulated by the so-called standards of a career-entry profile. Rather we might be prepared for discontinuities; for new and radically different experiences; for turbulence both between and within the pre-service, induction, and in-service periods of professional education. We might even acknowledge and learn from the fact that in some aspects of social life in some communities, initiation processes – rites of passage – are intended to disrupt, disturb, and radically change the outlooks, commitments, and even identities of initiates.

If that's too radical, perhaps we should at least recognize the view that 'crossing the ocean of existence . . . from the near shore which is fraught with dangers to the further shore which is safe' (Gethin 1998: 64) is both a desire and an illusion in a world where everything we experience is unstable and changing; and where experiences are gained through minds which are themselves 'fundamentally unclear, unsettled and confused' (Gethin 1998: 73). Rupert Gethin's words stem from a Buddhist tradition of many millennia, considering human experience in general, but they are mirrored by the International Study Association on Teachers and Teaching (ISATT), in its comment on recent influences in education, pointing out that:

> Pace of change, globalisation, market forces ideology, to mention but a few, have contributed to a 'manufactured uncertainty'. In this climate of unprecedented volatility, educators are challenged . . . to participate more actively in shaping educational theory and practice.
>
> (ISATT 1998: 1)

Similar perspectives on the dynamic of social life in general and education in particular (and on the grasping for order in the face it) have been represented recently as a feature of education in postmodern society. The search for stability in the face of turmoil, for security in knowing rather than satisfaction in speculating, for orthodoxy instead of creativity, is also a characteristic that Sanger and Tickle (1987) observed in the learning experiences of student teachers. What we saw as a matrix of certainty and uncertainty in student teachers' experiences can also be seen as a major conundrum of induction. This is the challenge of achieving educational conditions and states of mind which at one and the same time can handle and even create change, avoiding tendencies to become rigid and routinized in conventional and unquestioned practices, yet without being destabilized or destabilizing in a debilitating way.

It is difficult to imagine how that might be achieved, given the wider context of education. In much of the educational literature the picture is one of what Smyth and Shacklock (1998: 11) describe as 'dramatic, profound and far reaching changes . . . impacting on teachers and their work.' Describing the processes of economic globalization, international competitiveness, and national disintegrations, they detect moves within education towards annexing the curriculum to industry; the subjugation of teachers; the 'commodification' of learning; the routinization of teaching; more and more sophisticated surveillance; greater prescriptiveness; increased managerialism; and much more. These are manifest in multiple innovations and waves of reform, with a plethora of what they call 'official policy discourses' – effectiveness, partnerships, collegiality, international best practice, accountability, appraisal, competence, parental charters, league tables, strategies, standards, benchmarking, and much else (Smyth and Shacklock 1998: 35). Teachers are increasingly the subject of blame for perceived failings in society. Yet at the core of the job, it remains complex to the point of being undoable (Tickle 1987a). Citing Connell (1989) they dissect a simple piece of classroom instruction to reveal

> a complex inter-dependency of tasks: . . . preparing the lesson . . . getting the class settled and willing to listen . . . supervising exercises and correcting them; keeping order; dealing with conflicts between children; having a joke with them from time to time and building up some personal contact; discussing work with them individually; planning lesson sequences; preparing handouts and physical materials; collecting, using and storing books and audio-visual aids; organising and marking tests and exams; keeping records; liaising with other teachers, and so on.
>
> (Smyth and Sharrock 1998: 25)

Continuing with Connell's dissection, they move outside the classroom into the realms of playground supervision, arranging excursions and events, staff meetings, extraclassroom activities, counselling, liaising with other agencies, updating curricula and resources, attending courses, writing reports, and the rest. There is nothing new in this list of duties, of course. I use it simply as a reminder that the job of teaching has its own internal dynamic, which can become a maelstrom of events and interpersonal encounters within any one day. The turbulence is both within the mind, the immediate circumstance, and the wider context of the new teacher's experience.

Even without this turbulent perspective the notion that learning should be extended from the pre-service period in a sequential or continuous direction may be misconceived or overidealized. Rarely is there a direct logistical link between training and employment – from school practice placement to a job in the same school. Even in that circumstance, judging precisely what learning is necessary for an individual new teacher, or which aspects should have priority, are likely to differ among people they encounter. Or maybe the needs just cannot always be predicted. Commonly, new teachers learn from their contemporaries that what is needed for one particular job differs in some ways from other jobs in other schools or localities. They also report, as do their support tutors, the common wisdom that what is needed by one person differs from the needs of another. And they report being taken by surprise – ambushed even – by situations in which they feel inadequately prepared for judicious action.

So an agreed, standardized curriculum to be followed by all new teachers seems to be a kind of holy grail of policy makers. It might be achievable to some extent if it is based on certain kinds of generic qualities and capabilities which are core to all educational practice. The core might well include subject knowledge, pedagogical skills, curriculum understanding, and professional values (NSWDET 1998a). It might also include the capacity of professionals to manage changes in their circumstances and curriculum responsibilities, or to initiate change in their practices. I wonder, will it also include the ability to lead the planning and conduct of their own and their colleagues' professional development, and to bring about change in educational environments? That involves a more expansive conception of professional knowledge and capability than the definition of either minimum or optimum competencies in subject knowledge, classroom management, and instructional practices to be acquired, consolidated, performed, and assessed (TTA 1998c; 1999a). A more embracing conceptualization of induction is a celebration that the process of educating teachers involves the acquisition and use of diverse but complementary kinds of knowledge, and ways of coming to know. The explicit and the tacit, the demonstrable skill and the ineffably spiritual quality, the intellectual and the emotional, the conventional and the imaginative, are just a few images of that complementarity, of which I will say more later. This is probably the most difficult aspect of induction to be tackled because sometimes the impression is given that the knowledge and skills needed for an effective education service are well defined and measurable behaviours.

The scale of the challenge to our imaginations is represented by Elliott (1998: 2–3) in his conception of the social/educational context and ways of responding to it. In summary, his logic is:

- Advanced societies are open to continuous but unpredictable change.
- Social change has ambiguous consequences, opening opportunities for human fulfillment but increasing risk and hazards for those seeking them.
- Education must enable all pupils to become active contributors in shaping the economic and social conditions of their existence.
- Educational change requires a focus on curriculum and pedagogy, with teachers as leaders in innovations.
- Educational change depends on the reflexive and discursive consciousness of teachers.
- Different conceptions of education and curriculum presuppose different conceptions of society and the principles governing access to its 'goods'.

In contrast, a technology of teaching is how the Teacher Training Agency, through its promotion of an ideology propounded by Professor David Reynolds, among others, portrays effective teacher behaviours. The search for an applied science of teaching is based on the premise that 'our ignorance in the area of teacher effectiveness is virtually total' (Reynolds 1998: 26). While Reynolds claims that a 'codified, scientifically established body of knowledge' needs to be developed, he also argues that it is necessary to ensure that all new teachers are inducted into 'the technology of their profession', through a training cycle that is sequential:

> The training cycle should therefore go:
> - teaching of instructional theory;
> - teaching methods (that are only understandable if one can link them together theoretically);
> - practice of the methods;
> - re-teaching and coaching in the methods as appropriate.
> (Reynolds 1998: 28)

The contradiction involved here is neat and clear. The argument is that teachers need to be given something that does not exist. If there is no adequate science, no theory, there is no training base and no promise of effective practice being transmitted. The difficulty which that presents is compounded by the argument that the technology needs developing by research that will 'give us the teacher behaviours that are appropriate for children of different ages, subjects, catchment areas and districts [etc. . . . with] . . . a common core of effective practices throughout' (Reynolds 1998: 28). Presumably the 'etc.' includes gender, ethnicity, home circumstances, classroom environment and community, financial conditions and resources, the reigning policies on school visits, parental participation, and examination syllabuses – to add just a few of the material factors of schooling.

Perhaps it includes only a selective few of those material factors because the bid for a science of instruction is a curious attempt to overthrow those 'who celebrate a values debate and discuss the "ends" of education', in favour of a systematic search for the means of achieving some presumed but unstated aim (Reynolds 1998: 26). Writing as if scientists do not debate or depend upon values, the TTA is cited by Reynolds as having done 'sterling service' in insisting that teachers themselves should be able

> to use the empirical rational model [of scientific research] to create knowledge about effective practices that is better than that which they should have been given as their intellectual and practical foundation.
> (Reynolds 1998: 28)

Perhaps fortunately, a long history of educational ideas, research, and collected professional expertise shows that there are differences of view, within the social practice that we call education, about the nature and purposes of knowledge, the conceptions of teaching, and its practical performance. Fortunately, that is, partly because similar quests for understanding do exist in other branches of social life and community practices – in both the sciences and the arts. Indeed the attempt by Reynolds to divide the two is an unnecessary diversion, as Miller (1997: 40) pointed out when he asked, rhetorically,

'What did Albert Einstein, George Braque and Pablo Picasso have in common?' His answer is that each searched for 'new means to express the inner beauties of nature . . . While Einstein expressed himself in mathematics, Braque and Picasso applied paint to canvas' (Miller 1997: 40). Fortunately, also, because even within the social sciences to which Reynolds appeals there continues to be a productive and enlivening debate about its purposes, philosophical underpinnings, and related methodological issues which offer complementary approaches to the empirical rational model (Phillips 1987; Scott and Usher 1996; Brown and Dowling 1997). Perhaps more importantly it is fortunate because this combined history of education and research leaves open the route to enquiry, and allows space for curiosity and imagination. It invites rigorous self-scrutiny by educators and researchers (who are often one and the same) as well as scepticism towards prescriptions for the schooling of societies' young people in selectively ascribed knowledge, using ideologically prescribed pedagogical methods, based on notions of effectiveness derived from a narrow view of proof.

Of course there is a sense that the science is inadequate, as much of science is. It is inaccurate, however, to suggest that a literature on pedagogical processes does not exist. It is extensive, complex and contains its own frictions which are too broad to review here. However, if the call (in which I join) for teachers to become researchers of their practice is upheld, then it is necessary to ask how that might be possible, and how they can engage with that foundation of professional knowledge. It presumably means that all teachers, teacher educators, educational researchers and policy makers, including new entrants to the profession, need to engage collaboratively in the development of appropriate research aims and methods, which can lead to the further establishment of the body of professional knowledge. This places a quite different but complementary dimension of teacher expertise at the core of practice, to accompany what must then be seen as provisional views of what constitutes effective education. Such a claim on the professional dispositions, time, energies, and developing expertise of new entrants broadens the conception of teaching quality and into what that induction is to be very considerably. It is a breadth of view that is promoted elsewhere by the Teacher Training Agency in its subscription to a research based profession (TTA 1997; Cordingley 1998).

There is another sense in which conceptions of teaching quality and induction can be broadened to challenge the idea that new entrants are necessarily inferior in their contribution to the service compared with longer-serving teachers (Ingvarson 1998). It is a view in which the so-called novice is, in times of change, at least in some respects transformed into a relative expert alongside established members of a profession. There is a well founded recognition that many new entrants to teaching have higher standing over their predecessors with regard to some aspects of subject knowledge, pedagogical imagination, and professional capabilities. Their capacity to handle uncertainty and to bring about change – given appropriately supportive circumstances – can be equal to or better than more senior colleagues. In these senses they are potential or actual leaders and innovators as well as inductees, and are often acknowledged to be so by colleagues and pupils alike. These perspectives on induction require the extended core of qualities and capabilities to accommodate but also reach well beyond the minimum realms of teacher tasks and behaviours like those defined in career entry profiles.

Recovering the challenge

The more optimistic and expansive view of induction is a reminder to guard against the persistence of policies that adopt a predominantly minimalist perspective on the quality of performance by new teachers. That is exemplified in the approach to the treatment and assessment of probationary teachers adopted throughout the second half of the twentieth century, and rein-forced with the reintroduction in England of a probationary year (DfEE 1998a). In it, the gatekeeping role to prevent incompetence, which in itself is an essential part of the profession's responsibilities for quality assurance, displaces a constructive approach to maximizing the professional expertise of new teachers. The minimalist point of view has a tendency to reduce images of teacher induction to descriptions of subject content, curriculum specifica-tions, methods of teaching, and modes of pupil assessment. It is that which dominates the TTA career entry profile and induction standards (DfEE 1999; TTA 1999a).

The outlook associated with this and similar conceptions of teaching make educational discourse limited only to decisions about time allocations, new examination syllabuses, new curriculum requirements, proposals for the adoption of particular teaching methods, or ways of tabulating test results. Discussions are, understandably, mainly carried on at this kind of practical level in the pragmatic tradition of schooling. While that is not a surprise, it is a matter for mourning. The dominant themes of subject, methods, and assessment swamp some very important educational considerations such as:

- views on what we think education is for;
- what we regard as being educated;
- how we view and act upon social justice issues;
- our regard for the distribution of educational resources;
- perspectives on the construction of knowledge;
- evidence of educational policy;
- who should have the power to decide what we learn, and how;
- what we think about the processes of schooling;
- how we regard the nature of childhood;
- theories of learning;
- whether we see education as political or apolitical;
- the part that research evidence should play in our educational imagina-tions; and so on.

The minimal approach to education and to induction into it masks different conceptions of education and of teaching, which display differences of view about what kinds of teachers we want and the criteria against which quality of practice should be judged. We see bureaucratic powers used to override such healthy discussion, to impose upon teacher educators and teachers a presumptive view of the purposes, practices and consequences of teacher education and of teaching.

Despite the stealth of attempts to impose a narrow view of teaching, there are various beliefs about what knowledge (or skills, competence, qualities, capabilities, etc.) should be acquired by teachers, and how, and to what effect it should be put. Throughout a long history, arguments about appropriate teacher knowledge and induction methods have been rehearsed in many parts of the world. In England it is now constrained, although not entirely, by the Office for Standards in Education (Ofsted), the Teacher Training Agency, and the agenda of school standards, league tables, and educational effectiveness. Despite these restrictions, however, the Universities Council for the Education of Teachers (UCET), the educational research community, and the General Teachers Council, for example, continue to search for acceptable professional formulations of initial teacher education, induction, and continuing professional development, as do other bodies in the far corners of the educational world, with sufficient sparks of alternative thinking to keep fanning the embers (Mahoney 1998; NSWDET 1998a). As the OECD (1994) put it:

> The new challenges and demands on schools and teachers emerge from new and heightened expectations of schools, advances in research on teaching and learning and the need to manage classrooms that are increasingly diverse in terms of ethnic, linguistic and cultural backgrounds. These challenges and demands require new capacities and knowledge on the part of teachers. The current situation is both dynamic and varied.
>
> (Centre for Educational Research and Innovation,
> OECD 1994: 9; in NSWDET 1998a: 4)

The demands for regressive and conservative approaches to teacher training, which derive from governments and their agencies, present one face to those with a will to improve the quality of debate about induction (Tickle 1994). Another face is presented by the kind of challenge from the OECD. Together these represent the Janus-like dilemma between reaction and foresight that faces education in general. The strained character of teacher education was summed up by the New South Wales ministry in the following way:

> The differences between approaches on either side of the Atlantic serve to illustrate, inter alia, the extent to which discourse has been overlaid by a melange of theoretical, political and economic agendas. At its simplest level, this has led to a sharp divide between those who favour

a model of teachers as technically competent practitioners (technicians who implement government policy) and those who seek reflective, professional teachers, capable of thoughtfully evaluating their own work, adaptable, committed to equity and social justice and a process of lifelong learning (Schön 1983; Ofsted 1993; McCulloch 1994; Gore 1995). These models of course are closely related to perceptions of the fundamental purposes of schooling. The technician teacher is in a good position to protect and reproduce the social status quo; the reflective teacher is likely to be a better agent of social transformation.

(NSWDET 1998b: 32)

At the forefront of induction practice, then, the lack of sophistication and differences in views about professional knowledge are likely to result in variations of experience for newly qualified teachers, and quite possibly in vague, confused or unplanned experiences. Induction may well be encountered as discontinuities of experience; or conflicts of view about education; or indifference to role expectations; or puzzling about how to proceed in supporting new teachers to enable them to learn. Evidence shows that learning during induction is affected by different values and characterized in part by chance placement in employment, the happenstance of working circumstances, the views of senior teachers about their own roles as tutors, assessors, or managers, and their conceptions of newly qualified teachers' potential to innovate and lead as well as learn and follow (DES 1982, 1988a; Beynon 1987; Tickle 1994).

The central paradox of teacher induction is that so much attention has been paid, over generations, to making the experience positive, or at least less traumatic than it is often reported to be. Yet the 'problem' of induction remains – both for individuals entering the profession, and for managers of the education service. Perhaps, then, it is time to reconceptualize at least some aspects of induction as a period of opportunity for maintaining a sense of the problematic nature of education for those who will become its professors.

Living with the problematic

If we see induction as being and remaining inherently complex, and seek to understand it adequately, then we might be able to assert some educational principles for entry to the profession that will help newly qualified teachers. Their pupils might also then get maximum educational benefit from the induction process. A disposition of educational enquiry is therefore adopted in this book as a means of empowering those who profess education to do so not simply as teachers but as educators who can engage in debate, the development of practice, and the transformation of educating.

The distinction I draw between teaching and educating is deliberate and purposeful, and readers should be very conscious of it, because I have assumed in much of what follows that as teachers we are also capable of functioning in ways that are diseducational. That is not to say that we do so wittingly. It is, though, to argue that by becoming members of the teaching force we are drawn into a schooling system which in many respects is dysfunctional, despite our commitments and best efforts to the contrary. This perspective is a crucial part of the arguments I wish to address. It affects the interpretation which we give to the issue of what it is that induction is into, in terms of the role and function of teachers and schools.

A further problem of induction is that education's managers, in their desire to prescribe and assess performance, carry a quite different mantle from educators whose interest is to debate, counsel, facilitate initiative, and encourage self-appraisal. Part of that process of diseducation is the tendency to seek certainties, to know, which can outweigh our capacity to live with ambiguity, mystery, and inquiry. Induction is a period of disturbance and imbalance, in tension with a tendency to seek calm and equilibrium.

I don't intend to ignore the importance of material resources that are dedicated (or not) to induction, and conditions of education within which new teachers are obliged to learn and practise. They, too, remain persistently problematic, in ways that often adversely affect the learning experiences and practices of the newly qualified, and the possibilities available to their support tutors and their pupils. Finance is a major variable in the possible circumstances in which teachers find themselves. So let it be clear that the gap between the aspiration to provide systematic induction, and its realization in the lives of teachers, results also from the failure to fund induction programmes adequately, and the failure to change by funding both the learning environments in which new teachers are employed, and the opportunities to maximize the use of their educational talents and energies (DES 1982, 1988a; Ofsted 1993). This includes the need to fund those who support, educate, and facilitate the work of new teachers, in order that they themselves can develop the best possible conceptualizations and practices in their professional tutor roles (Tickle 1994; TTA 1998a).

To conclude for the moment this review of the problematic nature of induction, there are some other notable characteristics that are tied up in professional culture and the circumstances of schooling, particularly in the social conditions and physical environments of teaching which, for instance, result in the way:

- classroom practice is a largely isolated and individualized activity;
- teachers sometimes seek to be, or by force of circumstance become, autonomous and private in their work, and carry their responsibilities individually;
- the monumental demands of the job outstrip the resources for doing all aspects of it as well as teachers would like to;
- the shortage of time prevents discussion with others about education and its effectiveness, about the curriculum, or about policy;
- new entrants are expected suddenly, and despite sentiments to the contrary, to do the same job as experienced colleagues.

The background to and consequences of these conditions of education and associated professional culture add to the realization that to think of induction as being systematic on a scale wider than the provision made by individual schools may simply be misleading. Any thoughts in that direction are tempered by one experience (among many) of a three-teacher rural primary school that had not had a new appointment of any teaching staff for 15 years, let alone a newly qualified teacher. Suddenly it had both, in the same person. Teacher induction there, particularly for the rapidly designated teacher-tutor, meant something very different from a city high school with 120 teaching staff, regular appointments of several newly qualified teachers at a time, and a well tried, developed, and funded induction programme that had been devised and modified by senior staff over many years.

Both of these schools were working within an arrangement funded by a local education authority's in-service budget. Then, without warning, the provision of funded support for new teachers was severely amended, then rapidly abandoned, because of financial cuts and changes in grants for in-service teacher education.

Schools and local education authorities, in any case, differ markedly in their attitudes to induction and their provision for it. A simple review asking if designated posts of responsibility for overseeing induction exist in schools and local administrative bodies will reveal those differences. A review of the (non)existence of formal induction programmes draws similar results. Policy at county, state, or national levels has remained indecisive and turbulent for as long as there has been induction (Tickle 1994). Recent years show little sign of policies or provision stabilizing.

Amidst this view of induction, the most worrying aspect from a professional perspective is the deprofessionalization of the education services being brought about especially by the casualization of work; the disengagement of teachers from curriculum decision making; and the redefinition of teaching as a process dominated by testing pupil performance. The recognition of induction as the start of career-long learning does not take account of the employment conditions of teaching, or the employment paths of individuals who may have already had other careers, in which initiative was celebrated. Nor does the rhetoric recognize that some might be expected to move to yet other jobs in despair that schooling is dysfunctional, or simply in search of security and salary.

A research-based profession

Anarchic, volatile, fragmented or fractured, or maybe ignored by some, even in the face of attempts by others to gain central control, then, are better descriptions than systematic if one looks at teacher induction at its various points of provision, even over a short timescale. That situation can, I suppose, be regarded as allowing the conditions to foster creative solutions to the problem at a local level – more creative at least than imposition by stealth of a narrow view of teacher training. Yet such a narrow view may well prevail upon us by the power of assessment and profiling of teachers, definitions of teaching standards, and the assertions of classroom effectiveness research.

The ineffectiveness of policy, failure in local provision, and variable support for new teachers in schools is reflected in a disparate body of literature on induction. Fragments of this literature are laid down in the sediments of the past like educational fossils. They record the precarious nature of some of the many attempts to get induction right, evidence that the starting points of induction projects differ; that they are often small scale; geographically scattered; and their timescales short. These features are reason enough to ensure that the educational community is unlikely to learn from and apply their lessons to improve practice. This is a case of what Schön (1971) described as our inability to learn from investment in social programmes, because of our incapacity to deal adequately with the number of ideas vying for attention and funding. Schön was referring to competing, broad social agendas, of which induction into the teaching profession is a very minor one within the field of teacher education, which itself has not commanded much attention relatively to other aspects of education.

The case for the adoption of a view of teacher education that puts research-based practice at its heart has become a recurrent theme which contrasts with simpler views of competence. It comes from arguments for the continuing education of teachers to be based in action research (Carr and Kemmis 1986; Elliott 1991; McKernan 1991). The aim of research based practice is the development of active dispositions towards classroom and school research and its use in understanding the quality of teachers' own actions, and in maximizing educational progress for pupils. The idea of the teacher as researcher can be used as a basis for the development of new teachers, as well as those with more experience. Taking that approach, I believe, provides an imaginative solution to the educational problem of teacher induction.

Those principles can provide a particular and distinctive element in the generic professional qualities and capabilities needed for educational practice. They extend the purported core of instructional competencies to encompass all aspects of an educator's work. That is, they are inclusive of subject knowledge; awareness of the curriculum; pedagogical expertise; the capacity to manage and generate change; the ability to engage constructively in self-development as a teacher; and involvement in the research and development of schools and the education service more widely. They accommodate practical skills, as well as perceptual, imaginative, conceptual, emotional and spiritual powers. Those principles provide for professional learning needs in aspects of practice in which teachers are novices, and potentially lead to their development as experts, at whichever career stage they are. The importance of this perspective can hardly be overemphasized – in the building of a professional knowledge base; in complex practices; in situations that are changing rapidly; and where education is constructively contended in terms of both its ends and its means – the novice/expert relationship has to be unconventional and the usual image of induction reimagined.

The intention in this book is to illustrate research based practices in ways that newly qualified teachers themselves can use to guide their own experience and development. It is also my intention to convey the ideas and their practical implications to those who support new teachers, in one way or another, during their initiation into the profession. They will mainly be professional tutors in schools, or interested colleagues, or maybe headteachers, and teacher educators. I hope that school governors, local education authority personnel, and members of the policy bodies will also pay heed to the needs of new and changing circumstances and of new teachers within them. The ideas that are offered for supporting their development, and enabling their talents to contribute to the service of educating, need to be promoted within the profession simultaneously with their promotion among new entrants.

The case for induction provision that includes teacher research is based on evidence of new teachers' experiences of learning, and on underlying theories of teacher professionalism and teacher education curricula. The evidence shows that the problem of providing an effective, continuing, learning-based induction for newly qualified professionals is a universal one. However, albeit a universal problem, it is clear that the approaches taken to the question of what we learn or should learn as educators, and of what we should be able to do, differ among people even within various parts of the education service (Edwards 1998; Pring 1998; Reynolds 1998; Woodhead 1998). In recent years views about different kinds of teacher knowledge and competence, and associated conceptions of professional development, have been rather polarized and argued over (Doyle 1985; Shulman 1986a, 1986b; Sockett 1987; Elliott 1991, 1992). At the opposite extreme to the teacher-researcher notion for example, there is the view that teachers just need substantial academic knowledge in a specialist subject to be able to teach effectively, and that teachers' performance in transmitting subject knowledge should merely be assessed, rather than developed. That view is still explicitly rehearsed occasionally, and is implicit in teacher employment in some schools.

These extremes suggest that it is important to take an overview of research on teacher learning, so that it is clear where research based practice stands within the knowledge we have about teacher development. I am convinced that an approach to induction based on principles of research-based teaching can provide the benefits of complementarity for these seemingly different views on teacher education. It offers a distinctive answer to the questions raised about teachers' learning during induction, by potentially developing educational professionalism, and not just producing the instrumental outcomes of training associated with subject knowledge and classroom performance.

The overlap between an academic knowledge/skills-view of teaching and a research-based view is an important focus of the book. A purely academic, subject-expertise view of teaching, and the skills-based conception of competence have long traditions in popular and professional culture, and in policy. A broader notion of the teacher as a professional, which includes the development of personal qualities and dispositions, the place of the self in teaching, and a much broader sense of competence than just the technical classroom skills of instruction, can at best be described as an emerging tradition that is constantly threatened by the more dominant perspective on academic, skills-based instruction.

The arguments for a research-based profession, and for the use of critical educational enquiry as a basis for professional development, are relatively recent, though they are based on principles previously rehearsed by educators from Aristotle to Dewey. They are far from having widespread acceptance, though the associated but rather innocuously attuned notion of reflective practice is on the lips of many professional educators and policy makers worldwide (Schön 1983; Clandinin and Connelly 1990; Tabachnick and Zeichner 1991; NSWDET 1998a). Curriculum action research and research based teaching are increasingly being adopted and developed as more rigorous and self-critical approaches to professional development in international settings (Hollingsworth 1997).

Practical knowledge and professional support

Research that shows how induction is experienced by new teachers illustrates how they see the nature and complexity of the challenges they face. For example, discontinuity between pre-service education and induction is a problem because of the severe disruptions that come with the shift from studenthood to being a full-time teacher. This is characterized by:

- the shift in status;
- tension between expected professional performance and learning on the job;
- change of location;
- the fullness and complexity of new responsibilities;
- new school situation and organizational features;
- handling different curriculum content;
- getting to know resources;
- strangeness of new colleagues;
- meeting many (even hundreds of) young people who have suddenly become significant in one's life;
- isolation from other novices as soulmates;
- facing aspects of teaching which were never dealt with in training.

In these circumstances the notion of a research-based professional induction is an ideal – and its principles are unlikely to be hot on the lips of newly qualified teachers and their support tutors. Nor am I suggesting that it is the whole answer to professional learning for new teachers. In the mêlée of induction the very idea of principles and research might be like whispers from over the mountain top. Also, learning might come by a variety of means, in a range of circumstances, with regard to diverse elements of professional knowledge. So the search for complementarity meets another challenge: to ensure that these particular ideas on induction through research-based teaching can make practical sense. In the face of the real-life experiences of inductees and their school-based support tutors, within a range of contenders for their receptive attention, the case has to be convincing.

I have listed just some of the disruptions which have to be dealt with in those real-life experiences, where my notion of a problem is intended to represent challenge, motivation, matters to be solved, new learning to be acquired, new responsibilities to be adopted, new educational arguments to be rehearsed, new initiatives to be taken. In that sense this book treats induction in a constructive light, even though the individual experiences of it might not always be positive. At the same time it does not shrink from destructive experiences and negative aspects of induction. They provide a recurring reminder of the need to get it right, and a motivation for identifying what right means and how to achieve it. However, I hope the book displays and celebrates a way ahead where the constructive growth of the new professional is the foremost consideration and characteristic. Its aim is to contribute to the dissemination of that way, to bring about understanding and creative thinking which can achieve that development.

In so far as the question of induction hinges on the nature of what teachers have to know and be able to do, and the qualities and professional dispositions that they might have or acquire, then a picture of those matters is an essential starting point. An analysis of educational knowledge, based on the experiences of induction, on international research and scholarship, and on the content of policies for teacher education provides a major part of the book. The analysis is used to illustrate both the component parts and the holistic nature of educational knowledge and its contended nature. Initially I have concentrated on the more obvious dimensions of practice and practical knowledge – those simple categories of subject knowledge, knowledge of the curriculum and educational context, and the practical skills of pedagogy. That choice might be seen as confirming a particular definition of teachers' knowledge. I hope not. It should be self-evident that to function as an educator one needs to understand principles of education; to know about children and their modes of learning; and to appreciate the origin and consequences of a competitive system of compulsory, common schooling (among other things). Rather, I have sought to convey knowledge in those core domains as prerequisite to, but certainly not the whole of, what is required for an educative view of teachers' work, or of their own professional learning. It is also my intention to show how even those core aspects of professional knowledge should be considered from a problematizing disposition. At its simplest, for example, with regard to subject knowledge we need ways of dealing with:

- the expanse of knowledge content, which makes selection for curriculum inevitable, probably controversial, often outdated, and likely to result in irrelevance or disinterest for pupils;
- diverse ways of conceptualizing knowledge, from empirically demonstrated immutable facts, through theoretical propositions, provisional claims, interesting hypotheses, to ineffable mysteries;
- advances in knowledge, which need to be kept abreast of, over a career length of possibly 40 years.

With regard to knowledge of the school curriculum itself, an educative stance maintains that there are different ways of studying and understanding it, which affect the ways we think of designing, implementing and practising it. Again, curriculum knowledge is not simply a case of accepting and operating in accordance with someone else's view of what constitutes a curriculum. Rather, it is a continuous process of engagement with:

- educational ideas, and the possibilities and consequences of different forms of curriculum provision;
- debates about the way educational institutions are organized;
- the potentials and impacts of educational technologies;
- evidence and argument about the assessment of learning, its practices, and its consequences.

The same applies to pedagogical expertise, in which there are some techniques that can be mastered and performed, but also a range of possibilities that need to be tested and contested. For example, we know it is essential to speak clearly and coherently when explaining something or presenting an argument. It is obvious that time spent on the management and distribution of resources should be used efficiently and effectively in favour of maximizing active learning time. There is a clear case for providing feedback to students as soon and as comprehensively as possible after they produce evidence related to their learning, either within or after an activity, and so on. These are the elements of practice dealt with comprehensively by many analysts of the act of instruction (Wragg 1984). But also, for example, the possibilities that exist within a range of methods for teaching reading, mathematics, or particular curriculum content demand awareness, understanding, and judgement in their adoption and use. Our understanding of children's learning styles and of specific learning difficulties is still developing. The identification of appropriate moments for introducing new concepts to, or extending those already held by, individual students is a matter that depends on information, evidence, and judgement.

So educational practice resides in these realms of professional judgement and the use of evidence too. Furthermore, educational knowledge includes personal qualities, professional characteristics, and self-knowledge. That raises the profile of aspects of the self, and the importance of including the characteristics of being a professional and the place of emotions in teaching. Evidence shows how they can easily, and detrimentally, be disregarded (Hamachek

1999; Lipka and Brinthaupt 1999). I will argue that a curriculum for their development is necessary, and suggest ways in which it is achievable as part of teacher induction.

Identifying the nature of professional knowledge is one step towards developing induction, but working out how different kinds of knowledge are acquired and developed is just as difficult. So I will consider some ideas about how knowledge for educational practice is gained, and how best it might be provided for during induction. Different ways of imagining what teachers should know and how they might come to know it have resulted in the fashioning of different kinds of teacher education programmes. Some of these variants were described by Munro (1989), Tickle (1994) and Wilkin (1996). Each type makes assumptions about what kinds of education society should have, and therefore implies the kind of teachers to be produced. I have presumed that proposals for induction need to take account of those different orientations to teacher education curricula, or need to be understood in the context of their possibilities and consequences.

Assessment of professional performance is an aspect of induction that remains at the forefront of the minds of new teachers, their colleagues, managers, and policy makers. Its importance is emphasized with the reintroduction of a probationary period (called the induction year) in England (TTA 1999). Licensing and provisional registration have equivalents elsewhere (NSWDET 1998a). The renewed emphasis on teacher appraisal, the use of temporary contracts of employment, and the increasingly prominent use of standards and graded performance measures, also reinforce its priority position. Moves towards profiling the capabilities of new entrants to teaching is a particular formulation of the use of assessment criteria, and mechanisms for judging teaching quality are laid down in some induction arrangements, including those newly reintroduced in England.

Profiling and appraisal are not entirely built on promises to educate, however. They are intrinsically coupled with the professional and political need to assess the quality of teaching, and to prevent the entry of, or quickly remove, incompetent teachers. That combination of pressures to educate for competence and to eradicate incompetence is summed up by the notion of probation. This was explicit in the TTA's (1998a) consultation as a search for balance between mentoring and monitoring, support and surveillance. It has also been a characteristic tension in teacher appraisal since its introduction in the 1980s in Britain and elsewhere (Elliott 1991; Tickle 1994).

I have sought to include this theme throughout the book too, by way of an educative alternative which holds the prospect of regenerating educational competence and commitment. It can be presumed that particular uses of assessment criteria determine the kinds of learning experiences of new teachers. I will argue that collaborative, research-based induction can provide a climate of self-regulation and self-improvement, for both individual teachers and schools. It also potentially accommodates the external imposition of assessment and inspection, through the creation of a professional force that is more advanced than any inspectorate. The consequent model of an induction curriculum based on this broader perspective of quality is described. The proposals for research based practice, developed in collaboration with new teachers and their professional tutors, are placed in a context of first appointments, and the conditions under which those appointments are taken up. They present ways in which the research based practice of induction can be effected in institutional, local and national support arrangements. Perhaps a General Teachers Council in England will be capable of adopting this kind of educative and self-regulatory perspective on induction (Calderhead 1992).

The main players in creating provision for the implementation of an induction curriculum include government or state agencies, employers, school managers, professional support tutors, colleagues, new teachers themselves, and their pupils. Each carry responsibilities that contribute to the educational experiences of individual new teachers, and through them to the long-term development of the education profession. I think it is apparent that ideally induction provision by these various players needs to work in harmony towards creating opportunities (and expectations) for new teachers, but that harmony and coherence are likely to remain elusive. This does place the inductee in the eye of the storm, so to speak, with the challenge of steering a creative course through it, by adopting the principles of research-based teaching at the heart of, but amidst other modes in, their learning.

The image I have of induction is not so much a bridge, therefore, but rather more an outward access route, from the strength of initial competence to an open horizon of professional and educational adventure. It is an adventure that looks beyond the performance of individual teachers judged by pupil outcomes alone. As Simons (1987: 199) put it:

> many of the indices being sought focus solely on pupil outcomes. These are only one measure of the worth of a school. Much more needs to be evaluated including curriculum policies, learning opportunities, the interrelationships between levels (pupil, classroom, school) and forms of provision and achievements.

Approaches to the continuing professional education of teachers during the period immediately postinduction are an important consideration in working out how induction itself can best be understood, planned, and provided for. Only with a clear sense of what it is that educators are being inducted into in the longer term, and where they might journey next, can we have a sense of their professional development. Like initial training, the assumptions about in-service development are diverse, and sometimes at odds with each other. These are discussed, extending the theoretical and practical issues already introduced, in order to identify the values that lie in the immediate postinduction stages of in-service education.

The possibilities for providing structured teacher education programmes for teachers immediately beyond the first year, related directly to the development of practical educational expertise, is presented to show how that can be achieved. Drawing from developments and research in this early career phase, and locating the studies in the new contexts of so-called expert teachers, advanced skills teacher, and curriculum leadership proposals, a new outlook on teacher education for a period of teaching, which has tended to be overlooked, is presented. Indeed I will suggest that induction itself is necessarily rather more than a one-year process in which continuous self-improvement can be maintained. Of course there are reflections of that bridge here, presumptions that continuing professional development should build firm structures on the foundations of initial teacher education and induction towards the responsibilities of curriculum leadership in a managed way. I will need to remember my own appeals for a problematizing approach to the complex and agreeably argumentative world of the newly qualified educator. Perhaps Elliott (1998: 65) will help:

> The intelligent response to the complexities and paradoxes of living in advanced modern societies is one of imaginative experimentation based on a tolerance of ambiguity and risk. Increasing complexity and paradox in a society enlarges the social space in which its members can participate in the construction of their own and their society's future.

2   Professional knowledge and expertise

Defining teaching knowledge

What is the nature of knowledge that teachers have, or need to acquire during induction? It may seem obvious that the way knowledge is defined, and what each teacher might continue to learn after entry into the profession, are central to describing the kinds of opportunities and support that should be provided for induction. Yet in research literature and in policy documents on induction, professional knowledge and teaching quality have not had centre stage. They appear to be in an infant state, and somewhat contentious (NSWDET 1998a; Reynolds 1998; TTA 1999). As Hamachek put it: 'The question remains, how do we actually go about identifying those behaviours associated with good, or effective, or expert, or master teachers?' (1999: 191). This chapter considers aspects of professional knowledge centred around academic subject matter, learners, classroom management, pedagogical skills, the working context of the school, curriculum, assessment, and the routines and functions of being a teacher. The focus on the need to know specific content and where it fits in the curriculum, to be capable in classroom management, and to be skilled in methods of instruction, including associated assessment procedures, represent powerful constructs at the heart of that range of knowledge which teachers are expected to possess and deploy. These have become the centre of policies internationally, and the main platform of argument about teachers' work.

These constructs should not, though, be adopted at face value, nor taken for granted as the only way of thinking about professional knowledge. The curriculum model represented by these core elements is a simple competency-based one – and is not the only one available to us. Even within it, each of those components is compound, because decisions about the selection and adoption of particular content, modes of instruction and assessment, have different kinds of consequences for student learning. Furthermore, even that fairly lengthy list of elements of professional knowledge does not convey the idea that practical expertise is holistic in nature, rather than divisible into components.

Treating practical knowledge as problematic and considering different ways of thinking about it can counter a tendency to accept, and repeat, simple versions of what teachers know and need to know. Taking a sceptical disposition towards any particular knowledge construct and adopting a more expansive and open-minded view of professional practice can help us to appreciate its complexities. It can also create the space in which to revive the identity of teachers as professional educators – an identity that is increasingly being hidden by demands for their compliant, instrumental role in implementing prescribed curricula using particular methods of instruction. Different views as to the range of knowledge required by professional educators tend to be of three main kinds:

- educational researchers' classifications based on studies of practice;
- policy formats listing domains of expected competence to be acquired or proven;
- teacher educators' descriptions of curricula to be mastered by intending or practising teachers.

Indeed, the classification of types of research on teachers and their professional development offered by Hoyle and John (1997) includes three different perspectives that even underpin attempts to study teachers' knowledge. These reflect fundamentally different philosophical views of how knowledge is generated and acquired, or constructed. It is presumed or implied by Hoyle and John that different beliefs held by researchers reflect different kinds of knowledge that they expect to find. By implication the knowledge that teachers are expected to acquire and deploy will depend upon convictions and allegiances to one or other of these different positions. Such positions might be held by policy makers, teacher educators, educational managers, teacher colleagues, or new teachers themselves. This is a recipe for divergence and dispute, and in some contrast to attempts to simplify and standardize. Hoyle and John's analysis of the perspectives on professional knowledge is summarized by the following discussion.

The positivist tradition seeks the advantages of 'value-free, law-like generalizations [in which] the task of teaching and learning will be made more efficient' (Hoyle and John 1997: 54). A search for 'undisputed knowledge on a par with medicine' is engaged, as a basis for achieving professional standing and improving the status of teachers.

Interpretive research is based in the paradigms of existentialism and interactionism, seeking to 'understand, describe and explain the inner realms of human consciousness, and motivation, [and] intentionality' (Hoyle and John 1997: 55). These imply a humanistic approach, like that cited by Hargreaves

(1988) in which knowledge is not prescribed for purposes of efficiency, but rather constructed for purposes of creative problem solving.

A critical theory perspective seeks to understand and change teaching in terms of the way knowledge is 'socially, economically and politically constructed, and therefore tied to fundamental structural interests' (Hoyle and John 1997: 55). This approach is implicitly critical of the social conservatism of schooling, and asserts that it is necessary to bring about change among teachers by altering their appreciation of the consequences of their practices, and constructing alternatives. In some cases its proponents argue that change among teachers needs to be accompanied by changes in the social structures of schooling and society.

Hoyle and John point out that these different perspectives cohabit in an eclectic search to understand professional knowledge. Their delineation of frameworks into which various studies of teachers and teaching fit (see below) provide what they describe as a selected review of studies of teaching knowledge. In itself their review shows how difficult it is to pin down quite what new teachers are expected to grapple with as they learn their art. The argument about eclecticism appears to be a reflection of Popper's (1959; 1962) notion that human beings in general inhabit different knowledge worlds simultaneously:

- an external world in which states of affairs and objects have been defined by other people, a world of tradition and established disciplines;
- a social world in which norms, values, attitudes and beliefs of individuals are formed through interaction with others, or with groups, or belief systems;
- an internal world in which our ideas, emotions, imaginations, and thoughts play a significant part, an existential world of the individual.

(Popper 1959; 1962, adapted from Holub 1991: 13)

The traditional, the debatable, and the imaginable (as these might be called) make interesting and potentially lively cohabitees. The different emphases which we or others place on each of these kinds of knowledge as they apply to teaching might well explain the range of attempts to define what teachers should know and be able to do, and how they should develop their expertise. Hoyle and John's types of professional knowledge and the research on which they are based include the following:

- *cognitive* – studies of teachers' thinking, and of the cognitive processes used by teachers that underlie what they do, and concentrate on what they know and how they acquire knowledge, develop it, and use it;
- *practical* – studies of practical action and its underlying implicit theories, or tacit knowledge, and the ways in which rules of practice (or practical principles) and teachers' feelings, values, needs and beliefs underlie the organization of practice;
- *biographical* – life-history studies of the ways teachers' knowledge and lived experience relates to personal, social and economic circumstances in which they work, including studies that have moved into the autobiographical;

- *contextual* – the ways in which teachers organize knowledge by taking account of circumstance and experiences of situations, their craft knowledge, or strategies for responding to contexts and expectations;
- *subject matter* – studies of (or ideas about) the acquisition, transformation, and transmission of content.

(adapted from Hoyle and John 1997)

The common dimensions of subject, curriculum, and pedagogy are highlighted in many other sources in literature on teaching, as illustrated by researchers such as Elbaz (1985), Carr and Kemmis (1986), Wilson *et al.* (1987) and Tickle (1994). These examples show the place that that core of professional knowledge holds, but they also show significant differences of view, and the need to think beyond it in terms of the range of knowledge in which new teachers might become proficient. The common ground can be seen in the lists below:

- Carr and Kemmis: commonsense – folk wisdom – skill – contextual – professional – theoretical – social/moral theory – philosophical outlook;
- Elbaz: subject matter – instruction – curriculum – teaching context – teacher self – evaluation/appraisal;
- Tickle: subject content – curriculum – school context – learners – teaching strategies – evaluation – self – broad range of matters relating to ethical, legal, relational, and policy dimensions;
- Wilson *et al.*: subject content – pedagogical content – pedagogical methods – curriculum – learners and learning – school context – educational aims.

(adapted from Tickle 1994)

The differences between these sources are quite as striking as their similarities. While Wilson *et al.* orientate towards a subject-expert/skilled instructor view of the teacher, Carr and Kemmis come closer to the classical thinking of the philosopher-educator, while Elbaz and Tickle include the self as a significant dimension. My own analysis also extends to a much longer classification, reaching into a range of day-to-day functional knowledge – matters that are needed to be able to operate at all within a school setting. That reflects my own experiences and extensive observations of teaching, as well as the explicit concerns of the newly qualified teachers with whom I have worked in professional development projects over many years.

Another way of classifying those kinds of functional concerns and other knowledge that practical teaching represents was considered by Eraut (1994). He provides a detailed review of literature on the nature of professional expertise, among which he notes that Dreyfus and Dreyfus (1986) provide

> an analysis of skilled behaviour under conditions of rapid interpretation and decision making, in which the logically distinct processes of acquiring information, following routines and making decisions are fully integrated.

(Eraut 1994: 128)

This particular version of 'holistic' professional knowledge and practice is also explored by Eraut through the work of Hammond (1980), Schön (1971, 1983, 1987), and others, concluding by noting 'the revolution in thinking about professional expertise' (Eraut 1994: 157). The revolution, it seems, is born partly from reimagining the relationship between theory and practice, but is still in its infancy – described as fuzzy, incomplete, underconceptualized, and subject to the 'primitive state of our methodology for describing and prescribing a profession's knowledge base' (Eraut 1994: 102).

It is in that reimagining that the revolution has its greatest challenge it seems, because 'the process of interpreting and personalizing theory and integrating it into conceptual frameworks that are themselves partly inconsistent and partly tacit is as yet only minimally understood' (Eraut 1994: 157). The responsibility for extending the search for understanding is laid firmly at the feet of professionals by Eraut as a central part of 'ongoing evaluation of their personal knowledge base.' On the face of it this makes Reynolds and Eraut rather interesting bedfellows in the search for the creation of a sound professional knowledge base – until one considers the startlingly different starting point of the Teacher Training Agency.

While I will represent the latter in this chapter, it will be treated as something of a counter-revolution that would deny the opportunities for the development of professional education which taking on the 'fuzziness' would allow. In his response to that challenge, Eraut maps different kinds of knowledge within a broad framework, each with subcategories:

propositional knowledge
• theories and concepts;
• generalizations and practical principles;
• specific propositions in case-contexts.

Using the work of Broudy *et al.* (1964) Eraut outlines how propositional knowledge might be used in different modes:

• replicative – used in routine, repetitive tasks, working within rules and procedures;
• applicatory – translating principles into action within unfamiliar situations;
• interpretive – making judgements in practice situations, based on understanding and theoretical knowledge;
• associative – drawing on previous experience and images of teaching, as well as theoretical knowledge, in intuitive ways.

(based on Eraut 1994: 48)

personal knowledge
• impressions;
• schemes of experience;
• reflection and accommodation.

process knowledge
• acquiring information;
• skilled behaviour;

- deliberation;
- metacognition.

(based on Eraut 1994: 102–16)

It will be apparent already that these categories combine types of knowledge with modes of acquiring it, reflecting precisely the central characteristic of this problem – that we are engaged with knowledge that is based in social practice and personal performance. In its nature, its accumulation, its acquisition, and its use, professional knowledge is both a communal capital resource as well as a personal one. The challenge is to join Eraut in consolidating what I take to be a call to a professional equivalent to popular social revolution, in the search for the betterment of both personal performance and social practices, and the conditions in which they are developed and deployed. I will return later to the question of how proficient practice can be developed by new teachers.

Practising in-dignity

In the commonplace construct associated with a technical view of practice, subject content, observable actions for knowledge transmission to pupils, and measurement of their learning (in student test performance) are the main concerns. Such views of teaching, using taxonomies of behavioural objectives and techniques of training in classroom skills, are well known (Brown 1975). In England the Teacher Training Agency's version of teaching competencies, described as standards for the award of qualified teacher status in the Career Entry Profile, largely replicate that approach to curriculum and teaching (TTA 1997; 1999a). Intended as the basis for professional development during induction, its sections are almost entirely limited to subject knowledge and instructional know-how. Their flavour can be gained from Reynolds' (1998) lecture on teaching quality, in which effective teacher behaviours are claimed to have been defined in international research, including:

- lesson clarity;
- instructional variety;
- effective time management;
- high student levels of time on task;
- maintaining a high success rate for pupils;
- using and incorporating pupil ideas;
- strong structuring (of lesson content);
- appropriate and varied questioning;
- probing for knowledge;
- frequent feedback;
- high expectations of what pupils can achieve;
- clear, and restricted, goals.

(adapted from Reynolds 1998: 27–8)

Profiles have been created in various places as lists of competencies by teacher educators and administrators for pre-service purposes for many years. In the five years prior to a national profile being imposed in England in 1997 all teacher education departments had been charged with devising their own. Many had already operated profiling procedures as part of the assessment of professional practice. They were not all the same and they changed over time. In fact, in England the core of knowledge described in national policy changed from subject knowledge, pedagogical skills, and personal qualities, to leave the latter displaced by knowledge of assessment procedures (TTA 1997; 1999a).

In the USA, Canada, Australia, New Zealand, and other countries similar key elements are centre stage in attempts to define teaching. Though described with some variation in language, the assumptions of the subject/instructor/assessor are strong. Typically effective teachers:

- have mastery of content and discourse of their discipline;
- are expert in the art and science of teaching;
- are accomplished in assessing and reporting learning outcomes;
- manage the classroom in exemplary ways.

(adapted from NSWDET 1998a: 3)

This portrayal is the symbolic formalization of learning and performance requirements derived from the hot political and social contexts in which teachers' work is delineated and reduced to minimal descriptions. It is part of a long preoccupation, in social debate and policy making, with defining what a good teacher is supposed to be (Waller 1932; Lortie 1975; Elliott 1991; Sockett 1994). Those core qualities have not always been reduced to as little as three or four elements, as the following summary derived from a survey across recent research and policy in several countries shows:

- subject knowledge;
- pedagogic content;
- learning and learners;
- classroom management and instruction;
- classroom and school contexts;
- curriculum policy and principles;
- assessment policy and methods;
- evaluation of teaching;
- routines and functional know-how.

Seen through the eyes of Sharon Snow, a new teacher, the matter of what she knew and needed to know reads more like an exorcism of ghosts encountered during induction. Seven months into her first year of teaching she described confronting an overwhelming extent and variety of problems, such as 'which area of my course to begin with, which texts to use to best complement my objectives, where to find additional resources' (Snow 1988: 288). While she acknowledged that her pre-service training taught her the subject content and classroom techniques she needed, just one page of her description of experiencing induction shows how unprepared she felt. It includes the following:

> I learned very quickly to make adjustments to presentation of material . . .
> to . . . alter my plans for specific classes and specific pupils . . .
> I did feel unprepared in a variety of areas . . .
> I simply did not know . . .
> I felt the problem acutely . . .
> I felt overwhelmed . . .
> I simply did not have the experience . . .
> I did not know how . . .
> I did not know enough . . .
> I did not have the expertise . . .
> What I learned very quickly [was] . . .
>
> (Snow 1988: 288)

It is evident from recent increases in demand for the accountability of teachers that the contest for the right to define their knowledge in terms of their own learning, rather than performance, has been lost by the profession through the political reinforcement of a whole range of measures that control what teachers are and what they do (Hoyle and John 1997). Control has been extended dramatically in the 1990s over initial teacher education programmes, the requirements for newly qualified teachers, experienced teachers' duties and ways of assessing their practice, and the provision of in-service professional development. Like any form of assessment-driven curriculum, the way the standards are defined and their particular components applied as criteria, so teacher education and the roles and identities of teachers become defined. That in turn is likely to determine what it is that new teachers become inducted into, and thus become. Potential moves in the late 1990s create a perpetuation of the conservatisms of schooling in which the proof of capability comes first, almost in denial of the learning potentials that exist for teachers and the communities in which they work.

The problem with this and with the concept of effectiveness that underlies it is that they are based on a particular set of values. Elliott (1998: 86–7) argues that underpinning the school effectiveness research and its findings is a 'set of values that appear to be a constituent of a social control ideology'. If that model is adopted by new teachers the implication is clear – induction would be into a context, culture, and process of social control rather than a process of educational emancipation, based on an alternative 'vision of education as a highly personal transaction between teacher and pupil in collaboration with parents' (Elliott 1998: 89).

We are in danger of the portrayal of the teacher as the all-dancing, all-singing, all-knowing expert in subject content, instructional techniques and assessment methods becoming the dominant one. This development would miss one point that can be drawn from the description of experience by

Sharon Snow. Her account and many similar ones show that what teachers are engaged in is a process of learning, through multiple problem solving in complex situations. That is not to deny that they should have demonstrable capabilities by the time they begin to carry out their responsibilities with young people. Rather it is to re-emphasize that, to use Eraut's modes of teaching knowledge, the concurrent use and acquisition of routines, the process of working out principled actions, the making of judgements, and the reliance on and reconstruction of theories of teaching, all combine in some sort of conspiring whirl. At the individual, personal level, evidence of initial encounters with full-time teaching are demonstrations of experience in which a great deal remains to be learned. That evidence is an incitement to raise the status of those who are willing to say 'I do not know' because that is the foundation of all research, and a significant basis of learning. It is also an incitement to ensure that the narrowness of profiles is recognized as a minimal basis of proficiency, beyond which induction must reach for professional knowledge of a more substantial and educationally significant kind. The nature of that challenge was elaborated by Elliott:

> curriculum and pedagogical decision making only becomes a complex affair when teachers value their pupils as self-determining agents of their learning. This implies that learning is a dynamic and unpredictable process whose outcomes are not something the teacher can confidently predict or control. His or her responsibility is to establish the curriculum and pedagogical conditions which enable pupils to generate personally significant and meaningful learning outcomes for themselves. This is a very complex affair indeed and very context-bound. It explains why teachers should play a major generative role in determining the quality of the educational process . . . The implications . . . for schools are profound. Their future as traditionally bounded organizations is doubtful. They may have to reconstruct their role in society as the coordinating centres of electronically-based learning systems and networks which are flexible and open to inputs from learners faced with the task of constructing their own futures.
>
> (Elliott 1998: 101–2)

Routines and functional knowledge

Let me emphasize the daily realities of new teachers trying to function with dignity and a sense of order and stability in the mêlée of classrooms and schools. Throughout the previous sections there are frequent references to components of what I have called the routines and functional know-how that make induction what it primarily is. It is above all else a sudden immersion into administrative, organizational, managerial, collegial, legal, and traditional aspects of institutional life. Colleagues and most pupils are already inducted into these matters and have worked out their own strategies for living within them. Those multiple strategies make up the subcultures of a school, which themselves have to be perceived, responded to, and negotiated by new members. The appeals of Sharon Snow and other new teachers for this kind of knowledge are powerful and urgent. They represent the search for safety on that further shore beyond pre-service experience, in the desire to become capital T teachers (Tickle 1992b). It is primary knowledge, not lower level knowledge, as implied by Eraut's model of replicative routines. Yet it is just cause for concern that if it became the only or the major focus in the search for knowledge, then life in rule-driven, taken-for-granted, disenfranchised teaching will displace the potential breadth of expertise of a professional educator.

There is also another way of interpreting this hurried assimilation of functional knowledge. Dependence on the 'I' in the report by Sharon Snow makes her, the individual, the locus of accountability, performance, and success or failure. This dependence may be self-constructed, or it may be a result of the way teachers are held accountable independently of each other, and come to accept that precept. This seems to be Edwards' (1998: 30) concern when he points out that the educational prospects of pupils are affected by social determinants external to schools, by school-wide conditions and processes, and by teacher characteristics and actions in the classroom, each in relationship to the others. He argues that the concentration on attempts to separate out and measure a single cause of effectiveness (i.e. teacher behaviour) by Reynolds (1998) trivializes the debates that have taken place about the complexity of those relationships and their link with the consideration of ends, as well as means, in education.

Of course in some respects it is crucial to focus on the personal responsibilities of individual teachers. However, it is also important to see the education of the young as a collective endeavour. Young people themselves have major responsibilities for their own learning; parents and other teachers share those responsibilities; so does the wider community which establishes and maintains the forms of education on offer and allocates the resources for it. Teachers are a part of that collective endeavour. It is clear from social commentaries on schooling and the continuing search for solutions to education's problems that it is also we – collectively – who do not know enough, who do not have sufficient expertise in a range of areas, who have difficulty agreeing on what we think education is for and what forms it should take. If induction focuses on functional know-how to the exclusion of these other matters, and remains locked in the realm of the 'I', then the powers of new teachers will be locked in the unprofessional domain and their contributions to education will be restricted to maintaining the status quo.

There is a further incitement to professionals to recapture their role as educational experts who are capable of asking fundamental questions, as well as instrumental ones, about what it is that seems so dysfunctional about schooling; why it is that communities, states and nations seem so dissatisfied with what they have created; and what the alternatives might be that would better suit our young people and serve their futures.

Perhaps the central problem that we collectively, and such teacl
Sharon, face is that few people ask the fundamental questions.
another is that the lack of research on the one hand, and intensive demands
for skilled performance in teaching on the other, have not led to professional knowledge being neatly classified and tabulated. For the moment,
though, let us consider that extended core of teaching knowledge as if it was
both acceptable as a sufficient definition of what's required, and neatly
separable into component parts.

Subject knowledge

The simplest model of the mediating role of education is the academic/
vocational tradition, which asserts that teachers need to know the subject
matter that is to be taught. They are expected to know it, typically, to a
degree somewhat below that which is produced in the academies and commercial hotbeds where research, or intellectual reasoning, or the development
of new products, and the applied know-how of commerce is done by educated
élites. They need to know it to a degree above their students. Subdivisions
of subject matter make up the menu of content knowledge deemed suitable
for wider dissemination. The academic/vocational tradition is based on a
notion of cultural transmission in which a social group (or nation) has a
consensus about, or power over, knowledge into which its members should
be inducted. Usually dissemination varies in degrees according to social and
occupational statuses. That is, which groups should be inducted into which
parts of a society's cultural wisdoms, ways of understanding the world, and
means of functioning and developing technologically and economically, is
age, class, race, or gender divided. The knowledge involved is often represented as certain knowledge, or at least the work of generations of experts
whose ways of representing the world or functioning within it are to be
understood, adopted, and practised.

In conditions of rapidly advancing technologies, globalization of information, multiculturalism, and the diversification of specialist knowledge, that
notion of the academic teacher becomes both redundant and paradoxically
in greater demand. That is to say, the knowledge and information resource
is collectively so vast and volatile that an educated and informed society,
and its individual members, would be disenfranchised and put at risk if they
were merely inducted into traditional, canonical knowledge, and productive
practices. Yet to participate in society individuals need the cultural reference
points, the means of interpreting the world via the disciplines, the capability
to engage in argument, or the skills to join productive occupations, in ways
defined by the dominant discourses within areas of study or trades.

Being knowledgeable across a range of subjects, and more deeply knowledgeable in some specialism(s) is the quality expected of an educated person
in liberal democratic societies. This is accompanied by needing the tools of
participation such as higher orders of literacy, numeracy, and information/

communications technology, either as the means into the study of subjects, or as functional life skills. The vocational parallels involve the acquisition and development of applied knowledge, capabilities and values demanded in the economic, productive, or community services labour markets. These expectations make teachers the substantial guardians and disseminators of cultural knowledge for new generations. Induction into that role of guardianship is central to the process of becoming a teacher in the academic/ vocational view of education. The requirement to focus on the traditional subject approach is set out in the Teacher Training Agency's requirement that for provisional qualified teacher status teachers must demonstrate that, for the secondary level, they:

• have a secure knowledge and understanding of . . . their specialist subject(s) at a standard equivalent to degree level;
• know and can teach the key skills required for current qualifications relevant to their specialist subject(s);
• cope securely with subject-related questions that pupils raise;

At the primary level teachers should be able to:

• cope securely with subject-related questions that pupils raise;
• for English, mathematics and science, have a secure knowledge and understanding of the subject content specified in the ITT (initial teacher training) National Curriculum;
• for any specialist subject(s), have a secure knowledge of the subject to at least GCE Advanced level;
• have a working knowledge of information and communications technology to level 8 in the National Curriculum;
• for any non-core, non-specialist subject have a secure knowledge to at least level 7 of the National Curriculum.

(adapted from TTA 1997; 1999a)

Specifications of subject content and school-age levels in different nations and localities confirm both the common search for standards, and the diversity of situations which makes induction into school-based knowledge context-specific. The latter creates problems if new teachers choose career mobility. The recruitment of Australians into English schools (or vice versa), and trans-European or interstate American employment patterns, illustrates that problem. In these respects, yet again, we can see that the underlying capabilities needed by teachers are those that facilitate learning and the handling of change and diversity.

Advertisements for teacher vacancies are likely to convey the view that a teacher must be a subject expert. In its ideal type, knowledge content and procedures, or the capabilities deployed in pursuit of a discipline such as music, or occupational practice such as manufacturing capability or business management, should not just be acquired for subsequent transmission to students. They should be the centre of the educator's very being. This designates teachers as masters of cultural knowledge even though the knowledge for which they become the masters is usually not authentic knowledge, in which they are genuine experts engaged in knowledge creation or its use. Even towards the later stages of schooling, where specialist teaching asserts such an image, teachers are rarely first-hand experts in pursuit of their own research and working at the forefront of the disciplines.

The classical academic tradition represents teaching differently of course. It is commitment, inspiration, dedication to understanding the subject and conveying its passions. That designation of the teacher as subject expert has been complemented (or maybe disrupted) by other views of the curriculum and of the educator as a facilitator, enabling students to access other sources where knowledge and capabilities can be acquired. Yet by and large the subject expert is still defined within western traditions of nationalism, rationalism, and vocationalism – the histories and traditions of localities, the classical reasoning of the sciences, and the skilling of economic and commercial activities.

Even if this designation of the teacher were sufficiently viable for developed nations in the twenty-first century, the education of teachers, or time and resources needed to achieve the depth and range of expertise and the flexibility to handle multiple contents at both personal and pedagogical levels, don't exist. Teacher education's investments and products are respectively low cost and intended to follow traditional designs that presume academic/ vocational, and/or elementary traditions within limited course contact time. These restrictions and the problematic nature of content selection and adaptation are not necessarily overt in the educational experiences of new teachers. They become evident, even acute, at the point of classroom performance when the demonstration of expertise is required. Where expertise does not already exist, induction has three possible routes:

- into a sense of inadequacy, self-doubt, guilt, and coping strategies for compliance with curriculum content requirements;
- into acknowledgement of deficiencies, and a learning agenda that seeks to secure greater knowledge and expertise;
- into enquiry and openness centred around the diversity and dynamic of knowledge, its multiple cultural foundations, and its essential conventions and mysteries.

The idea of a single person performing the impossible is not an accurate reflection of how knowledge is generated, developed and used in society. Research, development and production are done often in teams, crossing boundaries, outsourcing some elements, consulting specialists, and so on. Knowledge is both vested in each person and in whole interdependent communities. It does appear that in these terms, what we call induction into teaching constitutes a process of the abduction of those who become teachers from the wider society. That abduction is then extended to students, who are held for the compulsory years of schooling in virtual knowledge worlds, with some curriculum attempts at the later stages of secondary education to reintegrate them into the world of 'work'.

What's more, subject content and vocational capabilities, as experienced by teachers and students alike, are largely sanitized from engagement with controversies and contentious issues that are part of the wider knowledge community. Intellectual élitism and protectionism, the appropriation of ideas and products, and the exploitation of labour for maximum private profit, testing the boundaries of ethical practices, industrial espionage, and other characteristics that can be found in the academies or in industrial and commercial settings are largely disinfected from school curricula. It goes further. The school curriculum pays lip service to the radicals of history, the politics of science, and the power of language, for example, rather than being radical or providing those powers to the disadvantaged. Teachers and pupils consider the work of avant-garde cultural performers at a distance, as spectators of some kind of professional curiosity. Information and communications technology is dealt with instrumentally, as a tool of access, rather more than it is dealt with critically as a mechanism for social divisiveness or of a corrupting nature.

So the definitions of knowledge and understanding which new teachers are expected to be able to demonstrate according to the profiles and checklists in various localities should be examined carefully. They need scrutinizing, alongside the curriculum specifications for subjects, for their implicit values and potential consequences. It is the capacity to perceive that need, to engage those values, and to act according to the ethics of education but within the politics of schooling, which would constitute an induction into being a professional educator.

Pedagogic content

A slightly more complex model of teaching as the mediation of subject matter is that which also requires the academic/practitioner to translate their expertise to make it accessible to pupils who are at different levels of familiarity with it. Shulman (1986a) and his colleagues claimed that this includes knowing how to reformulate subject knowledge into what they called pedagogical content (Shulman 1986b; Wilson et al. 1987). As is most demonstrable in primary schools where individual teachers cover 10 subjects, the kind of knowledge being managed is selected and refashioned to make it assimilable, at least by the more successful of the school's population. Teachers work to render it capable of being re-presented in classrooms and in assessment performance by students. It is what teachers give out as information or training, and what students are required to give back through recitation and demonstration, in the ritualized practices of schooling and credentialling.

In this model teachers do not necessarily learn at their own level, or engage in person with the discipline of a subject or the practice of a trade. They acquire packaged knowledge deemed suitable for pupils of different ages and capabilities (Bruner 1977; TTA 1997; 1999a). It is a corrupted version of the academic/vocational traditions, a derivative of the pupil–teacher system of the nineteenth century. Teachers in this view merely assist in the transmission of prescribed knowledge and skills, packaged in what are deemed to be assimilable segments.

So there are inherent tensions within society's knowledge creation base itself, and in the purposes of schooling, which underlie how we define what professional educators need to know and what they are responsible for doing. These tensions are one reason why we are faced with contradictions in expectations about professional knowledge and standing. We feel that teachers should be at the forefront through command of a subject, yet they can never be so because the job is to transmit a historical and general overview of subjects or occupational practices and their many divisions, at levels deemed appropriate to students. Or worse, they are asked to teach subjects that are tangential to their lives, in order to fill staffing slots on timetables (DES 1982, 1988a; Tickle 1994). They are at the interface between real knowledge and school knowledge – between social/cultural dynamic and the ossified matter into which the young are themselves initiated.

This position raises fundamental questions about the nature and purpose of schools in society, about the possibility that schools as presently constituted are outmoded and socially regressive, and thus the likelihood of these traditions of teaching not being tenable for future educational endeavours. However, our systems of schooling appear to be self-perpetuating. Radical de-schooling alternatives have been rejected or overlooked as if they are irrelevant, and formal systems modelled on western practices have spread like bushfires throughout the developing world. So the view that remains is a perception of new teachers being inducted into the improbable, in order to perform the impossible, as long as their role is centrally defined as subject expert.

We also expect teachers to be personally expertly literate and numerate, and, more recently, skilled in the use of information and communications technology. These realms of knowledge are deemed the essentials of participation in modern social life, and the basic exploitable human capacity of modern economies. Once again, the expectations are not for personal participation and expertise, but for pedagogical knowledge directly equated with whatever is prescribed for children.

Teachers are also expected to model citizenship and personal ethics (for example) because educators are supposed to maintain social norms and lead in the behavioural socialization of the young. It is not just the knowledge that teachers hold, then, but their performance in behaviour and manifestation of values, as defined and required by dominant social groups, institutional milieux, or managing bodies. These behaviours and values mainly exclude radical participation in citizenry. They are again referenced by traditions that maintain social hypocrisies, seeking to hide or ignore the playfulness of the aristocracy, the gambling and drunkenness of the yuppie classes, the infidelity of politicians, generic racism and sexism of many groups, and so on. Teachers in this sense are not expected to be real persons either. They are cloned, as if devoid of human frailties, in role (Beynon 1987). Their task is to convey what is expected of students, as if there is an artificial social norm.

There are differences, then, between real subjects and school subjects, and between real people and schoolteachers. In the broader curriculum of citizenship and socialization, real social issues are deflected, as politics, economics, philosophy, critical studies, or attitudes to social injustice, and values pertaining to the organization of social life (for example) are held at bay or filtered out in the processing of school knowledge. Radicalism, dissent and argumentation are the ingredients of social instability, and there is a tendency not to socialize the young – or their teachers – into the attitudes and conventions of the dissenters and levellers or their latterday followers (Hill 1976).

Public school teachers were always likely to be secondhand purveyors of other people's knowledge, translators in the transmission of culture, or occupational trades, or social capabilities. In the case of primary school teachers, the tension this creates is intense. The very idea of being an expert in, or even knowing secondhand, the content and principles of 10 different subjects is self-evidently silly. Yet it is maintained as an expectation in many nations, confirming that the academic/vocational traditions of schooling remain strong. In primary schools it combines with the elementary tradition that requires training in literacy, numeracy, and now information and communications technology, and ascribed social behaviours (Blyth 1965; Alexander 1995). It is joined by the pedagogic traditions of both primary and secondary schooling, which emphasize the characteristics of learners and the processes of children's learning, and the search for pedagogic excellence that depends upon that theoretical and practical knowledge (Blyth 1965; Hammersley 1977; Goodson 1983; Hargreaves 1985).

Which elements of content, skills, capabilities and values are included depends on the power and preferences of those who design syllabuses, or on traditional cultures, or on the winners among the constantly competing contenders for inclusion in curriculum content (Goodson 1983). This is partly because academic/pedagogical content knowledge, functional competencies such as numeracy and literacy, and values, are often culturally, context or time-specific. That is to say, subject knowledge inevitably rests in the curriculum content that is defined by particular communities within specific times and geographical locations, through their curriculum specifications, examination syllabuses or schools' aims. Some of what is required in England is not necessarily required in Scotland, Eire, France, or the USA. Some of what was required in England in 1997 was not included in 1987; in Hong Kong, curricula in 1998 were different from curricula in 1997; Roman Catholic, Muslim and Jewish schools follow different curricula, and so on. In this sense the task for new teachers is manifold:

- to steer a way through the continuous acquisition of subject expertise, ideally maintaining a closeness to the heart of a discipline or subdiscipline and its development in the wider world;

- to know what conventions and segments of knowledge have been selected or might best be chosen for students at different stages of their progress through schooling;
- to recognize (and if necessary challenge) the mechanisms of selection, distribution, and provision of access to subject matter in the school system;
- to be capable of handling complex and possibly conflicting approaches within the study of subjects, and the dynamics of changes in those approaches over time.

Learning and learners

Concern for pupils' successful acquisition of subject knowledge and vocational capabilities led to what is known as the pedagogical tradition of teaching (Goodson 1983). It involves concern to perfect the pedagogical skills that might be appropriate for different knowledge content or skills, for pupils of different ages, capabilities or diverse backgrounds, operating in different learning environments. It involves teachers in understanding how learners assimilate and internalize the discipline of the subject or develop particular capabilities, and gaining the know-how for facilitating the acquisition of a broadly defined base of knowledge, skills, understanding, or values in accordance with defined pedagogical principles.

The know-how for successfully initiating the young into the proficiencies of literacy, numeracy, ICT, citizenship, and so on, is also based on understanding the learners' modes of mental, physical, cultural, or interactional processing of information and experience. The academic, vocational and elementary versions of the pedagogic tradition are sometimes complemented by a constructivist psychology in which the learner is seen as actively curious and self-directed. That presumes less about the prior selection of subject knowledge or vocational proficiencies, and more about the teacher's need to know about children and how they are motivated, as well as how they process experience and information. Knowledge of learners and the management of processes of learning – pedagogical expertise – becomes an essential component of the teacher's armoury. So in some versions the management of learning is based on guiding pupils towards pre-specified knowledge by a variety of means. In others, the direction is open-ended, and curiosity is encouraged to roam the intellectual fields. In both, knowledge of learners and learning is deemed essential material into which new teachers should be inducted if their teaching is to be successful.

Understanding the psychology and sociology of learning, and of the effect of different cultural and material conditions upon it, are important parts of an educator's expertise. These lie in the realm of teacher education that has been called theory-based – an approach that in the past has curiously been condemned by some right-wing political activists (Hillgate Group 1989; Lawlor 1990). Those condemnations, to take Habermas' (1968) notion of the nature of theory as being based in practice, derive from a particular view of the traditional academic curriculum and limited perceptions of practical expertise. They also derive from crude political strategies to remove critique of schooling systems and the problems that they manifest. Belief in the status quo of privilege on the one hand and the reproduction of educational disadvantage on the other, seems to be defended against the possibilities of social justice and celebrations of cultural diversity in which knowledge of children and how they learn is the secret of successful teaching. At least in the view of induction implied in the Career Entry Profile the new teacher's task in relation to pedagogical knowledge is presented as full-square within the need to know theory – about learners, across a range of areas of human development:

Primary/Secondary
• know, for their specialist subject(s), pupils' most common misconceptions and mistakes;
• understand how pupils' learning in the subject is affected by their physical, intellectual, emotional and social development.

These specifications can also be read as evidence of limitation. The gaps are apparent. There is no mention of cultural difference, nor of social disadvantage or privilege, or of the effects of the material conditions of classrooms and schools. Even with that limitation, there is a need to recognize that these realms of practical theorizing have a significant and constantly growing data source. Like subject knowledge they are not stable and fixed, nor uncontroversial. Rather, they are exploratory and sometimes contentious. The wisdoms of psychology, social psychology, anthropology, and sociology, as they apply to learners and learning, are frequently contested from within their disciplines. Different orientations to the conduct of research in these fields display different implicit views on human nature, modes of social organization, and the processes of human interaction (Phillips 1987).

There is also a professional culture that transmits assumptions about pupils' capacities for learning. It carries notions of ability as a general defining characteristic of individuals, which is deemed to be normatively distributed. It conveys associated expectations of differential performance among students, according to ethnicity, gender, age, family background, or even place of residence. Educators individually have a variety of implicit theories that affect their interpretations of events in, and actions within, classrooms (Hammersley 1977). Perspectives and beliefs about the processes of learning and the characteristics of learners are central. In this sense, self-knowledge, recognizing where one stands in relation to theories of human potential, is essential in the reflexive pursuit of excellence in education. It is arguably central to induction, but by implication needs to be matched by the re-culturation of the profession. Access to theoretical and scholarly sources that form the bedrock of the work of professional educators needs to be matched by the development of practical theorizing based on the evidence of experience and observation.

All three of these sources of practical knowledge – the applicable disciplines, professional culture, and personal beliefs and experience – are part of the environment of induction in which new teachers roam. It is the expanse of that environment, and the instability and contestability of its elements into which inductees need to be guided. Without that, new teachers might come to take research, or professional norms, or personal beliefs, as truth. Or they might experience the contest of ideas as destabilizing and debilitating. Induction into a profession, on the other hand, will acknowledge the provisionality of ideas, the diversity of views, and the need to engage in and with research as the most productive and promising way ahead.

The idea of knowing children, or of having firm beliefs about their learning, has another dimension, with a double edge. Educators necessarily create images of individual students in the process of getting to know them. Mental constructs and identities, on which actions are constructed, are a necessary part of the armoury of instruction. This is also a potentially dangerous and damaging process – another professional paradox – because educational judgements have consequences for learners. Children and learning situations also inherently hold the possibility of being wrongly judged, especially in the hurried handling of impressions during daily classroom life.

Induction therefore needs to involve the development of a clear perception of the educational damage that such predispositions and judgements can do, despite the best efforts of teachers. It should include explicit acknowledgement that in the act of becoming a teacher, new entrants will be inducted into more than processes of educational enhancement. They will, albeit unwittingly, engage in activities that lead to the curtailment of life choices and chances, and the destruction of educational desire (Willis 1977; McFadden 1996). Is this sentiment too strong? Well, perhaps, to the extent that induction does not take the form of conscious collusion with these processes. Yet it is a persistent characteristic of schooling that it plays a part in the broader social processes which define identities and distribute knowledge, vocational proficiencies, values, and career opportunities in ways that privilege some students and disadvantage others.

Induction involves new teachers in becoming skilled in handling the inherent contradictions and dilemmas of schooling that its processes present, and in managing damage limitation of which they do become aware. So knowing how learning is affected by children's development means also knowing how development is affected by the judgements and the professional cultures of teaching, and the underlying dispositions towards human growth and potential. Race, gender, culture, social class, and the impact of the expectations of teachers upon pupils' learning, are issues – rather than simply some prior knowledge to be acquired by new teachers. It is the issues and ways of responding to them into which they should be welcomed – as well as into an appreciation of the failure of the schooling system to address those issues satisfactorily. It follows that if personal theories, professional cultures, or principles of pedagogy steer decisions and the formation of judgements to a considerable degree, then the capacity to explicate and examine those practical theories, and to re-search for possibilities for their development, should be an intrinsic part of induction processes.

Classroom management and instruction

Curriculum processes involve the translation of principles about learning and knowledge of learners into classroom practices (I am using classroom here in the widest possible sense to include all learning environments). Action is also based on beliefs about instructional strategies, which take account of the practical possibilities of material circumstances. Educational practice in this sense might be both idealistic and pragmatic, and thus built on compromises. The management of learning environments by acts of compromise represents one of the most fundamental generic professional capabilities. Instructional qualities and skills that are deployed in classrooms are another essential partner to the beliefs about learners and learning, and management capabilities. They combine to create coping strategies, as expressions of the contradictions that teachers handle, in the pursuit of ideals, and deployment of skill, within the material environments in which they work (Hargreaves 1978; Pollard 1985).

It is self-evident that there are some organizational skills that make educational encounters in any situation more likely to be deemed satisfying or successful if they are applied than if they are not. These are based on more than technique. They depend on dispositions and the capacity to judge the organizational opportunities of particular situations. That involves observation, assessment of evidence, decisiveness, and possibly risk-taking. It means being aware of the need to plan space and furnishings, and to moderate room temperatures or lighting. Methods of organizing, managing, and distributing resources – prerequisites in creating learning situations – also involve perceptiveness, requisitioning, knowing what's available, prediction, contingency planning, and so on.

The capacity to make judgements of this kind applies, in principle at least, in all manner of educational practice and circumstances. It is those decision making capabilities to which induction needs to attend, and the same can be said of instructional judgements. Describing educational goals clearly and succinctly to students and gaining their commitments to them – or else having them define their own – is common across different curricula and forms of instruction.

Once again, these essential prerequisites of management and instruction are laid out in school systems' proclamations in this realm of professional knowledge. However, although policies may pretend to encourage independent professional judgement, they often claim the superiority of certain kinds of teaching techniques. Primarily, given the knowledge-content assumption, methods are commonly based on a transmission view of teacher input–student output, or technical efficiency. In its extreme form in the late 1990s in England, policy makers have sought to dictate management and instructional techniques such as whole class teaching, literacy and numeracy hours for primary schools divided into portions of specified activities, and end of course, formal written examinations for some secondary subjects (to name just a few policy impositions).

The catalogue of these kinds of management skills and instructional behaviours is produced in many formats; their characteristics can again be gleaned from the work to be demonstrated by newly qualified teachers in primary and secondary schools in England, which include the following:

- planning their teaching to achieve progression in pupils' learning through:
  1 identifying clear teaching objectives and content, appropriate to the subject matter and the pupils being taught, and specifying how these will be taught and assessed;
  2 setting tasks for whole-class, individual and group work, including homework, which challenge pupils and ensure high levels of pupil interest;
  3 setting appropriate and demanding expectations for pupils' learning, motivation and presentation of work;
  4 setting clear targets for pupils' learning, building on prior attainment, and ensuring that pupils are aware of the substance and purpose of what they are asked to do;
- identifying pupils who:
  1 have special educational needs, including specific learning difficulties;
  2 are very able;
  3 are not yet fluent in English;
- provide clear structures for lessons, and for sequences of lessons, in the short, medium and longer term, which maintain pace, motivation and challenge for pupils;
- make effective use of assessment information on pupils' attainment and progress in their teaching and in planning future lessons and sequences of lessons;
- plan opportunities to contribute to pupils' personal, spiritual, moral, social and cultural development;
- ensure coverage of the relevant examination syllabuses and National Curriculum programmes of study;
- be familiar with subject-specific health and safety requirements, where relevant, and plan lessons to avoid potential hazards.

(adapted from TTA 1997; 1999a)

These lists bring into view another sense in which pedagogic knowledge forms the basis of expectations for teaching expertise and educational efficacy. That is the wider knowledge and understanding of different instructional strategies and their use in varying organizational arrangements or material conditions. I do not mean knowledge portrayed in the conventional practice metaphors and stereotypes of what works with certain kinds or ages of children in set-piece situations. Indeed, there is as much data of the kind that says 'that won't work for me in my school' as there are examples of 'what works' (sometimes called 'good practice'). What I mean is awareness of and a capacity to engage with and be involved in the debates about these matters, by reference to research, reasoned argument, and accumulated professional wisdom. Involvement in this sense might be based on educational action and experience, or on discussion about curriculum principles and their impact on practice, or on significant activity in carrying out research.

Deciding upon the best courses of action for meeting the educational needs of students in a particular context is a general capability that is indisputably a key to being a successful educator. It, too, is likely to involve the skills of evidence handling, as well as qualities such as empathy, responsiveness, and knowledge of a range of possible teaching strategies and their potential consequences. Again, these matters need to be known at the level of experience and underlying beliefs and principles – that is, the implicit values that underpin practice need to be explicated, and assumptions that reside in methods proposed by non-practitioners need to be tested in practice. The implication is for induction processes to be able to handle the acquisition and demonstration of such a wealth and range of capability. At the same time it needs to equip new teachers with the capacity to question their own practices and those propounded by others. More than skills, then, this constitutes professional, practical theorizing, or praxis.

With regard to teaching performance and classroom management the demonstrative capabilities required of new teachers in England amount to an extensive list:

- ensure effective teaching of whole classes, and of groups and individuals within the whole-class setting, so that teaching objectives are met and best use is made of available teaching time;
- monitor and intervene when teaching to ensure sound learning and discipline;
- establish and maintain a purposeful working atmosphere;
- set high expectations for pupils' behaviour, establishing and maintaining a good standard of discipline through well focused teaching and through positive and productive relationships;
- establish a safe environment that supports learning and in which pupils feel secure and confident;
- use teaching methods that sustain the momentum of pupils' work and keep all pupils engaged through:
    1 stimulating intellectual curiosity, communicating enthusiasm for the subject being taught, fostering pupils' enthusiasm and maintaining pupils' motivation;
    2 matching the approaches used to the subject matter and the pupils being taught;
    3 structuring information well, including outlining content and aims, signaling transitions and summarizing key points as the lesson progresses;

4 clear presentation of content around a set of key ideas, using appropriate subject-specific vocabulary and well chosen illustrations and examples;

5 clear instruction and demonstration, and accurate well-paced explanation;

6 effective questioning that matches the pace and direction of the lesson and ensures that pupils take part;

7 careful attention to pupils' errors and misconceptions, and helping to remedy them;

8 listening carefully to pupils, analysing their responses and responding constructively in order to take pupils' learning forward;

9 selecting and making good use of textbooks, ICT and other learning resources that enable teaching objectives to be met;

10 maximizing opportunities for pupils to consolidate their knowledge;

11 exploiting opportunities to improve pupils' basic skills in literacy, numeracy and ICT, and individual and collaborative study skills;

12 exploiting opportunities to contribute to the quality of pupils' personal, spiritual, moral, social and cultural development;

13 setting high expectations for all pupils notwithstanding individual differences, including gender, and cultural and linguistic backgrounds;

14 providing opportunities to develop pupils' wider understanding by relating their learning to real and work-related examples;

• ensure that pupils acquire and consolidate knowledge, skills and understanding in the subject;

• evaluate their own teaching critically and use this to improve their effectiveness.

(adapted from TTA 1997; 1999a)

Beliefs about the boundaries of responsibility and authority also affect what is expected of students, and how classrooms are organized. Such beliefs are complex and cannot be taken for granted or assumed to be stable and fully formed in the ideas of individual teachers at the start of a professional career. Whether one's classroom management operates in the mode of an autocrat, a bureaucrat, or a democrat, or some mixture of these or other modes, is entirely pertinent to the experience of pupils. These kinds of factors in the work of educators are represented by diversity, and even manifest contradictions and inconsistencies in practice. So how should induction processes handle this? A constructivist approach to professional development would involve new teachers in displaying and examining their own ideas about authority and responsibility in classroom management, and considering the options and potential consequences of these, as well as those that inform others' practices. The place of such personal theories or principles steer decisions and the formation of judgements about the management of learning environments to a considerable degree. For example, there are different perspectives on the place and purposes of didactic instruction, or the importance of practical experiment for effecting and maximizing learning towards different educational goals. The rules of social behaviour and conduct that should be followed in classrooms and schools are also based on deeply held ethical values, about relationships between people, and the rights of the individual in relation to the rights of social groups. They are also affected by the material conditions of crowded spaces and the pragmatics of order and safety, coupled with theories of human behaviour.

These kinds of perspectives do not come entirely ready-made for newly qualified teachers. The use of particular methods of organizing learning and of instructing pupils' needs to be learnt through rigorous practical application and critical reflection. Induction in this respect is into the testing of ethical principles and pragmatic proposals. The search for evidence of what is educationally successful, measured against carefully explicated criteria and values, ought to be part of that induction if we are to ensure the development of principled professionalism, rather than simply following unprofessional practices.

Values, judgement and decision making, then, as well as informed critique and professional action, are necessary complements to any consideration about how classrooms are organized and managed. Once again it is the sense of enquiry, the acknowledgement that practices are provisional in the face of competing possible courses of action, and the consequent curiosities towards practice that induction can embrace and enjoy. That is more comprehensive than simply becoming skilled in prescribed or conventional instructional techniques.

Analyses of the core elements of teachers' knowledge from several countries show a similar range of management and instructional skills. Some also make note of their inadequacies. For example, the New South Wales team point out in relation to the Scottish version of competencies for new teachers that, for example:

> what seems to be missing, in this otherwise comprehensive set of competencies, are those qualities of critical analysis, self-reflection, and those other characteristics of effective teaching associated with the 'interpretive' and/or transformative, as distinct from the merely 'transmissional' and/or reproductive, roles of the educator.
>
> (NSWDET 1998a: 34)

Unfortunately the elements of competence that the NSW team themselves come round to identifying for effective teaching require 'demonstrable and observable performance criteria' based on a largely transmission model of teaching. That is despite a laudable and inclusive review of international developments which mentions more radical components, and embraces the reflective practitioner.

In the interpretive and transformative dimensions of professional knowledge, about which the document laments the absence from Scotland's policies, teachers would engage in capabilities far beyond the designations of content, classroom management and instructional expertise. Distinctive and individual aspects of teacher knowledge in these core elements combine with personal values, with the capacity to search for evidence and analyse experience, with a willingness to take a stance towards policy decisions and other educators' views rather than just accept them, and with awareness of educational knowledge from beyond the immediate practice situation. Inevitably these associations involve bringing together complementary – or maybe conflicting – aspects of educational knowledge, in a process of analysis and synthesis. Potentially they lead to changes in practice and in policy with respect to the way methods of teaching are deployed and classrooms are managed. That is the anticipated process of transformative education led by reforming professionals.

Classroom and school contexts

Expertise in classroom management and the development and use of classroom skills is also partly dependent on acute perceptions of the contexts in which that expertise will be used. The ways in which physical space is allocated, including the claims to territory and allocations of responsibilities for its management, are characteristics of overcrowded places like schools. Ecological awareness – or the politics of space – is a part of what new teachers need to learn quickly. The expectations that pupils and colleagues have of the way new teachers should behave set limits on what might be done. Those kinds of expectation vary between peer cultures, from class to class, across departments and schools.

The broad ethos of a school, the specific policies and adopted methods of a department, the size, age, dispositions and previous experiences of a class, and knowledge of the individual children, for example, affect choices in the organization of learning environments and methods of instruction. The data that new teachers face in making sense of these kinds of matters are extensive, and not always explicit or self-evident. Since they can reside in the taken-for-granted worlds of school cultures they are potentially confusing or confronting. What new teachers need to be inducted into is the development of those perceptions and the sensitivities which a new incumbent might need in negotiating their way to understanding not only how things are in the institutional cultures of schools, but also why they are so. Contextual knowledge of that kind is a necessary part of appreciating what might be done on one's own terms, and where the space for negotiation or change might be in someone else's terms.

Carrying out the functions of teaching, then, involves deploying pedagogical skills within particular learning situations. Some aspects of management and methods may be used in a specially equipped classroom base that is occupied by a teacher and class for all their lessons. The same options are unlikely to be transferable to a situation in which a teacher meets the same class in several different rooms within each week (DES 1982, 1988a; Tickle 1994). Knowing what resources are needed depends on a knowledge of the syllabus in operation, or which parts of it are dealt with by which teachers, where classes are shared. The distribution and use of materials depends on knowing how to negotiate their availability, where to locate them, which are most appropriate for use in the physical space available, or for particular pupils. Ordering materials depends on knowledge of budgeting and the financial and administrative procedures of the school or department. Judging which equipment and materials particular pupils can manipulate, knowing which emergency exits should be kept clear (for example), and a myriad matters pertaining to the specifics of classroom situations all have to be processed. A great deal of complex contextual knowledge of this kind has to be acquired to function with even a moderate sense of being effective.

Functioning effectively also involves understanding the impact of those contextual factors upon the process of educating. It incorporates the capacity to critique the environments, and to amend them if necessary by professional actions. It involves, in other words, the development of prudent judgements for action both within them and about them. So for example the impact of class size or different ways of organizing groups on the achievement of pupils, and on the experiences of the teacher, are important areas of understanding that have been headline issues for some decades (Plowden Report 1967; Bennett 1976; Simon *et al.* 1981; Alexander 1995). They constitute specific aspects of classroom and school contexts about which new teachers need to be well informed, or at least be aware of and capable of studying. This is not just a need to know the rules of engagement in a given situation – though that will be needed. It is also to know how to justify and create new situations, how to devise rules of conduct within them, and how to measure their consequences.

Beyond the classroom there are contextual matters that impinge on practice in significant ways that new teachers need to know. This broader ecology of education includes essential legal matters such as those set out in the Career Entry Profile and that have equivalents in many countries:

- have a working knowledge and understanding of teachers' legal liabilities and responsibilities relating to:
  1 health and safety procedures and responsibilities;
  2 duty to maintain reasonable care towards pupils;
  3 anti-discrimination legislation;
  4 child protection;
  5 detention, physical restraints and chastisement;
- understand professional responsibilities in relation to school policies and practices, including pastoral care and personal development, safety matters, bullying etc.;
- be aware of the role and purpose of school governing bodies.

(adapted from TTA 1997; 1999a)

These are not simply matters of knowing legislation and policy. Rather they require analysis and application in practice, so that they provide principles upon which actions are based. In most cases the specific legislation is potentially also a source for debate about the educational problems that the legislation seeks to solve, and the educational and practical implications of implementation. Like many policies, some are matter-of-fact, common sense; others are subject to interpretation, variation, and even litigation, so that induction into their functioning involves a complex and subtle process of initiation.

The contents of schoolteachers' pay and conditions of service legislation in many countries set out the professional duties required and thus the standards of conduct expected of an employee. Knowledge of this legislation is another dimension of the context of which new teachers need to be aware. It provides information on roles and responsibilities, including such matters as participation in continued training, and involvement in meetings. It also ensures that teachers have some knowledge of employee rights, so that a balanced view of a professional life and career can be gained, and if necessary acted upon through participation in professional associations. New teachers are formally expected to demonstrate or rapidly acquire the capacities implied in areas like the following:

- have a working knowledge and understanding of teachers' professional duties;
- have established effective working relationships with professional colleagues;
- recognize that learning takes place inside and outside the school context, and liaise effectively with parents and other agencies.

(adapted from TTA 1997; 1999a)

It is not so straightforward to 'have' a working knowledge of one's duties prior to taking up employment – that appears to be a contradiction in terms. Working knowledge is necessarily grounded in experience, so that induction ought to incorporate the testing of those prescribed and documented duties that apply to all teachers against the specific cases, conditions and experiences of individual practice. In engaging in that test, compliance and conformity can become informed participation in the reconstruction of definitions of the professional responsibilities of schoolteachers.

Similarly, effective working relationships with colleagues are not so straightforward as to be simply demonstrated. The complexities of social interactions in institutions like schools show that they include a nexus of personalities, expectations, values, emotions, differential distributions of power, different role definitions, subjective judgements in the allocation of duties, and so on. New teachers in this situation inevitably face the need to assess situations, make judgements about the kinds of conduct that are appropriate, engage with people in different ways for different purposes. They will probably develop sensitivities to what it means to be professional in criticisms of situations or colleagues, or perhaps in being assertive in the promotion of educational values. The specific micropolitics and social networks and relationships of collegial groups are matters to be inducted into and to research. More pertinently, perhaps, is the need for induction into the manner of perceiving, assessing, judging and responding to such situations wherever they might be encountered.

That is also true of the need to build relationships with parents and other agents, where expectations, the boundaries of responsibility, and interpersonal relationships are equally if not more complex than those among colleagues. That means being inducted into a range of other matters – from knowing names and information about pupils in a thorough way, to handling the presentation of that information and discussion about it, to gaining a sense of the lives and family circumstances of parents as they impinge on educational progress, appreciating community subcultures, and developing professional ways of handling personal responses to characteristics within these situations that might be confronting or challenging to a teacher's own personal dispositions. Once more, new teachers are faced with the need to become acquainted with people in particular circumstances, and rapidly develop working practices that will benefit pupils within them. This cannot just be demonstrated on command.

Working with other agencies has similar complexities and subtleties, from getting to know the range of agencies – speech therapists, careers advisors, health workers, social workers, education welfare officers, police liaison staff, and psychologists, for example – the individuals who represent those agencies, and the procedural steps for referring pupils to them or involving them in school activities and procedures. To benefit pupils in need of such services means becoming skilled in listening, observing, understanding procedures, knowing when to be decisive and when to be more deliberating, questioning decisions, and acting on information. So understanding the need to liaise with others might be readily achievable in a theoretical sense, but practising those liaisons is a matter to be developed. Judging whether the liaisons are effective is, however, only possible through the evidence of experience. It is that evidence that will show the quality of the actions of the new teacher, as well as that of the others involved in what is inevitably a collaborative endeavour. Once again this is an aspect of practice in which new teachers might be inducted into ways of handling evidence.

Curriculum policy and principles

Professional knowledge is also about knowledge of and engagement with the mandated or manifest curriculum. Like subject matter, the curriculum is mostly held in schools as a second-hand construction, made up of other people's components. In England the foundation principles of the curriculum – breadth, balance, relevance, and differentiation (DES 1985c) – which are intrinsically problematic and potentially radical as catalysts for debate, lie in a legislative archive, bureaucratically prescribed but educationally forgotten and undebated. They are displaced by concerns with syllabuses, or programmes of study, in the subjects of the National Curriculum and religous education. The struggle for curriculum debate and reconstruction was barely fought and certainly lost by the teaching profession in England between the mid-1960s and the late 1980s. The extent of the victory is such that the designations of what teachers need to know for entry to employment don't even include the description and meaning of those foundation principles. They are limited to parcels of pedagogical content knowledge, skills of transmission, and dedicated methods of assessing pupils' performance. Segments of the Career Entry Profile demonstrate the limited horizons to which new teachers are expected to aspire in terms of knowing matters related to the curriculum:

Secondary specialized subject(s)
- have a detailed knowledge and understanding of the National Curriculum programmes of study;
- be familiar with the relevant syllabuses and courses;
- understand the framework of qualifications.

Primary
- understand the purposes, scope, structure and balance of the National Curriculum;
- be aware of the breadth of content covered by the National Curriculum;
- have a detailed knowledge and understanding of the National Curriculum programmes of study.

(adapted from TTA 1997; 1999a)

Teachers' work here depends merely on knowing which elements of content and skills are included in the official curriculum, and where the content 'fits' within a programme of study or syllabus. For the unprofessional teacher this may appear to be simply a case of knowing the prescribed requirements of a syllabus plan. But if knowledge of curriculum principles and design is also part of the expertise of the professional educator, then induction requires more than that. Even where a legislated curriculum exists, it is educationally necessary to understand the basis on which it is designed, in order to judge its underlying principles, their implications for practice, the reasons for content being deemed relevant to the community, and the potential impact of the principles, content selection, and modes of assessment on the educational progress of students.

This requires more than knowing which bits of content follow which, or whether one subject relates to another, or how to translate subject matter or skills into 'targets'. A tendency to think within the National Curriculum in England seems to have developed that way. What I mean is recognizing that subject content is socially and politically specified and specifiable, and changeable, within legislation that sets out the curriculum principles of breadth, balance, relevance and differentiation – and having the capability to debate those principles and the social processes involved in defining curricula. What I also mean, as that implies, is that professional expertise would rehabilitate these ideas from being rarely mentioned in discussion, and almost forgotten. Their philosophical basis is a crucial element for curriculum design and school timetables, and for judging the success or otherwise of the curriculum experiment undertaken by a national government (Elliott 1998). They are the real core of curriculum which professional educators would research, together with their community partners.

By focusing attention on the need to improve subject knowledge and pedagogical skills, those (such as Reynolds 1998 and Woodhead 1998) who have perceptions of a deficient education service may be wrongly locating the source of their problem. Deficiencies lie at least equally in the social and economic structures within which schools were devised and continue to operate. They include the way the curriculum is conceived, designed and mandated, and its delivery fixed by convention, material and cultural conditions, and sometimes by the coercion or persuasion of teachers by their managers and employers to implement policy without question. These affect the ways in which educational knowledge is conceptualized and its transmission is conducted. They in turn are reflected in the expertise expected of teachers. So, in so far as the knowledge and capabilities of teachers are part of public education services, it is important to get the conceptualization of curriculum right, to see *its* complexities in the right way. As the work of Blyth (1965), Stenhouse (1975), Eisner (1979), Goodson (1983), Hargreaves (1985), Alexander (1995), and Bush and West-Burnham (1995), among others suggest, there is a range of ideological orientations at work in defining curricula.

Eisner (1979) for example alerts us to the fact that the metaphors and images of schooling and teaching that we acquire have profound consequences for our educational values and for our views of how schooling should occur. The dominant image, he asserts, has been the factory (school) and assembly line (teaching). Rationality has been conceived as scientific, cognition as linguistic. The dominant framework for viewing the curriculum has consequences for the practical operation of schools. Eisner describes five basic orientations to the curriculum, each harbouring an implicit conception of educational virtue, each serving both to legitimize certain educational practices and to negatively sanction others. Each also functions as an ideological centre around which political support can be gathered (Eisner 1979: 70). The orientations identified are listed below.

- The *cognitive process* orientation aligns with a belief that the curriculum provided and the teaching strategies used should foster the development of the students' cognitive processes. The major functions of school are to help children to learn how to learn and to provide them with opportunities to use and strengthen the variety of intellectual faculties they possess.
- *Academic rationalism* is associated with a subject-centred curriculum in which the major function of school is to foster intellectual growth of the student in those subject matters deemed worthy of study.
- The *personal relevance* orientation is consistent with a child-centred curriculum, recognizing the primacy of personal meaning and the importance of the individual's construction of knowledge. School programmes that make such meaning possible are developed in concert with students.

- The *social adaptation and social reconstruction* orientation relates closely to a utilitarian curriculum in which the aims and content of education are derived from an analysis of the society that the school is constructed to serve. The main function of school is as an institution designed to serve the interests of society, particularly economic interests.
- *Curriculum as technology* is an orientation that is reflected in the 'objectives' approach to curriculum, in which planning is conceived as a rational, technical operation designed and implemented to ensure and achieve prescribed outcomes.

As observers of curriculum, we might recognize that each orientation carries with it particular assumptions about the nature of human beings, of society, of knowledge and its acquisition, of teaching, of education. As advocates of particular frameworks for curriculum practice, we would need to recognize which assumptions are implied within our advocacy, and what the consequences of each would be for the quality of curriculum – and of life-experiences. Other analyses demonstrate that need for awareness very clearly. Bush and West-Burnham (1995) for instance offer the following typology of curriculum perspectives, based on a review of literature, which I have adapted for the present purpose:

- The *neo-classical* perspective is represented by 'forms of worthwhile knowledge' and initiation into curriculum content; the guardian of authoritative cultural tradition founded on reason and defended via absolute values.
- The *vocational* perspective emphasizes instrumental values where the needs of the individual are seen as employability through the acquisition of useful knowledge, contributing to the economic requirements of society.
- The *meritocratic* perspective embraces the competitive equality of opportunity; this can be traced to affiliations with nineteenth-century Liberalism. With notions of minimal state involvement, it accentuates the need for pupils to acquire personal autonomy within a framework of freedom.
- The *progressive* perspective is an interventionist as opposed to a minimalist state to encourage tolerance and understanding rather than competition and élitism. It aims at individual development, self-expression and cultural pluralism and places personal autonomy in the context of social and cultural harmony.
- The *critical* perspective advocates that teachers, schools and the education system need to adopt a critical stance, believing that schools can and should change society. It defines curriculum in terms of encouraging social change through educational action.
- The *religious* perspective propounds the development within the individual of a system of beliefs and values, deriving from historic positions and seminal texts. Secular knowledge is viewed in the context of spiritual values and beliefs.

- The *pragmatic* perspective cites Dewey as the intellectual originator. A pragmatic stance to curriculum planning is seen as one that serves both the individual child and the needs of social democracies.

(adapted from Bush and West-Burnham 1995)

These analyses of different curriculum approaches help to put the formal curricula of local, state and national bodies in perspective. They also help us to detect the elements of different ideological orientations within those local curricula, to see what kinds of knowledge are valued and promoted, and to what end. Across several of these perspectives the place of outcomes-based (sometimes called objectives-based, means–ends, target-oriented, or input–output) approaches to syllabus construction, teaching methods, and assessment processes can be found. These are the approaches that have been widely adopted across nations in recent times:

The NSW Government's endorsement of . . . Profiles and Outcomes affirmed the prime role of syllabuses to describe the curriculum content, knowledge, skills and understandings in each subject area [which] should be the basis for . . . the collection of data on student learning achievements.

(NSWDET 1998b: 5)

Stenhouse (1975) took the objectives approach to curriculum design and evaluation to task, presenting an alternative view that represents the curriculum as a basis for research and evaluation.

This [objectives] model starts from a definition of the performance or attainment which students should reach at the end of a course, and proceeds to attempt to design a course which will deliver that performance . . . I want to treat that model as problematic: that is, I want to leave open the question whether it is a good one.

(Stenhouse 1975: 4)

Stenhouse offered the possibility that a curriculum should be a proposal, with a set of principles and features, content and method, capable of being translated into practice. It would be open to critical scrutiny, and the means by which the experiment is made publicly available would be intrinsic to the curriculum. This involves making clear the bases for planning, and for its empirical study. So the principles on which content is selected, on which teaching strategies are devised, by which experience is sequenced, and by which students are to be assessed, constitute the curriculum proposal at the planning stage. Implementation carries similar requirements in terms of describing the principles for testing its feasibility, and for working in specific school contexts with particular pupils. Evaluation in this scheme of inquiry is also to be based on principles for studying the progress of students and of teachers. Perhaps most important in this formulation is that the justification of a particular curriculum proposal should be explicit and accessible, and thus subject to debate.

Crucially, the point of this approach is that it would – in Stenhouse's terms, should – apply in all curriculum situations. As he said: 'In fact, when we apply these criteria, it is clear that neither traditional nor innovatory curricula stand up well under close scrutiny. Education is not in practice very sophisticated or efficient' (Stenhouse 1975: 5). Of course that judgement and the implications for curriculum are applicable to teacher education and induction programmes as much as they are to schools:

> The adoption of an outcomes approach in the school sector is not isolated from broader trends in education and training. Demands to identify and articulate course outcomes, adopt strategies to measure outcomes and to report on levels of achievement, are now essential features of the education and training sector.
>
> (NSWDET 1998b: 12)

However, the inadequacies of this approach were reflected in a comparison between what were called traditional and transformational outcomes, and the description of the latter as involving students in activities in which they:

> research, analyse, critically appraise and effectively communicate information, to exercise appropriate interpersonal and task-oriented skills in work-teams, to make imaginative and critical leaps in applying their knowledge to new settings and to carry a complex and relatively vague project successfully through to completion.
>
> (Forster 1996 cited in NSWDET 1998b: 11)

How can we explain the fact that this element of new teachers' work – curriculum policy and practice – is the shoddiest in the profile of proficiencies in England? Are we to presume that it is intended that teachers should not engage in the kinds of professional practices implied in the alternative offered by Stenhouse and others? Are we to accept that the investment of professional capital in these qualities is undesirable? I think not. In which case there is every reason to ensure that induction in this aspect of professional knowledge takes a transformational – and professional – route. The alternative is that within 10 years of the new millennium one-half of the teaching force in England will have been inducted into the shoddiness of policy and curriculum practices, and their consequent forms of unprofessionalism.

Assessment policy and methods

Lortie (1975), Lawn (1987), Grace (1991), Hoyle and John (1997) and others review the way in which the struggles between interest groups for the control of education – for the power, that is, to redefine curriculum and teaching – have been lost by educators as a consequence of deprofessionalization (Hoyle and John 1997: 38–43). The enforcement of the particular views of teacher education and educational knowledge continues through inspection, and through the funding of teacher education programmes and particular kinds of educational research, especially school effectiveness studies. This range of influences seem collectively to promote the technical achievements of classroom instruction, and designate teaching as an inexact science (Reynolds 1998). It is a view of teaching that is now being reinforced through induction, and by the designation of standards for stereotypical career stages.

The need for caution in accepting such conceptions of the work of educators is graphically illustrated by Salter and Tapper (1981) who argue, convincingly I believe, that the main political function of education is the legitimation of social inequalities. Their thesis is based on a premise that social inequality and social injustices stem from access to knowledge as measured by exposure to and performance in formal education. They do not discount the social integration function of education, that is, education serving the purpose of initiation or socialization of the young in the knowledge and values of society. They argue, however, that in advanced industrial societies the role-differentiation function of schooling – setting or keeping people on the tracks for different occupational and income positions – will increasingly become more pronounced than the social integration function. Progress appears to have occurred towards that point in England and elsewhere with the advance of formal assessment and testing, and the publication of school league tables.

Salter and Tapper claim that by organizing knowledge into status hierarchies, and labelling it and allocating it in ways that are judged to be rational, education controls access to scarce knowledge resources that are essential for an individual's occupational and social progress. It also performs an ideological function by persuading people that the process is legitimate, so that they come to accept their status. That is more possible when knowledge is set in a common framework and assessment of its acquisition is made against a common standard, or norm-referenced – a process that has been reinforced dramatically in the latter part of the twentieth century. The way in which this process functions is often couched in terms of individual merit and personal choice associated with targets or criteria, though these are illusory. As Bruner (1977) pointed out, even meritocracy has the inevitable negative consequence of promoting only a few learners to success, committing most to relative failure, and too many of those to failure at an abject level. The implications are that curriculum managers and teachers are mediators in that process, which could be said to be diseducational for certain groups within society. The place of this function in the work of newly qualified teachers in England, coupled with the integrative function, are described thus:

Effective teachers will:
• assess how well learning objectives have been achieved;
• mark and monitor pupils' assigned classwork and homework, providing constructive oral and written feedback;
• assess and record each pupil's progress systematically . . . and use these records to:

1 check that pupils have understood and completed the work set;
2 monitor strengths and weaknesses;
3 inform planning;
4 check that pupils continue to make demonstrable progress;

• [be] familiar with the statutory assessment and reporting requirements;
• where applicable, understand and know how to implement the assessment requirements of current qualifications;
• recognize the level at which a pupil is achieving, and assess pupils consistently against attainment targets;
• understand and know how national, local, comparative and school data, including National Curriculum test data, can be used to set clear targets for pupils' achievement.

(adapted from TTA 1997; 1999a)

From within the taken-for-granted, social integration view of the target-oriented curriculum, these aspects of the instructional process are an apparently unproblematic and necessary part of successful teaching. They are unavoidable, and proficiency in assessment is both an obligation and desire of good teachers. However, the personal and social consequences of a system of pupil differentiation are also unavoidable. In any case, it is evident that some behaviours and characteristics of pupils – and of newly qualified teachers – are simply not capable of being translated into objective criteria against which evidence can be quantified. There is a century or more of literature that represents the struggles that have been fought over the territory and the techniques of assessment, most recently over that associated with the National Curriculum in England.

A few of the difficulties of the objectives or outcomes approach are seen as the difficulty in deciding the number and range of outcomes, describing appropriate development sequences in relation to the stages of schooling, and the difficulty of specifying the kind of evidence to be used in judging standards of achievement.

Assessment serves contradictory and even mutually self-defeating purposes in education. On the one hand it advances learning for the individual. On the other it defines personal identity and educational failure. The search for precision has its own logic and force – to maximize the efficiency of learning and to give the impression of ensuring fairness. This is part of the fundamentally contradictory nature of schooling (Hargreaves 1978) and a major source of conflict and dilemmas for teachers (Berlak and Berlak 1981). To know how to assess is defined as an important aspect of teaching knowledge, but to understand the educational consequences of one's assessment practices is equally important. And to know how to manage the contradictions inherent in school assessment, and how to handle the dilemmas they create, could prove to be educationally more beneficial still for new teachers.

So, the question is: should teachers understand the diseducational consequences of assessment, or merely become proficient in perpetuating such consequences? When defining teacher knowledge we need to be prepared to understand just what knowing means, to what depth we should extend the meaning, and with what sort of complexity we should treat each knowledge construct. As in this example, it means rather more than merely becoming learned or skilled according to some checklist of technical operations.

Evaluation of teaching and curriculum

There is a distinction between the recital of curriculum requirements to be performed as an instructor, and curriculum understanding developed by an educator. If new teachers regard themselves as educational professionals they should not be engaged solely in relaying other people's selections from prescribed knowledge, or filtering it for transmission to the young. They might in addition be seen as the guardians and potential re-creators of the curriculum processes that are highlighted by the pedagogic traditions of education. They could also be the guardians of research into how they can maximize the potential achievements of individuals, and the advancement of learning communities.

That may be an implicit aspiration of the profession, though it appears to need revitalization to become overt. It is certainly not, apparently, the mainstream view of the primary role of teachers, either within or without the profession, that they should become experts in understanding curriculum processes. It has a glimmer in the supposed, and even proposed, instrumental use of other people's research evidence:

> [effective teachers are] aware of, and know how to access, recent inspection evidence and classroom relevant research evidence on teaching pupils in their subject, and know how to use this to inform and improve their teaching.
>
> (TTA 1997; 1999a)

Once again, the reinforcement of the academic/instructional assumptions of education is compounded by the spectre of the Inspectorate, and the assertion that it has the capacity and skills to garner dependable evidence on the processes of education. Further, this definition of the successful teacher has him or her as the recipient of others' research evidence – but only within the limitations of subject pedagogy. The supposition itself – that research done by others in different locations will be found to be a sound basis for change in their classrooms – has the potential for maintaining the theory–practice divide that was so long ago recognized as an impediment to educational progress.

The widespread desire that teachers should be reflective about their practice, the urge to spread the use of action research, and arguments for collaborative evaluation to be adopted, each represent strategies for overcoming those suppositions, and for bridging the theory–practice divide. Those strategies have been in the educational forum for a very long time. Eisner (1979) for example pointed out that the predominant model on which educational research and practice are based is probably inappropriate for most of the problems and aims of teaching, learning and curriculum development. The canons of behavioural science, he argued, have too often determined what will be regarded as important in education. He also argued that the procedures and criteria used in evaluation have profound effects on the content and form of schooling. Operationalism and measurement have focused on student behaviour, while quality of experience has been seriously neglected. The alternative is to see how knowing and teaching require the construction of meaningful patterns from experience, which he regards as an artistic activity – somewhat in contrast to Reynold's (1998) search for a science of teaching based on the isolation of teacher behaviours and the measurement of their impact.

Eisner argued that practical judgement based on ineffable forms of understanding should not be seen as irrational, and that the complexities and significant qualities of educational life can be made vivid through a method used to describe, interpret and evaluate other cultural forms. That method – the art of disclosure – is an empirical undertaking based on observation and enquiry. The qualities described or rendered must be capable of being located in the subject of the criticism, and good criticism thus affects the perception of education and helps us to understand its qualities, through the ability to perceive what is subtle and complex.

This is an important perspective, and aspiration, for the education profession's inductees as well as its more seasoned incumbents to grasp. Not to do so constitutes grounds for the charge of being unprofessional. Failure to acquire such perceptiveness leaves the dilemmas of schooling and teaching largely in the private domain, the admission of educational damage unspoken, and the experience of guilt among teachers commonplace. Specifically this aspiration means asking what precise disposition should be taken to the requirement to understand the purposes of the curriculum and the ways pupils' learning is affected by the material, social and psychological conditions of their lives. It also involves observing the actions of professional educators who are agents in the creation of some aspects of those conditions.

Eisner's version is not the only way of approaching evaluation from a disposition that appreciates both the lack of sophistication and the potential consequences of schooling. From a theoretical perspective on education and curriculum, Bernstein (1971, 1977, 1990, 1996) provided a detailed model for understanding the power relations in different versions of both content and pedagogy. He provided a way of conceptualizing the relationships between knowledge and knowers, and those who define knowledge and access to it, which appears to be very pertinent in the light of the developments of the late 1990s in the school curriculum and the curriculum of teacher education. He used the term educational knowledge codes to refer to the underlying power principles that shape the curriculum – that is, that determine:

- what counts as valid knowledge;
- what counts as valid means of transmitting knowledge;
- what counts as valid evidence of the acquisition of knowledge by learners.

Bernstein devised the concept of classification to denote the strength of boundaries and the degree of boundary maintenance between different knowledge contents. Strong boundary maintenance is exemplified by strict academic subject divisions, or subdivisions that exist as strong specialisms within a subject. Weak boundary maintenance is illustrated by the existence of integrated subject knowledge, or cross-curriculum and interdisciplinary learning.

Bernstein's work on pedagogy included the notion of framing to denote the degree of control that persons have over the selection, organization and pacing of knowledge acquisition. Strong framing is full teacher control; weak framing is pupil control of what, when and how learning occurs. In one sense the reference to teacher control needs modifying, given legislated curriculum contents, in which teachers are managers, or intermediaries, in the delivery of knowledge selected by others. Control rests in many respects with politicians, government agencies, examination boards, school managers, and others to whom teachers are accountable in their employment. The principle is clear, however, and suggests that now we could use Bernstein's concepts to consider divisions between the formal and informal curricula of young persons. We could of course apply it to the formally designated and the informally experiential curricula of beginning teachers.

These alternative approaches to the development of understanding of curriculum processes can be accommodated by – in fact are the basis of – an action research approach to the development of professional practice. That will be explored in detail later. For the moment I hope it will be sufficient to note how much they contrast with the simplification of evaluation as it is used in inspection procedures and in the construction of league tables based on test results. That contrast between prescribed and simplistic elements of teaching knowledge and a healthy, sceptical attitude towards the nature and application of expertise should be evident within the extended core of professional knowledge that I have considered in this chapter. Yet as I pointed out earlier, that core and its components were used as a convenience. There is a need to go further – to open the debate about what surrounds the core and how to approach the classification of professional knowledge.

3 Professional characteristics and personal qualities

Closer to the core

Notions of teaching as technical instruction are by no means new. They were the basis of Church and state elementary education in England in the nineteenth century, and the grammar school tradition from much earlier than that. They were reflected in the Tylerian rational-planning model of the curriculum (Tyler 1949), taxonomies of learning objectives and performance behaviours (Bloom 1956), and of microteaching in teacher education (Brown 1975). These were topical in 1950s America and are still evident there and elsewhere. As I showed in the previous chapter, the objectives model on which this form of curriculum is based, and its assumptions about teaching and learning, have many critics but remain a dominant force (Stenhouse 1975; Eisner 1979; Elliott 1998).

More recent policy in teacher education in many countries amounts to a reinforcement of that view of teaching. The tendency to prescribe knowledge as information and competence as measurable skills is its major characteristic. Instruction tends towards the didactic, and assessment tends to be based on the observation of practical demonstration. Performance is used to measure the extent of learning, or of failure to learn. This kind of competency model of teacher training is being reinforced despite a range of alternative conceptions of teacher education curricula (Stenhouse 1975; Carr and Kemmis 1986; Tickle 1987a; Winter 1989; Elliott 1991; Zeichner and Tabachnick 1991). The dominant themes of the teaching standards movement add to that reinforcement.

The endemic nature and pandemic spread of this curriculum/teaching paradigm in schooling and teacher education systems has resulted in the diminution or exclusion of other possibilities. Its persistence in perpetuating limitations in learning for individuals, from control of content to built-in guarantees of failure, rather than maximizing the achievement of educational potential for every individual and for learning communities, are of greatest concern to its critics (Bruner 1977). The constraints it places on the educational imagining of better alternatives has been recognized by many commentators (Young 1971; Stenhouse 1975; Eisner 1979; Adler 1982; Boyer 1983; Goodlad 1984). A history of those constraints as they were reimposed in national policy for teacher education in England is written elsewhere (Tickle 1987a, 1994; Wilkin 1996). In an extreme form, the consequences of this conception of teaching are powerful, because of the way it defines teachers as mediators of prescribed knowledge and learners as the unquestioning receivers. As an ideological force, it presumes a continuously re-forming élite–proletarian relationship. The social identities of teachers and students respectively as pseudo-expert and novices in acquiring and demonstrating knowledge and skills are clear. These are identities and social relations into which individual teachers will be inducted so long as that view of education prevails.

It is evident from the previous chapter that the core elements of classroom instruction are for some people more or less all of what a teacher should know and be able to do. The common ground that those elements occupy across research, policy, and teacher education practice is clearly demarcated internationally. I also accord them some priority, though they should not be taken for granted as unproblematic. Nor should they be granted higher status than other aspects of professional knowledge, which I will discuss in this chapter. That, though, is how they are commonly seen. In England, Ofsted (the Office for Standards in Education) is so confident of the simple view of teaching that it claims to be able to grade experienced teachers on a performance scale against its own norms of excellence, in a range of identifiable and arguably observable instructional competencies (Tickle 1992a). In the late 1990s the Department for Education and Employment and teacher unions promised a fast-dismissal track and a rehabilitation–recovery (or subsequent dismissal) track for teachers deemed incompetent on these kinds of measures of their practice.

Similar procedures are applied to the induction period in a number of countries, under regulations introduced to ensure that provisional registration and employment as teachers are accompanied by stringent assessment of observed performance. So we have the imposition upon communities and the teaching profession of legislated curricula and assessment regimes for pupils, with parallel systems for teacher education and induction. This provides a potent mechanism for defining what counts, and what does not, as legitimate matter for the curriculum and for teacher induction and professional development. Teacher knowledge and the assessment of induction in this limited form have a number of disturbing possible consequences. For example, they could:

• leave teaching depersonalized, handling only prescribed knowledge and particular technical skills of instruction;

- sanitize the experience of teachers and pupils from extraschool participation in the subjects or occupational practices;
- remove the sense of individualism from, and the celebration of personhood by, both teachers and students;
- encourage self-blame for deficiencies in academic knowledge and in teaching quality, rather than identifying collective social responsibilities;
- reinforce the difficulties teachers have in exploring and exposing their own values and attitudes, or the predominant ones of their institutions and governing authorities;
- increase the split between the public and private lives and attitudes of teachers, which is sometimes the cause of serious dilemmas, and even stress.

(Beynon 1987; Sparkes 1994)

Little wonder, given the range of professional learning and activities associated with it that have already been considered, that the heart of both the public's and the profession's own concerns with quality in teaching is the question of what teachers should know and be able to do. The question of what it is that new teachers will be inducted into, however, can take us beyond the acquisition of subject knowledge and instructional know-how, as I have already suggested, into understanding, reflexivity, critique and professional action. Between these two realms, it can take us deeper still, towards a view of what it is to become a teacher, not just gaining proficiency in practice but embarking on a professional life. At least, in following the relationship between personal identity and social structures, and regarding new teachers as creatively negotiating those relationships, I believe it is necessary to consider these complementary facets of induction.

There is a great difference between induction into a workforce operating prescribed curriculum content and techniques of instruction, and induction into a process of professional self-development, reconstruction of institutionalized practices, and active participation in reform of the education service. While the former might involve surrender to imposed ideas and the obedient use of method, the latter draws upon values, personal qualities, and professional characteristics of very different kinds. If these are essential then we might presume that they deserve to be identified and developed. While accepting the importance of practical efficacy in the narrower sense of teaching, effectiveness can be imagined also in terms that promote other qualities.

This broader view offers a more encompassing notion of teaching that includes personally reflexive and critically active teachers, among whom there is a sense of selves as well as service. Yet we cannot presume that selves are preformed and stable. Evidence suggests that induction is a period of rapid change in the development of the teacher-self. However, with that sense of both self and service in place teachers can become capable of bringing about personal, educational and social change, reflexive in response to their own and others' policies and practices. Given that some of those practices might result in the continuation of social inequalities, discrimination, injustices, and narrow world views, the focus for the reconstruction of education needs to include both self-critical and socially-critical dispositions, and the development of strategies for change. To achieve those possibilities, to turn the dream of a reflexive, educative profession into a reality, means among other things being able to deal with – and live within – paradoxes, contradictions, dilemmas, argumentation. An effective education, in this sense, lies in that realm of teachers' extended professional understanding and the handling of values, as well as the acquisition and deployment of other professional characteristics and personal qualities.

There can be little doubt that the core technical elements of teaching are at the heart of professional expertise. For new teachers their acquisition provides the key to that heart (Tickle 1987a). It is a key to professional self-respect and to credibility among the many clients and sponsors in the educational enterprise. Such proficiency is a basic characteristic of being professional. In the past decade I have drawn extensively upon evidence from trainee and newly qualified teachers that shows how they themselves come to contain their identities largely within the technical aspects of teaching, closely allied to a command of pedagogical content knowledge. I have also shown how they use and develop what Zimpher and Howey (1987) call clinical competence, in the form of practical problem-solving, which involves reflective action for the improvement of instructional strategies to fit the context in which they work (Tickle 1992b, 1992c). From that evidence I showed how subject knowledge and pedagogical skills are crucial to self-identity in teaching, especially among student and beginning teachers, who seek to become what one teacher called a teacher with a capital T (Tickle 1992). The capital T Teacher is one who has mastered subject knowledge, instructional techniques and classroom management to the point where they come naturally and equate with the proficient practices of more experienced colleagues.

For the aspiring educator who might want to introduce changes, being an adequate technician is crucial to the enterprise. A teacher does not help the disadvantaged or educationally disabled by being undisciplined in their subject, where one is professed, or by being technically incompetent in the classroom, nor by failing to have a thorough appreciation of the specific characteristics of the teaching and curriculum context, or the capability to define educational aims. It is not surprising then that those core aspects of teaching feature large in research and policy on teacher knowledge and in the aspirations of new teachers. However, becoming an educator is conditional upon the adequate technician distinguishing the relationship between technical acts, educational aims, and educational consequences. It is in understanding each of those and the relationship between them that the teacher has the potential of becoming an educational reformer as well as being technically proficient. This involves different kinds of educational knowledge that can be brought to bear on curriculum situations, and on the understanding of one's self as a professional educator. An alternative perspective on quality in this respect is presented by Mahoney (1998) who sees teaching as:

- complex, involving sophisticated understanding of what promotes and inhibits learning;
- political, in its distribution of life chances to pupils;
- based in values which inform practical activity.

(adapted from Mahoney 1998: 2)

Another image of teaching, which incorporates the dominant technical portrayal but extends the range of characteristics, sees high quality as:

- working equitably, caringly, and respectfully with all students;
- developing and using curriculum knowledge, instruction, principles of learning, technology, and evaluation towards effective learning;
- adopting professional principles, ethics and legal responsibilities;
- a reflective activity in which learning from evidence is lifelong;
- collaborative and communal;
- contributory to social developments.

(adapted from OISE/UT, cited in NSWDET 1998a: 25)

There is another clear sense in which the content/curriculum/pedagogical skills view of teacher knowledge is insufficient. The expectations and responsibilities set out in contracts of service show counselling, policy making, community relations, leadership of colleagues, administration, and self-evaluation as just a few of the task-related aspects of professional educators' multiple roles. If one adds to that a sufficient knowledge of the psychology of children's learning, and understanding of pupils' special educational needs (for example), then the technical aspects of professional knowledge merge with the practical and theoretical in a considerable extension of the dimensions of proficiency.

To engage the issues of race, gender and social disadvantage as they affect educational activity and its goal of bringing about and maximizing educational progress for individuals and communities is also an expected part of the professional role. To analyse the values underlying matters of diversity, equity and social justice, one is moving further into the realms of educational contest and critical reflection about the purposes of schooling, and the way the curriculum is organized and transmitted. These are areas that have often been denigrated as theory by those who prefer the pragmatic approach to teaching. They are especially sensitive among some activists and their advisors on the right of the political spectrum, who also appear to prefer that teachers should avoid an emancipatory view of knowledge (Cox and Dyson 1969, 1970; Hillgate Group 1989). To others it seems self-evident that there is a need to examine the social values that underlie educational problems – indeed to explore and define those problems adequately in the first place in terms of broad social issues (Young 1971; Elliott 1998).

In that sense, the broader perspective means that the personal beliefs, dispositions, theories, and practices of professionals need to be taken into account in the process of educational problem-solving, since these are likely to constitute some of the problems. The underlying values and overt practices and qualities of teachers, induction tutors, and others who claim expert knowledge (such as inspectors) should be open to (self) scrutiny and debate. Change, if it is determined that they do not provide the best notion of efficacy or the most educative experiences for teachers and their students, is then a possibility at the level of both policy and practice. It also means that these broader aspects of professional life can be taken into account by new teachers as they interact with and learn from others, and that they will themselves be encouraged to display and, where necessary, develop these elements of working effectively as professionals.

According priority to those core elements of practice on which I focused in the previous chapter might be read as buying into traditional transmissive education. It would be convenient to give way to them on the grounds that not all matters can be attended to in the crowded experience of teacher induction. Even worse would be to give way because values and personal qualities are harder to define, develop, and assess. There are, though, real dangers of entrapment in the process of building flimsy structures without solid foundations. The classifications of professional knowledge by Carr and Kemmis, Eraut, Hoyle and John, Tickle, Zimpher and Howey, and others, all illustrate that the simple linear relationship of 'input–output' teaching is by no means the whole picture of the knowledge base into which professionals need to be inducted. The curriculum and organizational life that I represented in the previous chapter also make it clear that induction needs to be into the search for teaching quality which acknowledges that other kinds of professional and personal characteristics and capabilities matter greatly in the professional enterprise of becoming an effective educator.

It should be clear, then, that I do not seek to undermine or deny the importance of knowledge and competence in those areas of subject, curriculum, and instruction. On the contrary – I agree that conceptualizing the complexity of teachers' knowledge and work has these in centre place for some purposes. There is this stronger foundation, however, for the ways curriculum knowledge is selected, organized, transmitted, and assessed, to use Bernstein's (1971, 1977) terms, are value driven. They are also affected by complementary, personal and critical dimensions of being an educator. These qualities and capabilities are not, and cannot be, the characteristics of millions of animateurs, performing someone else's script. They need, rather, to be the foundation of educational reconstruction conducted by one of the largest graduate workforces in our communities, one of humanity's main investments in professional capital and educational energy.

So, as Chapter 2 suggested, the very content that is available to teachers as well as pupils, and how they respond to it; the way the curriculum is framed, and how they respond to that; and the ways classrooms are managed, and how they respond to those; are all dependent upon the quality of thinking, the intensity of that creativity, and the qualities of professionalism that teachers develop and deploy. If that is so, the experience of learning to teach must include a process of induction into the kinds of thinking, creativity, and professional characteristics involved. Unless, of course, teachers are to be unprofessional, unthinking, and uncreative – and hence become a missed investment opportunity.

If the nature of the curriculum and its impact on pupils and teachers are suitable subjects for healthy dissent and the potential rehabilitation of the educational endeavour, then the subjugation of values is undesirable. Their explicit inclusion and the place of debate in the educational arena, with the raising of their status, and recognition that they are intrinsic to education, would add quality to the induction of new entrants. The power to argue about the nature of education, curriculum, and pedagogy rests in the professional will to do so and the quality of understanding of these matters. That quality needs to be based in evidence of professional practices and their consequences, and adequate conceptualization and articulation of educational issues.

That premise suggests that professional knowledge must include an understanding of the values, beliefs and attitudes that are brought to bear in educational argument, policies and practices. In that sense, what was once attacked from both within and outside the profession as educational theory can be recast as a prerequisite – professional practical theorizing. It is the foundation, the complementary, not just the supplementary, adjunct to subject knowledge, curriculum knowledge, and instructional skills.

In an unprofessional surrender, success for entry into teaching might be judged by levels of individual knowledge and skill in those instructional domains considered in the previous chapter. Performance in that regime is defined, observed and recorded by managers and supervisors, or by teachers themselves working under such supervision – the technically competent. However, quite what teachers' powers of personal agency should be in relation to educational change, and how they should exercise those powers as professionals, needs to remain an expansive rather than a closed question. The aspiration to keep the specification of teaching quality more open does survive in some places. According to the New South Wales Department of Education (1998a) for example, definitions of teaching must be framed as:

- broad areas of knowledge, skills, understanding and professional values;
- interrelated and written in prose – not taxonomized as checklists.

However, this kind of language will not in itself accomplish the inclusiveness of understanding, values, professional characteristics and personal qualities as part of induction. These appear to be more difficult to define and convey than knowledge and skills framed in the specification of observable performances. Values, professional characteristics and personal qualities are also more difficult to handle, even at an interpersonal level, precisely because they involve different views of what education might be about and how it might be managed. What is more, new teachers can find professional values difficult to analyse in the work of other teachers because:

- it may not seem appropriate to question experienced colleagues;
- the profession works in customary, taken-for-granted practices;
- new teachers are not necessarily equipped with values-based questions and don't necessarily know what to look for in the underlying assumptions of practice.

Professional status

There are also strong messages in competence-based teacher training about the power relations between policy makers, curriculum planners, academics, experienced teachers, and NQTs. Views of what knowledge is defined by whom as legitimate or worthy, and who holds the key roles in providing access to it, and assessing it, are central in these messages. This is partly about the nature of professional knowledge, but is also about the presumed status of new teachers in relation to more seasoned colleagues. The status hierarchy implied in these relationships is especially acute within teacher induction, in which experience is deemed to reign over novicehood, and supervisory experts sit in judgement on new practitioners. Also, the emphasis tends to be on individual responsibility for learning and performance, in which technical skills or problem-solving are the focus. Representations of collaborative, participatory and collective educational endeavours are not easy to find where these assumptions are strong. The hierarchical and individualistic construct is reinforced in cumulative models of expertise such as that described by Dreyfus and Dreyfus (1986), who hold that professional knowledge and development, and the location of new entrants to the professions, occurs in stages of:

- novice;
- advanced beginner;
- competent;
- proficient;
- expert.

In policy and practice in England the hierarchy is extended in the march of national professional standards and qualifications, from recommendation for qualified teacher status (QTS), provisional teacher registration, induction standards and credits, confirmed registration, advanced skills teachers, national professional standards – subject leaders, and national professional qualification – headteachers. Ingvarson (1998) also models a career trajectory, from an Australian/international perspective on teaching, with the characterization of stages as:

- provisional registration/QTS;
- entry/survival;
- confirmed registration/QTS;
- stabilization;

- master teacher;
- experimentation;
- leading teacher;
- serenity.

This list, like other attempts to formulate distinctions between beginning and advanced standing in the acquisition and demonstration of professional capabilities can be interpreted too simplistically. Huberman (1993) distinguished phases and stages in the lives and careers of teachers, pointing out that while the so-called exploration and stabilization periods at the beginning of a career could lead to rewards and responsibilities incrementally for some, for others these might take a long time, be temporary phases, or never happen. 'For some this process may appear to be linear, but for others there are stages, regressions, dead-ends and unpredictable changes of direction sparked by new realizations – in short, discontinuities' (Huberman 1993: 4). Evidence of the experiences of established teachers facing new influences and interventions in their work, or in contexts of rapid change, suggests that any notion of hierarchy might sometimes be turned on its head (Tickle 1994). It also suggests that a focus on experience needs to be complemented by attention to the qualities that new teachers can bring to their schools. These hierarchical career stages stereotype and threaten the complexities of professional characteristics, learning, and practice, and downgrade the potential contributions that newly qualified educators might make. They presume that teacher educators and more experienced teachers are somehow superior to those deemed to be novices. Heretical it may be, but I want to raise that assumption as a problematic one and argue that it may be so only in some respects. It may become especially dubious when we consider the place of understanding and values and the role of personal qualities and professional characteristics in the process of educating.

The world of practice involves qualities which, for example, are brought to bear as capability in analysing classroom and school situations. Analysis is matched by a capacity to synthesize information and orchestrate judgements based on the synthesis, in order to effect the most prudent course of action, or to engage in intelligent practice (Stenhouse 1975). Such qualities are not the sole province of experienced teachers. Nor are encounters with new knowledge the sole province of beginners, particularly in periods of change brought about by external events, or in self-motivated searches for new approaches to education. Huberman offers a view of career entry as a combination of survival and discovery, the former involving adjustments to the complex demands of teaching, the latter enthusiastically celebrating participation as a professional. Even within this time, individuals experience fluctuations, where indifference ameliorates both survival and exploration, or frustration tempers idealism, and thankless tasks are shared equally with more experienced colleagues.

The difficulty of plotting generalizable career trajectories is consistently identified in this work. In a review of literature Huberman (1993) notes others' views of a stabilization phase following career entry, where consolidation of practice is detected. Then experimentation, diversification and activism are said to follow. Reassessment of role and crisis in careers is followed for some by changed states of mind, and establishment in the profession. A stage of serenity might be matched by distancing, conservatism accompanied by complaining, disengagement followed by withdrawal. Huberman's project was to test these kinds of schemata in a longitudinal and complex study. He and his colleagues considered factors such as commitment, the place of new challenges, worries, harmony, self-doubt, dissonance, disenchantment, self-realization, liberation, wisdom, dwindling enthusiasm, stagnation, isolation, bitterness, renewal, immobility, tension, fatigue, pedagogical mastery, and more. The manifestation of these characteristics is portrayed among subgroups of teachers and individuals in complicated configurations. However, this parade of responses to the experiences of teaching indicates that no matter how much attention is given to technical mastery, we cannot ignore professional characteristics and personal qualities. Nor can we defer thinking about the implications of this kind of taxonomy for new teachers' experiences of joining their longer-serving colleagues. So I would like to hold in suspension the supposed relative statuses of new and experienced teachers, their knowledge, characteristics, and qualities.

Understanding and values

Redefining the teacher as professional educator, and the newly qualified teacher as someone engaged in the construction of their own knowledge and experience, as well as the reconstruction of education, looks wildly optimistic in the face of Huberman's work. That study reinforces the question of what, or who, the educator should be as well as what he or she should be able to do. So I am not just thinking about knowledge and knowing (epistemology) but about identity and being (ontology) (Sanger and Tickle 1987; Nias 1989; Holly and MacLure 1990; MacLure 1993). This clearly involves adopting an even more complex view of induction into educational knowledge, practice and professional life. For example, a conception of professional knowledge and educational life cannot be divorced from a critical appreciation of the curriculum and the social purposes of schooling. The social compact involved in becoming a teacher means that new teachers act intentionally in becoming a part of those purposes. Schooling is not simply a benign agency, though that may be the way education is portrayed, what we are supposed to believe. Its purposes are directly connected to the interests of social groups who define the nature of education and the way it is conducted. Among these groups there are competing claims as to what kind of curriculum experiences are appropriate for the citizens of a national and international community. Those claims relate to the images that people hold of their communities and their desired futures, and presume that education plays a part in the achievement of social goals and dreams. So, for instance, modern communities can be seen to exist within a global economy and communications network. Among its many characteristics the global network can be seen as exploitatively capitalist, fiercely economically competitive, environmentally destructive, fearful of social freedoms and unrest, and determined to exploit resources and information management to the advantage of privileged groups. Communities can be seen as socially intolerant and unjust, and aggressively militaristic. The global environment is filled with contradictions, and power can be seen to be used to ensure that societies are protective and selective in controlling access to knowledge.

In these circumstances it is not difficult to imagine why national governments or more local education authorities might reach out for traditional and unimaginative views of curriculum knowledge and of teaching – those that offer some sense of anchor to the intellectual and productive capital on which such societies and economies were built. Curricula in that unimaginative view, and teachers as functionaries of them, are seen to contribute a stabilizing form of maintenance to the status quo. They engage in the initiation of the young into the sacred conventions of knowledge and dispositions that underpin past histories. The idea that a teacher is a social instrument in the processes of knowledge mediation and allocation of life choices and chances is not, however, the one conveyed in recruitment campaigns or interviews for entry into teaching. It is hidden from view.

Nor is the usual image of the teacher one of a citizen committed to educational leadership and the political actions that that might involve. Yet education authorities could also appeal to innovation and debate about the kind of learning opportunities which communities jointly and concurrently construct and inhabit. However, regeneration is often subversive of former values; developments more than likely involve conflicting interests of different social groups; and new knowledge and its acquisition frequently confronts the perceptual, conceptual, ethical positions and views on authority of previous generations. So we might look to new teachers for the means of accommodating new ideas and transmitting emergent knowledge in the processes of economic and cultural reforms. They might be the leading edge in what has been labelled the information society of the future. However, the regeneration of intellectual and cultural capital needed for an imagined but unpredictable future mainly falls to those few at the forefront of research and development in the academies, industry, social agencies, politics, media and the arts, and so forth. It is an élite participation in which the status hierarchies and differentiated distribution of knowledge is perpetuated, to the advantage of some interests and the exploitation and exclusion of others.

In societies with formal school systems the mediation of both the traditional realms of knowledge and unequal distribution of opportunities, and the negotiation of access to that regeneration of knowledge and of social life, falls to the community's professional educators. Knowledge, its applications, and its distribution through the schooling and higher education system are not value-free; thus nor is the role or even the identity of professional educators, and their place in these knowledge communities, value-free. The very concept of teacher is itself socially defined, subject to change, and located within the social hierarchy as an instrument of cultural management. Our perceptions of the concept, location, and instrumental purposes of teaching affect our appreciation of the nature and purpose of the socialization or induction of new entrants to the profession. In one simple, face-value, sense induction entails becoming the mediator in that tense position between curriculum traditions and knowledge futures. It also means learning to live in the tension between the re-creation of élites and allocation of proletarian statuses on the one hand, and the desire to maximize achievement for all pupils.

These questions about the nature and purpose of schooling, the construction of curricula, and the role of teachers are the kinds of real issues that underlie the questions about professional knowledge and induction. They are issues that smoulder away largely unfanned, maybe showing an occasional wafting of the embers through serious commentary by the likes of Boyer (1983), Goodlad (1984, 1994) and the National Commission on Education (1993), or through glances further back to the work of authors like Dewey (1912), Holt (1964, 1967) and Freire (1972). They are moderately represented in additional areas of mastery in those profiles of teacher knowledge across the world, summarized, for example, as expectations to ensure that all effective teachers:

- are committed to their students and their holistic development;
- are reflective practitioners and embody the qualities of the educated person and exemplary citizen;
- are leaders of learning communities.

(adapted from NSWDET 1998a)

These expectations clearly incite the mind to ask about the nature of the educated person and exemplary citizen, to imagine where leadership in learning communities will lead. Similar incitements exist within the following professional qualities. Good teachers should:

- set a good example to the pupils they teach through their presentation and their personal and professional conduct;
- be committed to ensuring that every pupil is given the opportunity to achieve their potential and meet the high expectations set for them;
- understand the need to take responsibility for their own professional development and to keep up to date with research and developments in pedagogy and in the subjects they teach.

(adapted from TTA 1997; 1998c; 1999a)

These sorts of challenges mean becoming inducted into educational values and curriculum issues, and not just acquiring knowledge of syllabuses. Take, for instance, the foundation principles of the curriculum in England. Relevance as a curriculum principle is inherently disruptive to the idea of prescribing a common curriculum. So is differentiation. This apparent contradiction may be why these principles lie dormant in England's education policy, under the weight of common, prescribed subject content and assessment procedures in the National Curriculum and religious education. Those concepts are central issues for disaffected youth, who recognize the irrelevance of much of that which is packaged and transmitted in schools, and whose judgement of relevance and exercise of choice over what they study is restricted to their acceptance, compliance, or rejection of the formal curriculum.

There is some evidence that teachers also experience curriculum disaffection, where the meaning of and engagement with subject knowledge recedes along bureaucratic corridors, away from their energies and educational commitments. Bruner (1977) said that a curriculum is first and foremost for teachers, that if it cannot excite teachers it has little hope of enthusing their students. Herein lies a central and inherent problem of the subject-based curriculum – the reconciling of personal and communal interests, of traditional knowledge and the emergence of new perspectives, of local community cultures and participation in a more global world. These tensions, however, are both philosophically and organizationally extraordinarily difficult to cope with, either for each teacher as educator, or for schools as educational institutions. While subject knowledge is dislocated (or should we see it as complemented?) in these ways, teachers are faced with increasingly prescriptive projects and policing procedures to ensure they maintain elements of elementary, vocational and the academic curriculum traditions.

The tensions are intense. For instance, what is deemed personally relevant and of educational interest might be more idiosyncratic than communally valuable. Equally, short-term relevance might displace longer-term interests and benefits for both individuals and communities. Perhaps the very idea of 'relevance' is an illusion based on the psychology of motivation. Perhaps it is a device to persuade us that we should transmit knowledge that is utilitarian and economically productive, rather than merely intrinsically interesting: a mask of education over a face of training. Or, in cases like the 1944 Education Act in Britain, it could be the basis of a system of socially divisive schooling masquerading as education.

Enshrined in that Act was the creation of a tripartite organization of secondary grammar, technical, and modern schools, for pupils of supposedly different aptitudes and occupational futures. Deemed to have parity of esteem (equal status) no one was fooled by their social divisiveness, and some were (and still are) in favour of it. In Hong Kong, even after the 1997 transfer of sovereignty, secondary schools have designations in five bands of student ability, defined by tests. Some band one and two schools are designated to use English language as the medium of instruction, the rest are required to use Chinese. Status, life choices, and chances, are organizationally constructed and teachers operate the policies. These kinds of structural arrangements inevitably create tensions for teachers whose values differ from those underlying such arrangements. At the level of classroom organization more local tensions arise, from differences in perspective about how pedagogy itself should be managed.

Such broader issues and the debates they create are for elsewhere, and another time, but it seems clear that being inducted into teaching is being asked to engage with such tensions. Indeed it may be that some of those career experiences identified by Huberman (1993) stem from a clash of values, or the success in pursuing some of them in practice. Engaging the tension can be done by default, left to chance, or it can be an explicit part of professional development programmes.

Some other paradoxes faced by education authorities, and by implication being handled by educators, were illuminated by Delors (1996). They suggest that it will be teachers in the new millennium, in the schools across the global network, who will need to be inducted into handling those paradoxes, which are said to include tensions between:

- global–local perceptions of community, knowledge, and values;
- universal values–individual, personal identities;
- maintaining traditions–encompassing modernity;
- imagining/maintaining long-term strategies–short-term fixes;
- competitiveness for credentials–maximizing individual potential;
- expansion of knowledge–(in)capacity to assimilate it all;
- spiritual and moral aspirations–material goals.

(adapted from Delors 1996)

A more extended list of contenders for the title of dilemmas of teaching was created by Berlak and Berlak (1981) as a result of classroom observations and discussions with primary school teachers in England. Hargreaves (1985) also identified a number of fundamentally contradictory goals that teachers face and have the task of trying to reconcile, including the conditions of change that confront professionals in both social and personal terms.

The point emerging from these analyses is that there are a range of issues here, topics worthy of debate, about who defines what curriculum is educationally worthwhile and accessible, and what the role – and even the life – of the educator should encompass. These debates extend to the purposes of schooling in general, but also lie at the heart of questions about what it is that beginning teachers are to be inducted into. Paradoxes, dilemmas, tensions, change – all suggest that induction needs to be into a culture capable of handling these external and intrinsic conditions in educational and curriculum environments. That is very different from the search for certain knowledge and proof of its mastery, and it requires different psychological conditions and professional orientations among new teachers and their support tutors. Among a group of new teachers with whom I worked, every one talked of matters that were dear to their hearts as well as their minds:

- Richard's problems were about being constrained in implementing what he believed to be good educational practices.
- Mike had a firm commitment to a set of ideas that he proposed to take to another school if he could not implement them in his present location.

- Anna eventually did just that, but she also had to formulate her ideas and aims for the low achievers in mathematics, as well as her teaching strategies, because encountering such pupils was a completely new experience for her.
- Richard questioned his beliefs as a result of comments from colleagues and examples of their 'beliefs in action' as he put it.
- Diane had difficulty formulating and articulating any aims for her reception class: a problem exacerbated by a breakdown in relationships with the headteacher, so that the very idea of remaining a teacher deserted her.
- Lesley seemed to be constantly seeking practical strategies to help her realize her aims of equality of provision for pupils within an activity-led, enquiry-orientated classroom, demonstrating a determination to maximize achievement for every pupil.

(adapted from Tickle 1994: 46–103)

However, we should be aware that one of the features of newly qualified teachers' work is a lack of opportunity to make explicit their educational aims and values (Tickle 1992a, 1994). Reviewing and developing these kinds of personal and professional traits is a difficult area in their work. Nor are the aims and values of colleagues, or the curriculum policies of their schools, the starting points for deciding what to do or how to do it, for judging how it was done, or for dialogue about the education on offer to pupils. In some cases the desire to explicate, explore and expand these aspects of being an educator is frustrated by circumstance or by school cultures. In others, subject content, teaching skills, the invention of activities for pupils, or ideas about 'what works' form the images and metaphors of decision making and of evaluation. Either consciously or unwittingly new teachers get easily trapped in particular conceptions of the curriculum, and of the knowledge needed to put it into effect. The process of becoming unreflective, and settling into habitual actions in response to the intensity of work, might be judged as only reasonable. Routinization and a tendency to be conservative are part of the coping with the complexity of professional life and its gamut of responsibilities (Lo 1999).

It is also a feature of the professional culture of teaching, in which tacit, craft knowledge is the main currency (Elbaz 1983; Brown and McIntyre 1986; Clandinin 1986; Tickle 1992b). That may also result from the intensity of circumstances, and the demands of sometimes overwhelming social interactions. There is a certain irony here, in that many teachers articulate discomfort with the requirements of curriculum content, allocations of subject time, prescribed teaching methods, and formal modes of assessment. When circumstances deny personal values in the curriculum and in the conduct of teaching there is the possibility of reaction from compliance to disaffection (Butt *et al.* 1990). However, in a climate of change and evident need for educational reconstruction we might expect proaction in the demonstration of the values, aims and principles of the profession. So, beyond efficacy as it is commonly and simply defined, there is a need for, and sometimes a desire among, teachers to develop and sustain a broader sense of educational knowledge that includes aims and values, and critical awareness of pedagogical practices.

Professional characteristics

These wider traits of professional life reach even beyond the core of professional know-how and capacity for understanding and debate, into aspects of teaching that have been noticeably side-stepped in policy documents and in teacher education. From 1984 the Council for the Accreditation of Teacher Education (CATE) required applicants for initial training in England to be assessed to ensure they had the 'right' personal qualities before acceptance. The nature and characteristics of personal qualities were undefined, nor were they seen as matters worthy of development within teacher education programmes (Tickle 1991, 1994, 1999). Somehow it was presumed that new teachers come readily equipped with whatever these characteristics are. Institutions were commanded to assess applicants to confirm the existence of these qualities prior to entry into pre-service courses. Furthermore, when the Teacher Training Agency took over from CATE in the mid-1990s personal and professional qualities were largely excluded from the designation of courses, criteria for inspection, and profiling of individuals' teaching knowledge and competence. This is particularly surprising because at the extremes of this issue, while surveillance over instructional quality has grown, so has concern with issues of child protection and child care. A criterion of 'fit to teach', that is, suitable to work with children, is widespread, and rightly so. As Zehm (1999: 44) puts it:

> Teacher educators do need authority to screen prospective teachers they know are unfit from the teacher ranks. It is their moral responsibility to make decisions based on solid evidence about who gets into and out of teacher education programmes.

The gatekeeping function is a collective duty at the induction stage, too. Zehm contentiously goes so far as to say that potential or beginning teachers who themselves were raised in dysfunctional families might join the profession for the 'wrong reasons', and bring undesirable characteristics into their work. While the extremes are covered by legislative frameworks, other aspects remain undefined and sidelined, as noted by the Parliamentary Select Committee on Education in England in its 1997 report:

> While we agree with the TTA on the crucial importance of would-be teachers having a sound knowledge base in their subject, we also recognize the need for teachers to have appropriate personal qualities.
> (Parliamentary Select Committee 1997: para. 31)

The TTA appears to agree – professionalism is said to reside in appreciation of 'the creativity, commitment, energy and enthusiasm which teaching demands' (TTA 1997: 2). However, these too are standards to be met, and have a minor place. They are aspects of professional development that need opening up, in more than one sense. Since educating is an interpersonal and interactional activity, and its conduct and consequences are both personal and political, that would seem to be unavoidable. Yet there does appear to be an avoidance culture operating in the profession, which leaves us largely unable or unwilling to confront the personal and political dimensions of induction into education.

Their inclusion in pre-service development and career entry provision might have been sidestepped because they are an especially difficult area of induction to deal with, both conceptually and practically. Perhaps they have remained implicit and in some senses elusive because they involve attitudes and dispositions, and even factors of personality. Where they have maintained a profile within teacher education or in teacher assessment practices, it appears to be because teacher educators and teachers recognize their importance. Even in their practices, however, the identification, and more crucially the development, of this realm of professional knowing and professional being remain problematic, with a range of consequences. Zehm (1999: 49) pointed to one of these consequences in the American context, in his report that about 20 per cent of beginning teachers leave the teaching profession after their first two years of teaching. He argues passionately for positive measures to be adopted at the earliest possible stage of teacher induction:

> We are convinced, however, that this loss of young, idealistic teachers will continue until teacher educators begin to reeducate themselves regarding the importance of focusing on the human dimensions of teaching and learning and find time, places, and resources to focus on a self-development perspective for preservice teachers.
>
> (Zehm 1999: 49)

If nothing is done in pre-service programmes, then it is likely to be an acute issue during the induction year when the intensity of both intrapersonal and interpersonal dimensions of teaching are met by new entrants. The avoidance of these matters may seem even more surprising, because common sense suggests that who a teacher is makes a difference to the educational experiences of students. It is also the 'who' that denies the possibility of standardization and ensures the rich texture of educational encounters. Surprising or not, at an international conference on professionalism in teaching in 1999 an appeal was made to pinpoint research in this area because it had proven hard to locate in the search for standards (Marrin 1999). Zehm (1999: 42–3) confirms that difficulty, with a demonstration of how the dominant interest in instructional techniques in the USA since the late nineteenth century has only occasionally been punctuated by an interest in personal qualities.

So what are the traits that are desirable in these terms? At the heart of this are the questions of what it means to be a professional educator, and what the idea of developing as a teacher could and should entail beyond those core instructional competences. It is complex terrain – theoretically and in the experience of individuals becoming professionals. It has been acknowledged at least since the mid-nineteenth century that only the 'right kinds' of teachers should be selected for entry into the profession – another measure of standardization and in some senses a contradiction to the aspiration for a rich texture of personnel in the profession. In those early days diligence and sobriety were identified as desirable traits.

Lo (1999: 5) points out that in China a code of practice requires teachers to possess

> strong moral and political rectitude, loyalty to the course of social reconstruction, fairness and patience towards their students, and respect for the work and for the parents of their students.

Tsui (1999) reported that in Hong Kong after the Tiananmen Square protests in Beijing in 1989 the code of practice for teachers required them to respect the civil rights of students. These examples illustrate how professional characteristics and personal qualities, where they can be detected in policy, or in conventions of professional values or community expectations, are likely to be diverse, context specific, and changeable. That they are culturally, politically, communally, or personally defined means that they are likely to be contestable and contested, rather than simply testable and tested. So educational discourse is invoked in a search for understanding and agreement about what it is that teachers should be in their ideal type.

In educational research the study of these aspects of professional knowledge and practice has its own landmarks, from a range of perspectives in sociology, social psychology, teacher-thinking, life-histories, teacher education, fiction, and autobiographical literature. Confronting the topic here is a celebration of its importance, especially for the development of effective educational practice. My view is based on a simple hypothesis – that these more problematic professional characteristics and personal qualities of teachers have a transformative power in the education of teachers themselves and of their pupils, that they are central to the educative process and to the development of the education service in our communities, and that they are therefore worthy of attention, clarification, and potential development during induction in ways they have not enjoyed sufficiently so far.

The work of Clandinin (1986), Nias (1989), Huberman (1993), and others include aspects of what I have come to call personhood, as part of teacherhood. In the academic educational community there has been a veritable growth industry in this field of interest (Holly and MacLure 1990; Lipka and Brinthaupt 1999b), which should remind us, in the search for complementarity between theory and teacher education practice, to ask what 'the induction project' can gain from such work. The growth in interest in these dimensions of induction and of teaching more widely is for good reason. What we assume about teacher knowledge is likely to influence what we do to develop it and determine the kinds of teachers new entrants become.

In the practice of teacher education, there are also questions of interest in children's learning, dedication to teaching, and commitment to the service of education and the community. Enthusiasm for life, and involvement in a range of activities other than a curriculum subject, or a good sense of humour, are telltale signs that candidates for becoming a teacher may be expected to display. Advertisements for posts in schools invite applicants who are industrious, willing to take initiative, resilient, able to work with others, and so forth. In practice the implicit expectations and obligations that teachers meet, and that they have of each other, extend the range of those sorts of characteristics. In often subtle ways, but also sometimes explicitly, they encompass attitudes, values and beliefs – whether a person is likely to fit into the ethos of a school, whether they share particular religious or sectarian affiliations, the way an individual is 'persuaded by' particular methods of teaching, and such like.

Lortie (1975) in his classic work *Schoolteacher*, said that personal dispositions stand 'at the core' of being a teacher. More recently the importance of this broader view of professional knowledge, at least for my present project, was summed up by Swanson (1989: 4) when he wrote:

The newer studies of 'emotion' are broader than that word suggests. They have also to do with values and attitudes, motives and motivation. More generally they concern the meaning of social relations for people's fulfillment as persons or selves; a renewed interest in affective connections between personal functioning and social structure.

Nias (1989) too wrote about teaching as an activity that is personal, with strong investments of self. She identified commitment to, and by implication effectiveness in, the job as being writ through with:

• perceptions;
• attitudes;
• hopes;
• interests;
• intellects;
• aims;
• knowledge;
• qualities;
• ambitions;
• loves;
• values;
• experience;
• enthusiasms;
• politics;
• hates;
• beliefs;
• wisdoms;
• dreams.

The premise is that the satisfactory induction of new teachers into the profession, and their professional development, has this additional foundational dimension which at best is currently based on chance – which in turn means that a central part of the educative process for pupils is also deeply chancy. Furthermore, it means that the future development of education is itself chancy – and probably a chance missed. Responsibility for this does not rest solely on the shoulders of inductees. On the contrary, it is for the education service, and the professionals within it, to imagine the investments they need to make in shaping the experiences of inductees towards developing the potential of these qualities and capabilities.

These broader aspects of quality are part of what teachers depend upon in their professional lives, but evidence suggests that they are foundations of education that are not always very dependable – or why would we have that language of survival, of coping, of trauma, stress and industrial ill-health? Yet, if an induction curriculum that includes the development of professional characteristics and personal qualities is both necessary and achievable, we have first to explore its foundation in professional culture and in the standards agenda. We need to raise awareness, and then I trust, to reconceptualize induction in a constructive light in this direction. Only then might it be possible to find ways to make these characteristics and qualities more dependable, to develop and enhance their trustworthiness, with and on behalf of individual new teachers, and with and on behalf of the communities they serve. This is attempted here in an exploratory rather than a conclusive way, laying no claims to answer a universal, collective educational problem, but opening it up to stimulate the search for a range of possible solutions. New teachers will have a major contribution to make in that quest.

If the emotions also have a claim on centre stage, Swanson (1989) reminded us that they share that place with other aspects of character and attitude. What I have in mind are qualities such as

- empathy;
- compassion;
- the ability to manage frustration and impatience;
- understanding and celebration of cultural variations;
- tolerance of sexual orientations;
- love;
- the capacity to assess social situations;
- a mastery of reflective thinking;
- flexibility in the application of teaching techniques;
- tolerance of ambiguity and of conflicting interests and expectations;
- sensitivity to the needs of others;
- assertiveness in the face of abuse;
- an ability to share others' grief, sorrow, pleasure or delight;
- the capacity to manage guilt, anger, and contempt;
- ambition.

This list is not complete. It is offered to open the gate of consideration, in a concrete and illustrative way, to the affective realms of professional practice which have a bearing on the educative experiences of the teacher-self and student-self, and on the development of individual identities. For Sockett (1993) the elements of professionalism are constituted by 'virtues'. Centrally, these virtues include:

- honesty;
- care;
- fairness;
- patience;
- respect for others;
- empathy;
- courage;
- determination;
- practical wisdom.

Together, the professional virtues are said to constitute character, to which should be added a commitment to change and continuous improvement, but which incorporates the holding of substantial knowledge and understanding of the world (presumably via subject disciplines) and good standing in pedagogical expertise. Once again we see the inextricable combination of academic subject knowledge and practical know-how, with dispositions that foster self-confrontation (presumably towards achieving an ultimate self-fulfillment in the virtues). Various extensions to that list of virtues might be argued, as suggested by a view of the effective teacher that I discovered recently on a chart lying around in my department. It included the additional qualities of:

- flexibility;
- alertness;
- enthusiasm;
- sympathy;
- being inspirational;
- diplomatic;
- humorous;
- sincerity;
- sensitivity;
- consistency;
- being a 'listener';
- with-it-ness.

An antipodean version of such lists includes:

- trustworthiness;
- honesty;
- reliability;
- sensitivity;

- compassion;
- respect for others;
- imagination;
- enthusiasm;
- dedication.

(adapted from New Zealand Ministry of Education 1997)

Of course this approach runs the danger of analytic checklisting, just as the identification of instructional behaviours does. So it is necessary to draw back from that route, and move forwards instead towards the synthesis of holistic practice. Hamachek (1999: 190) reminds us of the need to combine considerations of teaching quality with those of learning quality, arguing that the characteristics of 'good teaching' and of 'effective teaching' are blended by the expert or master teacher. He also points out that 'there exists no well-defined standard that all experts meet and that no non-experts meet'. It is here, in my view, that the concept of practical wisdom (Elliott 1991) and that of prudence (Stenhouse 1975) can be of greatest help in establishing standards of practice.

Self and teaching

The notion of professional development associated with the personal qualities and characteristics, including a capacity to engage in reflective practice and critical inquiry/action, is based on a comprehensive image of continuous, professional self-appraisal. I do not see self-appraisal simply as appraisal of practice by oneself, though that certainly is part of what I imagine. By itself that has the danger of being taken hostage in ways that the Teacher Training Agency has displayed in its flagship *Teaching as a Research Based Profession*, where the approval of projects has remained largely in the domain of classroom management and instructional effectiveness (Cordingley 1998; TTA 1998b). Self-appraisal could become a self-blame game, or a part of a process of legitimation of the narrow conception of curriculum, driven by a technicist and narrow teacher effectiveness mentality. Or it could reside entirely within a particular countenance of educational action research (McKernan 1991) devoted to an individual's classroom activity without examining personal qualities, without extending to autobiography, or without incorporating studies of the conditions of schooling, the impact of policy, or social critique. In the focus on personal qualities, I want to include aspects of one's self as educational professional dispositions towards the purpose and consequences of schooling, and the use of personal agency in the pursuit of personal and educational reconstruction. The reason for seeking a deeper view of the teacher-self stems from a concern for a more tolerant, humane, and person-centred kind of education for both teachers and pupils. It is a bid for a more inclusive notion of professional development, in which the essentials of being an educator, and the bases of personal growth, perspective, and identity, can sit alongside subject knowledge, instructional strategies and curriculum organization as worthy of attention.

There has been some recognition, mainly among academic researchers interested in teachers' lives, that the person a teacher is matters in the drive for teaching quality, and in understanding teaching knowledge. That recognition comes from different perspectives. For example, the place of religious commitment or something close to it that underlies a sense of serving others has been identified as commonplace in the work of teachers (MacLure 1993). MacLure also recognizes that self and identity are a central source (and resource) for undertaking teaching and engaging in professional development. She argues that identities are used by teachers to explain, justify and make sense of themselves in relation to others and to the world at large (MacLure 1993). However, she says that the social perception of the teacher, the category of teacher itself, is undergoing changes of such magnitude that it amounts to a crisis in the profession and society. That crisis, when transferred to the individual teacher, results in spoiled identities, or even the denial of identity, as esteem, trust, authority, and expertise, are undermined by changes in the broader socioeconomic, technological, and political contexts of teaching. Consequent changes in social perceptions of teachers, she asserts, are undercutting old virtues and the basis of professionalism on which identities might once have been formed.

This view can be linked directly to the experiences and working conditions of newly qualified teachers, who are starting the job as it is defined according to these social perceptions, material circumstances, curriculum ideologies, and the social market of education. They are joining longer serving colleagues who are sometimes in those states of disaffection and cynicism, brought on by changes in identity, created by the nature and direction of the demands and requirements being made on them. Maybe some part of the cause is the displacement of attention to educational practice in favour of technical instruction. Or perhaps it is the amount and rapidity of reforms that teachers face, coming from political imperatives, so that alienation displaces the commitment to change for which policy makers hope. What is more, new teachers are often entering the workplace and the labour market on short-term, temporary contracts. This may well be coupled with existing financial debts incurred during training, further demeaning the social commitments to, and perceptions of, their identities of teachers as professionals.

The various perspectives adopted in studies of teachers and teaching show how broad are the approaches that can be adopted in considering the matter. Historians show how teaching is predominantly and traditionally an occupation for women of lower middle-class backgrounds, which itself has a significant impact on the social and self-definitions of teachers and their status (Grace 1991; Lawn 1991). There are studies of individual teachers engaged in the passion of their work, studies of the experience of lesbian and gay teachers, of those who are disaffected by being ignored in the processes of organizational change, of teachers' professional dispositions at different ages and career stages, and so on. There are, too, studies of the experiences of newly qualified teachers contesting and surrendering to the values and conditions or interpersonal grief of their situations (Beynon 1987; Hannam *et al.* 1988; Tickle 1994).

These different experiences all lead that step further into considering not just the nature of the knowledge of teaching (epistemology), but the very nature of becoming and being a teacher (ontology). Occasionally both have been addressed. Elbaz (1983) did go beyond what kinds of knowledge are involved in teaching, to the kinds of personal characteristics that were evident in the teacher she studied. Her analysis of teaching knowledge moved in that direction by taking an holistic view of one teacher's life and work – seeking to understand the connections between aspects of self and the processes of classroom instruction. McLean (1999: 58) articulates the case like this:

> Images of self-as-person and self-as-teacher are critical to the process of becoming a teacher because they constitute the personal context in which new information will be interpreted, and are the stuff of which a teaching persona is created . . . self-images are important not only in terms of visions of the future, they also guide one's experience of the present. For example, Britzman (1991: 6) claims that for beginning teachers, the most powerful self-image is one that captures self as 'the author of the teacher she is becoming.'

The worth of different kinds of self-image in helping to author personal and professional development becomes a crucial factor in this process, as McLean (1999: 58) points out, arguing that some images:

> do not help a beginning teacher imagine herself coping with ambiguities, negotiating conflicting demands, managing the inevitable dilemmas, and picking a path through the minefield of power relationships that together constitute the working environment for teachers.

Dadds (1996) provided a detailed view of the person-centredness of teaching, with insight into the ways in which teachers' work, teacher development, and school development link together in 'passionate enquiry', in which the self-image is one of emotional response and professional commitment to research educational events with a view to the improvement of practice. So the sense of personal experience and what personal qualities are used as resources during induction, and how these are handled in support programmes are matters in which, perhaps, changes are afoot. Maybe those changes are related to the status and esteem ascribed to the role of teacher. Recognition of the lower order of the status of teaching, or lack of professional standing, is not new. Lortie (1975) demonstrated how it is a lesser professional occupation than, say, medicine and law. The campaign to create a General Teaching Council in England is evidence of attempts to change from low to high status by ascribing self-regulatory powers, independent of political agencies. That campaign is one example from the teaching qualities movement around the world, driven by a combination of external demands for professional accountability and internal professional attempts to raise the status of teaching.

My own research with students and with new teachers considered the realm of the emotions in teaching situations and in learning to teach (Denzin 1984; Sanger and Tickle 1987; Tickle 1987a, 1991, 1994; Franks and McCarthy 1989; Clark 1992). The initial focus of my research with new teachers in this respect was the recognition of the failure of the technicist and clinical views of teaching to acknowledge, let alone provide for, the development of the emotions associated with being a teacher. Here, I realized, there is a need to extend the substance and methods of professional development, to accommodate the person within the role of teaching. New teachers reveal the importance of the emotions, both in terms of their relationship to judgements, actions and events and in terms of how they handle that relationship through greater self-awareness. As they reflect on their experiences, they identify how the professional self-development of that aspect of personal life is intrinsically linked to the qualities of caring and commitment, conscientiousness, and educational desire. Some reveal the importance of the emotions and their relationship to personal confidence and classroom practice, the 'things which cause emotional disturbance in the first place', as Debbie, one of the teachers, put it. These include judgements and misjudgements within the problem-solving elements of practice, in the point and counterpoint of learning from experience.

Drawing upon the substantial theories of social psychology, especially the symbolic interactionists Cooley (1902), Mead (1934), and Kohut (1971) Nias argued that self-concepts and core values are sources of stability for teachers, through which they maintain a sense of purpose in their life's work. However, stability does not mean stagnation, for she asserted that the concept of self also includes the process of adapting to new ways of perceiving ourselves, and to how we think others perceive us. This process of reshaping and rebuilding selves in ways that maintain 'self-regard and self-regulation' (so as not to become dysfunctional or damaging) can be seen as a critical part of interactions that new teachers face. According to Nias (1989: 26), the process includes a 'well defended relatively inflexible substantial self into which we incorporate the most highly prized aspects of our self-concept and the attitudes and values which are most salient to it'. However, she alerts us to the humanness of teachers in another way, by saying we must acknowledge 'teachers as persons with the urge at times to be impulsive, angry, rebellious, creative . . . the elusive and often disorderly identities of individual men and women'.

There is a deep need in induction programmes to take aspects of self in professional development seriously. The dearth of interest among policy makers and teacher education curriculum planners in such aspects of education, which are additional but closely related to aims and values needs to be challenged (Nias 1989; Dadds 1996). In policy and practice the identification and development of personal qualities at the interface between aspects of one's personal virtues and professional life, between personhood and teacherhood, has had very scant attention. Yet it does seem to be the key to aspirations of reflective practice and action research. It is, in my view, the route by which the compliant technician can escape to become the critically active tactician, equipped with a sense of purpose and with political strategy for bringing about both personal and social change. For unless one has a sense of self-development and the expertise to examine, develop and appropriately deploy professional characteristics and personal qualities, it seems unlikely that the adoption of a critical perspective on teaching and its circumstances will carry very far.

I believe that Nias's representation deserves revisiting in the light of those long lists of virtues that teachers might be expected to display. She appears to start from the premise of the existence of a pre-formed core self that teachers defend against change, with a more modifiable surrounding self based on secondary values. Her study was carried out with experienced teachers, and raises the question: is the theory sustainable in general, and in particular in relation to the life and work of new entrants to the profession in the twenty-first century?

Gethin (1998: 146–7) points out that an alternative view of self

> rests on the claim that we never in fact experience an unchanging self, and there is therefore no reason to posit an unchanging self underlying experience . . . This notion of self is born of delusion.

That delusion leads to attempts to lay claim to aspects of experience, through an attitude of 'this is mine, I am this, this is my self'. The dangers of this social and psychological construct of self and personal identity reside in seeking to appropriate things as one's own rather than seeing them as someone else's, 'leading inevitably to self-*ish* concerns'. It is the core self, in Nias's terms, which becomes vulnerable and is defended by individuals who adopt and seek to maintain the personal identity of teacher – and it is that sense of self which MacLure sees as becoming spoilt in the present, dynamic, social context of education.

An alternative to this is for educational communities to realize and rehabilitate the value of selflessness (Gethin 1998: 147). This has two dimensions, the first being for individuals to learn to live with both psychological and social change:

> The point that is being made is that reality is at heart something dynamic, something fluid; however one looks at it, reality is a process; analyse reality down to its smallest possible components or constituents, and what one finds are, not static building blocks, but dynamic processes.
>
> (Gethin 1998: 155)

The second dimension is that the ethical practice of education can be conceived as something depending on more than the character of individuals.

It can be seen as a human inheritance, in which individuals participate as contributors to a common good and to the well-being of others. Teaching becomes an holistic practice in quite another sense in that kind of construct. In it lies the possible foundation for honourable professionalism, which is radically different from the promotion of an élite core of individual 'experts', or the concentration on individuals as a point of blame. The complementarity that can be detected in this view is similar to the interactionist and post-structural views of the relationship between identity and social structures (Denzin 1989; Giddens 1996). Gethin offers some ways of resolving the paradoxes of the collective–individualist relationship, pointing out that actions are not the work of an autonomous self, but the outcome of 'complex interaction of diverse impersonal conditions' (Gethin 1998: 156). Yet, properly grasped, actions still involve personal conduct with moral consequences.

The result is that neither absolute free will, nor no choice whatsoever, are adequate representations of the relationship between the ecological and the psychological conditions in which new teachers find themselves. For educators the logic is simple: 'If I were an unchanging self what would be the point of trying to change myself?' (Gethin 1998: 157). These principles, derived from considerations of spiritual life, do seem to have profound messages for professional life. Both paths are chosen ones, courses of purposeful action, with an inherent sense of deficiency and will to develop – not just by solitary individuals, but by whole communities.

Beyond the self

Research on teachers' work shows how the characteristics of our educational environments and the demands that conditions of work place on us lead to our interpreting, making sense of, and adjusting to what we see as possible in our circumstances (Lacey 1977; Pollard 1985; Zeichner and Tabachnick 1985; Hargreaves 1988). These circumstances are cause for critique and inquiry, as well as social action, for those with curriculum imagination and those who value a transformational stance towards education (Freire 1972; Stenhouse 1975; Eisner 1979; Carr and Kemmis 1986; Elliott 1991). One of those conditions derives from evidence of teachers becoming 'locked into a view of themselves as technical experts', certain of their own expertise, and unreflective about their practice (Schön 1983: 68). This suggests that it is the qualities and capabilities beyond technical and clinical proficiency that are crucial to educational development, of both a personal and a communal kind. That is the common ground of educational action research, which is seen as a way to bring about personal, educational and social change (Elliott 1991; McKernan 1991; Tabachnick and Zeichner 1991; Carr 1995). So how far can we pursue this broader conceptualization of teaching knowledge?

The theoretical constructs of practical knowledge, in which the relationship between instructional technician and educational tactician needs to be considered, can be extended through a view of educational action in the form of social strategies. Lacey's (1977) study of student teachers recognized that induction into teaching (he called it socialization) involved a process of negotiation in which individuals can actively, and creatively, influence events and situations as well as passively respond to them. Lacey claimed that three types of response occur, sometimes singly or in combination:

- compliance with others' definitions, even though one holds different values and beliefs;
- congruence with the others' values and expectations;
- active pursuit of one's personal goals, and attempts to redefine circumstances to allow that to happen.

A similar interactionist perspective was also adopted by Hargreaves (1978) and Pollard (1985) in relation to teachers' coping strategies more generally, while Lacey's study of students was extended by Zeichner and Tabachnick (1985) to the work and lives of teachers in their first job. They showed how teachers variously adopted and adapted compliant, congruent, and redefinitional responses to specific aspects of their work and their situations. The level and range at which they were able to introduce and use new and creative elements of practice into their schools depended in part on their perceptions of opportunities and the powers exercised by the colleagues, managers, students, or parents who they encountered. Central to the process is the way in which individuals define their aims, articulate their hopes and expectations, and negotiate and carry out justifiable educational actions.

Perhaps it is possible to appreciate, from a quite different angle, how power and negotiation works in relation to professional practice, by considering Habermas' (1968) analysis of different kinds of knowledge. This was expressed in terms of the interests served by knowledge and what he had to say seems particularly pertinent in current circumstances of teaching, where dominant conceptions of technical knowledge are detectable, whereas in the informality of the information society access to knowledge may be taking us in a radically different educational direction. Habermas was concerned with the relationship between practice and theory, demonstrating that in its ancient Greek origins theory was supposed to comprise practical efficacy. In that sense theory is not value-free, nor detached from social life in the way theory has been represented in the sciences in our own times. In his attempts to rehabilitate practical efficacy to its original (Greek) status, Habermas postulated three kinds of knowledge, which correspond with different human interests, that is, which serve different purposes and different groups in society (Habermas 1968: 313). These kinds of knowledge, and hence the purposes, can be related to the practical knowledge of teaching and the notion of competence discussed above, and which have implications for education and for teaching, in the sense of what we teach and how we teach it.

Knowledge concerned with technical control is used to describe our understanding of the world and our control over it. This serves a technical interest of managing our daily lives. In teaching it is knowledge that provides control over the management of learning – how to organize a class, discipline, the structuring of knowledge content, the formalization of assessment. These are the areas of technical expertise that enable us to achieve specific goals. Usually that expertise is deployed as required, in a predefined curriculum, towards a system of instruction and assessment in which social selection for adult occupational routes is a major goal.

Knowledge that involves problem-solving, usually carried out through judgement in social situations, serves our practical interests according to Habermas. It includes intersubjective interpretations of social situations and problems. This kind of interpretive knowledge is encountered in pursuing the social purposes of daily life. In teaching, deciding how best to marshal and utilize time, space and available resources in the pursuit of educational aims would exemplify this kind of knowledge.

Habermas identified emancipatory knowledge as being concerned with reaching understanding and analyses of situations in ways that free consciousness, and enable us to reflect critically on our circumstances and our presuppositions about them, potentially leading to action for change. In teaching, the parallels are in questioning why we teach some content and not others, or why we assess pupils on a scale of achievement that systematically instills a sense of failure for many. Even more radically, perhaps, it might involve redefining the nature of the educational problems of the twenty-first century, to which the continuation of nineteenth-century mass schooling is the apparently unsatisfactory answer. Unsatisfactory, that is, since it appears already to have failed generations of learners during the twentieth century, so that existing modes of education continue to be seen as a most pressing social problem, while new modes are predictably necessary for the information age.

These different kinds of knowledge, and the interests that they serve, are according to Habermas related directly to different kinds and amounts of social activity, and the social relations that surround those activities, especially in the exercise of work, of language, and of power. So it is possible to learn, and be engaged in the application of technical knowledge, carrying out instructions without fully understanding to which problem the actions are supposed to be a solution. It is possible to learn how to observe and analyse social problems and articulate solutions to them, and even to engage in implementing and assessing the progress of the solutions in a practical day-to-day working environment, without inquiring into or taking a stance towards the social origins of the problem being solved. Or it is feasible that an individual will bring new perceptions to the way problems are perceived and identified, or to their origins, such that the problems themselves are reconceptualized, and alternative dispositions to the search for solutions are adopted.

The implication of these ideas for the present discussion is to recognize that the elements of teaching knowledge are defined by professional traditions, and by powerful groups can be represented, subscribed to or complied with in these different terms. Professional culture may define teaching in

the technical sense, and it is considerably more powerful than newly qualified teachers are. However, that does not make it unproblematic, or put it
out of reach of critique and argumentation. Nor does it mean that new
teachers should simply, solely, and unquestioningly be inducted into technical knowledge. Becoming problem-solving professional educators capable
of curriculum dissent and critique of ideologies framed in educational policy
is an essential complement to the potentials for educational reform. Thinking
of professional characteristics in these terms puts the educational aspirations
of new teachers at the forefront of practical action, and at the forefront of
their personal and professional development. That results in a major tension
and conundrum for teachers – to be confident, respectful, and respected in
their proficiency and their personal esteem, while remaining consciously
insecure in what they do and what they are, willing partners in an emancipatory educational adventure.

The differences that can exist in the orientations taken towards these
qualities, aspirations, principles and actions were illustrated by the notion of
competences adopted by Zimpher and Howey (1987). They devised a framework based on an analysis of the expectations which supervisors had of
novice teachers, and that they used in tutoring and assessing them. It is a
framework that certainly includes the technical and problem-solving dimensions of teaching, but extends to a more complex image of competence and
of the support that teacher-tutors could provide for new teachers, including
personal and critical dimensions. These are summarized below in a way that
outlines key characteristics of teaching and the sorts of supervisory support
that relates to those characteristics.

> *Technical competence*: the employment of craft knowledge and effective
> use of instructional strategies.
> Determines in advance what is to be learnt, how it is to be learnt, and
> criteria by which success is measured.
> Mastery of methods of instruction – specific skills: how to ask good
> questions; how to apply teaching strategies; how to select and organ-
> ize curriculum content; how to structure the classroom for learning;
> what techniques to use to maintain social control in the classroom.
> Supervision provides for skill development and efficient and effective
> use of resources in the classroom; translates theory into technical
> rules for application in classrooms.
> Knowledge is in the form of technical guidelines and analysis from craft
> knowledge of what constitutes 'good practice'.
> Learning is an applied science with linear problem-solving to determine
> how to accomplish given ends.
> Instrumental reasoning is applied to ensure that specific techniques
> help reach stated objectives.

> *Clinical competence*: ability to make judgements about problematic situ-
> ations and to solve problems through reflective action.
> Instructional problem-solving, involving inquiry and reflective action.

Supervision focuses on action to solve practical problems, and its relationship to theory; encourages reflection about the relationship between aims and actions based on evaluation of events, and with reference to theory.

Involves synthesis of normative, interpretive and explanatory knowledge to form intellectually and morally defensible practical judgements about what to do in specific situations.

Inquiry involves planning, monitoring, and reflecting on the processes and consequences of action through research to improve practice. This involves practical reasoning regarding best courses of action 'under the circumstances'.

Personal competence: the achievement of 'self-actualization', especially in terms of a willingness and capacity to develop values through self-confrontation and dialogue with others.

Kind of teacher envisaged is one who understands her/himself, and uses 'self-actualized' qualities as an effective and humane educator.

Supervision focuses on increasing self-awareness and identity formation, through self-confrontation, values clarification, and the development of personal style in teaching.

It provides expertise in theories of human development, through supportive tuition that explores and analyses teaching episodes and responds to new teachers' defined needs.

The knowledge involved is analytic and interpretive theory, drawing on self-reflection and ethnographic observation, and used to understand events in classrooms and school.

Interpretations of intentions, actions, events, values and meanings are related to self-awareness and identity as a teacher.

Critical competence: capacity to engage in critique of social institutions, social structures, and the norms and values, or ideologies, which operate within them.

Teaching is a rational, moral and socially conscious attempt to bring about change.

Guidance is aimed at developing reflective decision making and action to form more rational and just classrooms and schools, to critique undesirable consequences of the curriculum, and to overcome inequalities, injustices and forms of social oppression.

Supervisors collaborate in self-reflective dialogue and critical examination of educational practices, drawing on philosophical analysis, interpretive social science and critical theory.

Group inquiry is focused on conditions and processes of social interaction and social control, and the organization and practice of education. Reflexivity seeks to uncover the contradictions and inadequacies of different conceptions of educational practice as reflecting values within society.

(adapted from Zimpher and Howey 1987: 101–27)

The implications of these perspectives led to my own view of a curriculum for supported self-education that needs to be developed, to include a curriculum for the emotions (Tickle 1991). If the curriculum for the emotions is directly linked to the agenda for the development of personal competences more broadly (in the sense of teachers' personal meanings), and to the enhancement of repertoires of technical and clinical competencies, then we might gain a sense of 'holistic' appreciation of the complex practical activity and personal nature of teaching.

The notion of professional characteristics, personal qualities, or virtues, including the willingness to examine and develop one's values and beliefs, falls very clearly within Zimpher and Howey's notion of personal competence. It is not clear in Sockett's (1994) model of professionalism where the somewhat more contentious elements of teaching lie, those of engaging in social criticism – that which Zimpher and Howey call critical competence. They associate this aspect of professional practice with the twentieth century critical theorists and with certain countenances of action research (Carr and Kemmis 1986; McKernan 1991). Social criticism of that kind requires not only the sense of self-criticism (and self-regulation in the performance of practice) which personal qualities encompass, but the will and skill to engage in actions to change social institutions. Such will and skill are seen as necessary to participation in educational institutions and communities.

Those qualities take the teacher one step beyond the personal, into the communal aspects of knowledge, competence, and political action. They underlie much of the argument for teachers (and other professionals) to engage in reform rather than merely surrendering to other people's ideas. Action research, however, has never been homogeneous. It can be read, for instance, as serving the instrumental needs of instructional efficiency, if research on teaching is limited to examining the efficacy of a particular method of delivering someone else's prescribed curriculum. It can be read as serving the needs of personal fulfillment as educator and self-educator, if the concept of self is narrow and if research is limited to investigating one's personal life-project in being a teacher. Or it can be read as serving the interests of a community if the combined social purposes of professional groups and communities are the subject of investigation (McKernan 1991; Tabachnick and Zeichner 1991).

So far as the efficacious and self-fulfilling dimensions of professional reflection and action research are concerned there is much still to be achieved in establishing this as a central element of professional knowledge with a communal dimension. The central plank in teacher induction as it is leaves the focus on individual (self) development with the prevailing orientation of teacher training, induction, and formal teacher appraisal attending to individuals rather than communities.

4   Learning from induction

Perspectives on learning to teach

If there is difficulty in articulating a coherent body of teaching knowledge, then not surprisingly that is matched by differences of view about how teaching should, or could, be learned. Reviews of literature on teacher learning display a range of perspectives on the acquisition of educational expertise, and uncertainty in the state of the art of educating teachers (Tickle 1987a, 1994; Eraut 1994; Calderhead and Shorrock 1997; Hoyle and John 1997; Cochran-Smith and Lytle 1998). These differences are often represented in terms that relate to either formal and theoretical knowledge, or to practical knowledge, or to a synthesis that eliminates these distinctions – known as practical theorizing (Carr and Kemmis 1986; Elliott 1991; Eraut 1994). In research about the process of becoming a teacher, the pursuit and adoption of identity as a teacher, and the life experience of being a teacher, there has been rather less consideration of the process of development (Jarvis 1983; Huberman 1993; Harland and Kinder 1997; Hoyle and John 1997; Cochran-Smith and Lytle 1998).

The different perspectives held by social scientists and teacher educators are reflected in teacher effectiveness and school development paradigms. On the one hand much of the effectiveness literature sees research and teaching as empirical projects aimed at securing a validated body of educational practice which can be disseminated to and applied by practitioners. Teachers would behave in ways prescribed by researchers in order to ensure that practical effectiveness is achieved in classrooms. On the other hand, in paradigms that see research and educational practice as one and the same thing, in which educators ask questions and seek evidence about the nature and consequences of their actions (whether this is teachers in classrooms, managers, or policy makers), the implications for the way we learn and practice are very different. Where the motives of becoming, and the life-project of developing as a professional educator are to be considered, we might expect to find 'learning' reaching into the realm of personal change and growth. If that is extended to questions about the aims and consequences of schooling, the implications for the methods and organization of educational knowledge would reach into the development of both personal and professional agency.

Each of Zimpher and Howey's (1987) types of competencies, in other words, can be expected to need different methods for transmission or acquisition. That is clearly indicated in their consideration of different kinds of supervisory practices, and supported by Wragg's (1984) study of teacher education. It is also in evidence in studies of the organization of teacher education curricula. Calderhead and Shorrock (1997: 18) for example, claim that:

> Learning to teach involves the development of technical skills, as well as an appreciation of moral issues involved in education, an ability to negotiate and develop one's practice within the culture of the school, the development of personal qualities and an ability to reflect and evaluate both in and on one's actions. Each of these areas may make quite different demands upon the learner and entail different forms of professional growth.

The interpretive, interactional, constructivist, and transformative views, in which self-formation contrasts with replication of externally defined practices, is a declared bias of the previous chapters. In that bias, practice and its development are conceptualized as a research venture with the purpose of both personal and social reconstruction (Warnke 1987; Carr and Kemmis 1986; Schön 1983, 1987; Tickle 1987a, 1987b; Elliott 1991). In contrast, the most recent national developments of policy and recommended induction practice in England hold true to the kind of social control persuasions discussed by Elliott (1998). These put an emphasis on the external definition of teaching behaviours, with supervision and observation of practice by school managers and inspectors, making it very plain that external and expert referents for acceptable performance must be satisfied by new teachers.

Differences in perspective about the means of learning teaching and its organization have as long a pedigree as discussions about the nature of teaching knowledge itself. In England there was, for example, correspondence on the matter between Joseph Lancaster and Andrew Bell, the respective Quaker and Anglican founders of the monitorial system of elementary school teaching in the early nineteenth century. At that time both foundations operated in the same way: monitors (children aged up to 12) were trained in the content of lessons and classroom methods, using demonstration, observation, and instruction in the rules of teaching. Their job was then to deliver the content and check that it had been received by pupils, while being observed and assessed by supervisors. Lancaster later wanted to introduce personal education for the monitors, through what he called lectures on 'the passions'. Bell wanted them only to learn the subject content and instructional routines of the system, under supervision in the schoolroom (Rich 1933; Dent 1977). Debate about both ends and means of teacher training resulted.

The monitors' successors in the later part of the nineteenth century, pupil teachers, worked independently in separate classrooms but their tuition in content and method was given by headteachers, using the medium of a lesson plan journal. Journals were checked for accuracy of content and appropriateness of pedagogy, with time spent each day by the manager on monitoring through observation and testing of pupils, and mentoring based on the journals, observations and results. Residual elements of the assumptions underlying this kind of training exist in the conventions of student–supervisor relations in present day teacher education. They exist, too, in the experiences of teachers in schools in which the headteacher insists on regularly checking and commenting on lesson plans, pupil records, and evaluations of every teacher.

Arguments grew out of the monitorial and pupil–teacher systems with the emergence of training colleges in the nineteenth and early twentieth centuries being one of the results. In the colleges the curriculum was extended, and new methods of learning introduced that did not depend upon being in the practical context all of the time. Consequent changes in the ways teachers are educated have taken numerous twists and turns since then, which have been documented elsewhere (Taylor 1978; Alexander *et al.* 1984). In England more recent highlights in these developments are associated with a menu of policy and methods, including:

- all-graduate entry and required certification (from the 1980s);
- increase, then depletion, in disciplines of psychology, sociology, philosophy, and history, applied to education;
- the use of simulation and video-replays of personal performance, known as micro-teaching;
- observation of children in classrooms;
- the emergence of centralized training curricula;
- attempts to move training onto a basis of apprenticeship carried out within schools;
- increased observations of experienced teachers;
- direct entry into the profession, with learning on the job;
- policing of the time spent in school placement practice;
- increased use of fieldwork assignments and tasks;
- direct ties of teacher training to national curriculum content and assessment;
- increased use of mass lectures in higher education on school curriculum components and teaching behaviours;
- the elimination of critical educational perspectives from pre-service programmes;
- interest in reflective practice and experiential learning;
- the use of distance education, instruction guides, self-help manuals, and satellited school-based courses;

- use of journals for documenting experience and responses to it;
- mentor guidance as a basis for reflection and review of practice.

This pedigree of tradition, trial and error, tension and change is important to note, lest I or anyone else should assume that a consensus on how professional educators learn their trade can be either easily achieved, or, perhaps worse, imposed. As Hamachek (1999: 192) puts it:

> Indeed there is no single pathway to good teaching because no one set of teaching behaviors is clearly related to student performance outcomes in all situations (Brophy 1992; Leinhart 1992) and, in any case, achievement is only one of many student outcomes that is important in assessing teacher effectiveness.

From that pedigree it is easy to see that a range of assumptions about teacher education methods make it impossible to represent induction as systematic or agreed. If Reynolds (1998) had a problem about a science of instruction, he surely has a bigger one in claiming his 'training cycle' to be grounded in professional wisdom. There is a real problem in seeking the science and art of teacher education (Wragg 1982, 1984; Zimpher and Howey 1987; Munro 1989; Eraut 1994; Tickle 1994; Wilkin 1996; Calderhead and Shorrock 1997; Hoyle and John 1997). The process of argumentation and change derived from the different views on how teachers should be educated has left a legacy of curriculum models for teacher education programmes which are often a blend of different aims and assumptions about the processes of professional learning. Just as schools' curricula have come to serve a mixture of purposes, contain amalgams of content, get variously organized, and use a range of teaching methods, so too has teacher education developed that way. Wilkin's (1996) study of programme submissions for accreditation of courses show how they changed over three decades. Munro (1989) and Tickle (1994) summarized the diverse assumptions in teacher education curricula as reflecting:

- *apprenticeship* – where it is assumed the novice will be placed with an experienced mentor and gradually learn to model his or her practice;
- *experiential* – in which personal resources and images of teaching are used to help in devising lessons and testing out classroom strategies;
- *skills/performance based* – with instruction for classroom behaviours, which are carried out as prescribed by the instructor;
- *theoretical disciplines oriented* – pursuing understanding through studies of teaching and learning and their underlying principles, prior to or alongside the design of curriculum proposals based on them;
- *reflective practitioner* – where other routes to learning are accompanied by a reflective attitude which helps raise awareness through self-monitoring of practice;
- *critical revisionist/action research* – which assumes that teachers and pupils are located in circumstances that need reform, and sees them as con-

tributing to change in practice by developing and researching new forms of education.

In their review of research on early professional development, Calderhead and Shorrock (1997: 11) claim to have identified five models that characterize these sorts of different orientations towards professional learning:

- enculturation, or socialization into the professional culture;
- technical, training teachers in knowledge and skills;
- moral endeavour, the ethics of a caring profession;
- synthesis, involving personal development and professional work;
- reflective practice, drawing upon hands-on experience.

(adapted from Calderhead and Shorrock 1997)

Learning centred teaching

Induction projects that have been recorded suggest that they have drawn mainly on a model of learning from experience, with some elements derived from beliefs in apprenticeship, and occasionally some experimenting towards the development of reflective practice (Tickle 1994). The ad hoc emergence of induction schemes and persistence of make-do-and-mend arrangements indicate that most newly qualified teachers experience a hunter–gatherer, subsistence curriculum in which their hunger for knowledge is fed by their native cunning and limited pre-service training (DES 1982, 1988a). Gleaning advice, information, ideas, know-how, methods, and experience are the self-constructivist means of attempting to secure skilled performance in the management of educational environments and the conduct of professional action. In these situations, securing the tools and carrying out the job of making those environments safe, well-tended and productive depends largely on personal reserves and the unstructured familial support of colleagues. Of course, there is evidence that neither the psychological conditions of new teachers nor the environments in which they work are safe, well tended and productive (Tickle 1994).

In one illustration of the creative/survival/constructive responses to those conditions and responses, a group of new teachers who discussed their own learning from experience identified some key elements in the process. These were summarized (Tickle 1994: 208) in the teachers' own metaphors as necessarily involving a process of:

- being en route – embarking on the road to full proficiency;
- going through it – having personal experience built over prolonged periods of time;
- playing the hunch – testing ideas and taking risks without that experience to draw upon;
- playing it by ear – fine-tuning, adjusting or abandoning events as evidence emerged in response to actions;

- mental gymnastics – handling the multiple guiding ideas, classroom procedures, interpersonal encounters, and sources of evidence inherent in classroom and school environments;
- minding – or caring, the persistent ethical dimension of ensuring that educational responsibilities were fully carried out;
- monitoring – searching constantly for information, or data, from which to interpret events accurately, to measure consequences, and evaluate the achievement of aims or the practicability of pedagogical procedures.

I interpreted these descriptions as somewhat akin to the process of practitioner research discussed by Schön (1983), though I recognized that they could eventually lead to what he called unreflective (i.e. in my terms, unprofessional) practice if the aim was to eliminate risk, remove ambiguity, and create certainty. It was easy to see that the instabilities within which the teachers lived because they were newly en route would make it unwise to further destabilize their values and beliefs at this stage – that is, what is needed is a constructive process based on principles of procedure which support risk taking and their existing capacity to explore educational issues through reflexive thinking. The capacity for utilizing learning opportunities is evident in the following conversations between that same group of teachers and me:[1]

LC: I don't think we only learn by mistakes, that's one way of learning.
DD: But you do definitely learn by mistakes – learn from experience.
LC: And from observation, coming here, talking to others – you know.
SP: Mistakes are just more apparent, more immediate.
LT: Why are they more apparent?
SP: Well, if you do something that's wrong it comes back almost immediately, you realize that almost immediately, and I think we're all fairly critical of what we do, that's why it becomes apparent because we're critical of ourselves. When we do something that's good and that works well you still think that you can improve, you accept it and don't get too big-headed about it, you can see that you could still improve it. But it's the idea that if it is a mistake – it's there.
DD: It could be a mistake with the type of work, or the order of the work that it is done. It could be easy, it could be too hard, but it could also be mistakes in the way that you organize the work. If it's the organizational problem then it very much becomes apparent, if you suddenly discover you haven't got enough scissors or you haven't realized there is a certain piece of equipment that they actually did need, those mistakes very, very quickly are apparent.
LC: Everyday mistakes that we are always going to make, aren't we, not the bad mistakes concerning our teaching. But I've made organizational mistakes, like the way I set up the spelling scheme, which has now run in chaos for the last few weeks because I

hadn't done it properly. I know how I'm going to do it, well, I think. I've started getting the first half of next term planned . . . I think it's something we've got to go through and find our own method – I know teachers have talked to me about what they do, and I haven't been able to take it in because it's not my way, and I think I can only find out my way by trying what works and what doesn't . . . I mean, they could have told you that as a tip, but don't you think that you would have needed to have gone through the first year . . . for you to get through it?

DD: Yes and no, because I do very much rely, and get on very well with the other two members of the year team, and our year leader says things in such a nice way and our personalities are fairly similar, so I don't mind taking what he suggests because I can see that applying to me. If it had come from another member of staff that has a totally different approach from me then I'd probably feel I couldn't do that – that isn't me. So I rely very much on him. Often it's very much after the event, I have dealt with the situation, you can't know a situation is going to come up before you deal with it, and then you think, 'Well, yes, I dealt with it, but was it really the best way for the long term, or even, a short term remedy of that situation?' And I can't know, so I have to ask.

LT: Can you relate those questions about expectations and standards and so on to the exam groups that you have, Sue?

SP: Well, I chat to the head of department, and say to him, 'Look, I'm going to do this, or this. I'm doing it in this particular way, I'm using this strategy', and he goes through it, and says, 'Yes, I agree', and if there is something missing he will say to me, 'Look, this might come in'. I think the problem is all groups are different. So that is the problem there, you can anticipate certain things happening, but at the same time you always have to take into account what might happen with one group, a different group might have something totally different; you have to play it by ear.

LT: Play it by ear, does that mean, in a sense, guess work and judgement?

DM: I think it's important to distrust what you're doing, but sometimes it's also just as important to say, 'No, I won't do it that way'. I think experience can be learnt by being told, not by doing it, and it's always the chance that if you've been told the way you can do it, it might work – that doesn't mean it's the best, and I think that that is probably the most difficult thing to find – the difference between what works and what is best – that I think you need to look at people – for getting as many ideas as you can, and then assimilate them and reject some, and take on others which you find out yourself. I think it's building up a body of experience that is your experience rather than secondhand information, and once you start doing that then perhaps you become, with a capital T

Teacher – but I think in anything you can make improvements, even if it isn't a mistake, you can make improvements.

LC: [The difference is] I could go to [a university tutor] if I was worried about how to approach language, plus my teachers at school and there they were supervising me, plus my [practice] tutor, all those people to talk to, whereas now, although everybody is there to help me, and they are always lovely after the event, I still somehow feel that I've got to get through as well as I can without bothering people, you know, I've got to try because otherwise it looks bad or it's not fair on the parents if I can't do it – they've got their children in a beginner's class and she can't teach. Nobody's ever said that to me, it's a pressure I've put on myself probably, but I am noticing it now that the problems are coming. Well, this week I've had these two problems that have made me realize . . .

SP: I think the problem if you're on your own as well, is you can blow them all out of proportion . . . it suddenly seems worse than it actually is, maybe people aren't that concerned about it, but *you* are, and you've got nobody to talk to about it.

LT: I'm interested in looking at what the nature of the learning has been that you've experienced, and how that learning has seemed to you.

LC: I don't know whether to say learning to be more independent, or self-sufficient, perhaps that's a better word, not having to rely, not being able to rely so much on having other students.

DD: Being faced with something that you know nothing about and then, there isn't really anybody that I can talk to, how do I go about finding out about this thing before I'm faced with having to tell the children?

LC: Well, knowing that your staff can be very helpful, very happy to talk to you about it, but they've got so many things to do, they do the same job as you do, but it's very difficult for them to sit down in the way that a student would, a friend would or a tutor would because it's their job to. That's what your tutor does and as a friend you share it automatically . . . as a teacher . . .

DD: We have a meeting every half term as to what we are going to do in each of the subjects, and I will submit a forecast book outlining the schemes of work, but after that, how you do it, even some of the subjects that you do, it's down to you.

SP: I meet my head of department once every fortnight and I'll go through teaching strategies, materials – he's very supportive, and I also, on odd occasions, see the woman who is in charge of me as well, and she'll go through things with me. So I get that kind of feedback and that kind of support. Um, well, I feel that perhaps even on teaching practice I was self-sufficient.

LC: Yes, to be honest, Sue comes across as a lot more self-sufficient than I am – from what you've been saying in other meetings. I still feel quite unsure about a lot of the things.

SP: I've learnt on my own terms and not on somebody else imposing
         ideas and strategies and everything upon me. I've learnt them
         myself, rather than on teaching practice somebody sitting in on
         the lesson, whether it's going in the right direction or the wrong
         direction. So, that is independence – that's self-sufficiency maybe.
         I think I'd probably feel a lot more insecure if I had to teach eight
         subjects, 'cos I'm not an expert in eight subjects, I'm just an expert
         in one subject.

In some contrast, the dissection, checklisting and prescription of instructional methods used in profiles carries a very particular view of the acquisition of professional knowledge and identity. It is one based on the expert
to novice assumptions of apprenticeship and instruction in specific skills.
The conception of knowledge held in self-constructivist psychology, on the
other hand, sees the knower as an active creator rather than trained per-
former of professional practice. This distinction is crucial to ways of thinking
about learning professional practice. Hargreaves (1988: 216) describes the
social interactionist view of teachers succinctly: 'In this view, teachers, like
other people, are not just bundles of skill, competence and technique; they
are creators of meaning, interpreters of the world and all it asks of them'.

This puts the learner at centre stage. The individual is a self-reflexive
person, for whom the metacognitive layer of puzzling about what she or he
knows, and needs to know, and how to develop it, are essential components
of professionalism. It imagines the role of new teachers as defining aspects
of their own curriculum, and devising elements of their own learning experiences. Responding to the world and all it asks of them includes responding
to others who define what they should come to know and how they will
come to practice. So new teachers would, necessarily, take account of the
externally defined skills, competence, knowledge, understanding, and values
that exist in the worlds of teaching. They would also acknowledge the
realities of the conditions of their learning – whether in trial and error isolation, in guided supervisory relationships, in observational peer groups, and
so on. McLean (1999: 60) makes clear that these conditions are not solitary
or self-contained, that while personal choices are made there are also past
histories which guide images of teaching and decisions about practice, and
others who 'are bent on "constructing" you, in an image they value'. The
intensity of these processes can hardly be overemphasized:

SP: There's nobody you can trust in school, I mean, there's nobody I
         don't think, well, I'm very friendly with two of them, having said
         that, there's nobody, I mean, they know how I feel, [the rest] I
         wouldn't trust them as far as I could throw them, that's just my
         impression of the type of individuals that may be some teachers
         are. I wouldn't trust them. I mean, this is what I was saying today
         that this woman being in on my lesson, and she sort of made
         positive comments to me, and positive comments to somebody
         behind my back, also she just said something like, 'Oh, they were

too quiet in the lesson' and the other chap in my department said, 'No wonder, with her in the lesson they would be'. They worked in silence for the whole lesson, I thought, 'Oh, God, somebody . . .' They were just obviously scared to death because this woman was in the class, and she didn't say anything to me, you know, and that sort of feeling . . . what else is she going to say behind my back?

DD: I haven't had that sort of pressure, nobody has watched a lesson, to my knowledge, unless they've peered through the door without me looking, they've left me totally alone, I'm in a far corner of the school anyway, by myself.

LC: I must confess, it seems a bit of overkill – being observed in the staffroom.

LT: Can we give some attention to the idea of your self-concepts as teachers?

LC: Well, I don't know if it's because I'm very conscientious and worry too much, perhaps overworrying, but I'm the whole time thinking 'I haven't done full-stops with them – I haven't done paragraphs with them, the handwriting isn't very neat – am I doing enough maths' – the whole time worrying. I'm so inexperienced in so many ways. I know I can't be a bad teacher because I care about my children. I think more about them as individuals, I take home all their books and look through all of their work, I'm doing as much as I can but it's very difficult when I've got nobody there to compare with, to sort of say, 'How much English have you done?' or 'Should they really be knowing this, or is it my fault that they don't?' . . . I have always been quite self-critical though – people who have assessed me have said that your assessments of your lessons have been self-critical. I found out today the head takes in books and he likes exercise books that are full. Am I filling the books up quickly enough? Should I just set them stories to write? I've got the head's concept of what a teacher – I don't even know what his real concept is, I'm only guessing at it, but I'm trying to work to that as well as what my tutor said, what I've observed and liked, what I've found out for myself from actually teaching, so I'm still very confused about the way I want to go, not confident enough to say, 'I believe in . . .' There are some things I do really believe in and I wouldn't let anyone put me off it, but there are so many things where I can see how traditional teaching works, you know, I don't really know where I stand so – yes, that is a problem.

LT: Are you self-consciously exploring those questions? Do you self-consciously think, what kind of teacher am I?

LC: I do at night-time, in the holidays, at weekends, talking with friends on the phone, but this is where I really miss PGCE students, and this is why I like coming here and meeting people, but you don't get it enough, because once you are in that classroom all you can think about is that that child is at your desk, the child with their hand up, and you can't sit and think, 'Now is this the way I want to be able to have . . . ?' It's too much going on and I can't think of it in the classroom, and I haven't really got enough time to think about it or explore it fully.

For new teachers models of learning represent a potentially bewildering – certainly a multidimensional – array of knowledge and the means of acquiring expertise. Different means of learning teaching might be useful for different kinds of knowledge, skill, understanding and dispositions. As Sockett (1986: 15) pointed out:

We can shut ourselves in an empty classroom practising our blackboard writing. We can have critics or supervisors watch out particularly for the way we handle children's answers . . . but if we must use our judgment when we apply our skills the route to improvement in performance lies first in practice with judgment and critical reflection, and later in systematic self-analysis accompanied by trials of alternative practical hypotheses.

Elliott (1978) presented a view of the acquisition of teaching expertise in which he argued that intelligent practice amounts to tacit knowledge, which is held intuitively, and cannot be easily translated into forms specified or conveyed in words, for others to follow successfully. In this sense it does have a certain mystique, but it is more the mystique of the artistic synthesis of the many elements of teaching knowledge – those holistic qualities about which Elliott has written extensively. This means that the concept of expertise and the development of the expert are matters for representation in synthesized forms. If expertise is defined and gained within this conception of teaching as an holistic activity based on practical wisdom, it is likely to be gained by guidance in the application of professional judgement in practice, by trial and success, and the scrutiny of evidence of both practical actions and the ideas and principles that underlay them. In Calderhead and Shorrock's terms, the reflective, personal, ethical, and technical will be part of professional enculturation. But, as I have said throughout this book, the concept of socialization is problematic in the face of the tensions between reactionary traditions and dynamic needs for reform. It also serves to reconfirm those status hierarchies that prevent us from maximizing returns on, and making the most judicious further investment in, the professional capital that new teachers represent.

According to Elbaz (1983) the difficulty in articulating educational knowledge may also be because we have little experience that is truly shared. This suggests that teamwork, and the incorporation of inductees into a team that recognizes their strengths and contributions, offers a productive way ahead, for individual new teachers, for the principles of induction arrangements, and for educational reform. This seems essential, if, as other observers confirm, there is a profound difficulty in articulating intuitive, professional knowledge. Converting knowledge into a rational and analytical form, for the sake of helping others to understand its nature and acquire its skilled performance – if indeed we can agree on what skilled performance means – misrepresents its nature and potentially misleads new teachers (Elbaz 1983; Brown and McIntyre 1986).

Perhaps more worrying is the possibility that so long as they are treated as individual, novice performers, new teachers will handle their confusions, dilemmas and problems by remaining silent (Lipka and Brinthaupt 1999). There is a culture of privatism in teaching anyway, by way of which many teachers prefer to keep their practices hidden from public view. This may imply a lack of confidence in those who observe their practice, or in their own capacity to describe and justify classroom processes. It might stem from widespread beliefs in the autonomy and personal responsibility of teachers working in physical isolation, or the sheer necessity of acting autonomously in order to get the job done. There is little opportunity, given the material conditions and physical locations in which teaching occurs, to spend time in joint decision making, articulating reflections upon practice with others who are engaged in learning the same practices. Sometimes, communicating at all is difficult:

> *SP:* Yes, I told the head of department how I was feeling and he was very unaware of what I was feeling because I was covering it up so well, and he said that he had no idea because I seemed so confident and fairly happy with the situation, and I said, 'Well, no, I'm not'. And I explained everything to him – I went into detail and it just seemed to lift a whole weight off my shoulders, and that's made me feel much better at school, and I feel much happier in front of the children, I feel I can relate to them better. Other members of staff, again I seem to be getting on better with them, and I feel more established and I think this all arose through just telling my head of department. I said to my head of department, 'Don't tell the head, will you? Don't tell the woman who is in charge of me'.
>
> *LC:* It's quite difficult to start off with, to admit you've got a problem or a worry or that everything is not perfect, isn't it, it's so much harder once you've been given this label of a teacher. I don't want a halfway stage where as you said that you've still not passed yet, I definitely think we ought to be seen as teachers, but that people should be there to help as much as possible, because it is such a difficult year. You can't bare your soul, can you, because it gets trodden all over, everybody says, 'It's so good to be able to talk . . .' but it is so difficult at the same time and yet important.

Processes of demonstration, discussion, instruction, guided reflection, and other modes of considering practical actions and the beliefs that underlie them can be and are involved, in some school climates. Cochran-Smith and Lytle (1998: 19) argue that we should extend those climates and take on what they call the knowledge question. They suggest we 'open the conversation to provocative new avenues of investigation' with regard to the nature, purpose and acquisition of knowledge for and about teaching. The analyses earlier suggest that teaching knowledge is treated as incoherent, both when it is encountered by new teachers, and in the international efforts to define quality. Yet it is not so, it is argued, when it is choreographed, in its holistic and tacit forms by individual expert practitioners. Here is yet another paradox of educational knowledge – that its dissection detracts from such coherence yet may be necessary in order to make sense of it and find a way towards that coherence for new teachers. That means that new teachers must engage concurrently in the processes of analysis and synthesis, even if experienced teachers find it difficult to do so (Elbaz 1983; Brown and McIntyre 1986). In this sense, too, the period of induction may be unique and deserving of special measures for the development of teaching over a longer period than a year, and in synchronization with a team or community approach to educational development.

If traditional craft knowledge constitutes a limited realm into which new teachers are inducted, then ways of coming to know it are anyway redundant. There is little point in seeking or devising effective measures for transmitting outdated expertise, based on models of apprenticeship, which presume a gradual growth of individual skilled performance at the workbench. Equally, if there is widespread scepticism about theory that is divorced from experience, there is a need to accumulate theories of practice among all professional educators. The belief system in which gaining experience in the first-hand practice of teaching is the supposed guarantor of expertise also represents a failure to consider the nature of theory itself in relation to a practical, ethical profession, and an unwillingness to discuss the purpose and value of theory within the collective endeavour. This means researching the processes by which teaching knowledge is transmitted, acquired and improved. That is to say, the provocative new avenue (Cochran-Smith and Lytle 1998) is one in which the collective body of professional knowledge should be under construction through research, engaged in by all educators, including those who are formally designated as newly qualified to practice, and those who support them or claim to act as model practitioners.

The new approach is to:

- hold open the approach road to the reconceptualization of expert professional knowledge;
- reconsider the assumptions of mentoring and the processes of acquiring expertise;
- reinvigorate the relationship between proficient practice and perpetual development.

Such a view was summed up by Cochran-Smith and Lytle (1998: 22) after they concurred with numerous analyses that show how the transmission of teaching knowledge based on external research failed as a mode of teacher learning. They assert that 'inquiry approaches to teachers' learning across the lifespan are particularly promising for meeting the changing needs of an increasingly diverse society'.

Multidimensional learning

If that is reasonable, the inquiry needs to start among those involved in providing for teacher induction. If opening the conversation is the way ahead,
there is good reason to engage with their assertion that inquiry approaches
are particularly promising. They may be, for some purposes. There are other
possibilities, which might be illuminated, and become refined (or challenged)
within each of those elements of practice delineated in career entry profiles,
and beyond them. For instance, if the functional know-how of a specific job
in teaching is unsystematic, fragmented, extensive, and complex, as I argued
in Chapter 2, then it is just as likely that gaining such knowledge will be a
fairly chaotic business. How does it occur?

Within the conventions of the academic/elementary/vocational curriculum
(which is, remember, treated here as having inherent problems) gaining
knowledge of subject matter is seen as a critical feature in the early stages of
teaching. It may be similarly perceived in later years by experienced teachers
as changes in the subject knowledge base, or in curriculum content, provide
the challenge of keeping up to date or as they extend their interests into
new branches of their subject(s). For the conversation to proceed with regard
to induction, we need to ask: how is that subject knowledge extended during induction?

In the same tradition, adapting new knowledge to the curriculum needs
of students – transforming it into pedagogical content knowledge – is a
closely related feature. We need to know how that happens – what are the
sources and mechanisms of gaining pedagogical content knowledge?

Understanding the characteristics of children's learning processes adds to
the potential for successful management of learning environments and of
the process of ensuring effective student learning. How do we acquire knowledge of our students' capabilities and learning processes from a practice
situation?

Knowledge of the range and operation of instructional strategies, appropriate to different kinds of curriculum and particular pupils, is necessary for
effectiveness in teaching. During induction, how is expertise in the selection
and deployment of pedagogy gained, and where from?

Gaining appreciation of the curriculum context in which education is to
occur raises a similar question. The peculiarities of, provisions within, and
possibilities for action in a particular school or department compound the
need to ask: how is appreciation of an educational context arrived at, and
what kinds of appreciation are developed?

Knowing the technicalities of how to assess, going beyond technique to
understanding, and handling the conflicts and dilemmas of assessment are
equally complicated matters to acquire. How is that knowledge developed
and what are the practices that arise among new teachers?

The relatively unexplored realms of personal qualities and professional
characteristics leave us wondering how these might be supported and developed. Perhaps it is necessary to look elsewhere, outside of teaching, in

the personal development literature, to help to answer the question: how do we gain and sustain the capacity to engage in the processes of development of aspects of self?

A critical view of schooling assumes that the capacity to identify its problems is a necessary part of bringing about changes to improve the schooling process. Seen this way, the question is: how do we acquire and use a critical stance towards our own practices, the nature of what we profess, and the circumstances of schooling?

These are research questions for the induction community, based on a search for the means of effective induction. They presume that the practice of educating is an ethical activity based in deeply held values. Its practical and distinctively personal characteristics mean that communally as well as individually we continue to review and reconstruct different kinds of motives, as well as technical knowledge. Seen this way, the process of knowledge construction is likely to be complex, diverse, difficult and perpetual. That is true for individual new teachers and it is true for the educational community in finding the best methods of induction, developing clearer aims for it, and gaining a better appreciation of its consequences. For both inductees in relation to pupils, and for professional tutors in relation to inductees, this is not merely about the learning of content, the management of programmes, or the practice of discrete skills – though they play a part. Nor is it a simple apprehension of syllabus sequences or assessment agendas. These too play a part but they are elements of the activity of educational practice about which a research stance can be adopted, as part of the larger project of education and social reconstruction. Experience for new teachers, though, is rather more localized and pressing at the early stages of induction:

DM: Well, the staff tend to hide in little cubbyholes, so I've got to know the science staff quite well. One or two of the other staff I've got to know because I've joined clubs and stuff.

DD: I was just surprised by myself that I wasn't thinking about what I was going to teach, like schemes of work or anything like that, but, 'I've got to organize my classroom, I've got to set it up how I want it, now, how am I going to do that?' And I spent three days in school actually so I got to know the school, I felt I was like a fish out of water the first day I went in – sort of wandered around . . .

LC: I spent about an hour and a half in my classroom, sitting at the desk, not knowing what to do – these blank walls around me, all the desks everywhere, not having a clue how to sort them out, where to start.

DD: Yes, that's sort of how I felt, and you just fiddle around . . . and you think, 'Fine, now what?' I just felt totally disorientated, it was the most unusual experience – the most unusual feelings, 'This is my classroom'. I must have spent half the day just moving furniture and testing all the tables to see if they could see me, how many people I'd got with their back to me, anybody got their backs to the blackboard, where I was going to put resources so the children wouldn't be all crowding in on one area . . . how was I going to use that space, and where was the blackboard going to be, what am I going to put on the walls? That took me three days, and at the weekend, I thought, 'I'm teaching on Monday – what am I going to teach? What are they going to be like? How am I going to deal with the first day?'

LT: Sue, how do you relate to that?

SP: Well, it's a bit different because I'm moving around and teaching in different classrooms some of the time, I've got my own base, but I share it with somebody else, so it means that although I've put wall displays up and everything it's not that important to me, and I had to have the desks set out how they are in the department, you know, rules and regulations and everything, so I can't really move the classroom, that hadn't really crossed my mind.

DM: I think there are always one or two children who just want to get their own back on someone. There is one girl who has got this really bad home life, and she's getting her own back on the teachers. You can't really sort of come down too heavy on her because of the problem but you've got to come down heavily enough because you've got the whole class to realize this group is not the best working group so you've got to almost say, 'Well, I'm coming down on that person, remember the example'. Maybe it's one of those things that grows with you, that the more you actually acquire the more you actually see is needed.

LC: [David] is just unbelievable – he just does not listen to a thing – doesn't do a bit of work . . . made it really clear now: 'Right, all write your name in the book, write it in pen, I want you to write your name'. I've written it up on the board . . . he has got drawings all over it, he's miss-spelt, he hasn't done any work, he annoys the other children . . . I've had him up at my desk working, but he thought it was a treat, I've moved him around, I've sat him by me, I've kept him in, I'm running out of ideas. He's got special needs, he goes for help. The thing is he's clever, he's smart. He obviously needs help, he has problems with his reading, but I mean, a lot of children in the class do have that – there's four special needs children, he is only one of four, and he does less than he can do, I know, because when I have been really cross and made him stay in and do it he will do a perfect piece of work. I won't accept children coming up to me saying, 'Miss, I only need to do the answers for this because I go to special reading'. [I say] 'If you are careful you can do this . . . you've got to try.' And it is that sort of thing, pushing them to their limit, though obviously not too far.

SP: Yes, mine is slightly different though, mine is just sort of like, a fairly intelligent typical sort of teenage girl, it's just the look, the sneer, every time I ask her to do something, the sneer on her face,

I just don't know what to do with her. I've split her up from her friends now, I've asked other people what they'd do, and they say split her up, at least she does the work now, but she has started calling across the classroom to her soulmate . . . I don't want to send her out. I think that would just alienate her . . . and it's too easy to do that . . . I don't want to give her too many chances either, she is so off-hand, and so anti-me. She irritates, she is fairly popular, it surprises me that she is actually popular with the other pupils. I don't like her basically, but I try not to show that, I give her plenty of opportunities, I could easily have sent her out – I haven't sent anybody out.

DM: I've got a similar one in [year 11], and she has actualiy said to one of the teachers, 'Look I'll do the work, but I'm not going to like it, I'm going to make it as awkward as I like for any teacher.' That's been her – she has actually said that to teachers, this is her mani-festo, if you like, and you can see it. I've walked into the class and the look she gave me just walking into the classroom, I thought, 'I've never known anybody just take an instant dislike just because he walked in somewhere.' The funny thing is every now and again she enjoys the lesson, or enjoys what has been done, or enjoys something that has been said, I can see her smiling and then you look at her, and instantly her face will freeze into a scowl, this sort of . . . funny sort of thing that she is not going to allow herself to get involved, allow herself to enjoy school.

DD: I'm thinking of the interpersonal relations between you and the children. What do you let them get away with? Do you accept a certain way that they will talk to you? I like a laugh and a joke, I don't mind that but then I think well . . . Then you think if you let them do that, and perhaps you don't stamp on something, how will the way that I'm treating them now affect them later, how they treat me when it comes to the final term? I can't know that. What your expectation is about homework – we have homework set as policy, and about getting that in on time, because if you don't expect that in, if you let that lapse now, it's going to be horrendous in the third term, and I can see that one fairly easily. Another is the standard of work. I'm quite pleased that there are some of them that are coming on very, very well, and they have made real strides in some work that they found very difficult last year. Others I think, 'Well, my goodness, how can I tackle this now because if it's left much too long that's again going to cause a problem.' Or an attitude to work. And that is very difficult because you can't know the consequences really. Getting to know the children is so difficult to describe because your relationship changes so much from initial reaction and relationship with them, to when you get to know them a bit more and they get to know you a bit more and obviously being new they are always trying you out and seeing what they can do. The hardest thing for me is how do you get the balance that is needed between them working for you because they'd like to work for you, and actually working for you because they've got to work for you? And it's very, very difficult to walk that tightrope, and several conversations I've had and I've thought, maybe I should have reacted this way, is the way that I dealt with that the best way that I should have dealt with it? And I'm constantly turning over in my mind situations – should I have done that in that situation? Or said that? Or dealt with it in that way? It feels a continuing puzzle. The only thing I think I've learnt is to treat each child differently, you can't say that that will work, it will work a certain way, it will work with one person, but it won't work with another, and when you've got 30 of your own children, and I take not only my class, but I take another six classes, so, my relationship with my class is obviously different from my relationship with the other classes.

LC: I do feel guilty sometimes that however I try to be friendly, try to get to know them all it's very difficult and when you've got so many other things to think about, you've got to get the register down to the secretary, some child is coming in with a message, all those sorts of things that you forget little David, who's standing there, has got a new briefcase and wants to show it off, it's something I've always worked at before and always enjoyed, and yet I'm finding I'm having less and less time, and it's something I've really got to work at, to remember not to snap, or if I get cross then I mustn't shout at the next child who comes up just because they are unlucky enough . . .

DD: But it is so difficult when you've got the classroom management, the organization, the marking, the problems, you're dealing with everything from level 2 to level 6 in my class, and you all know that is a so wide ranging from special needs right to high-flyers, and it's mental gymnastics . . . trying to talk to the children, deal with them as people, plus interruptions.

Perhaps this is why Eisner (1979) refers to education as like art, ineffable in its character, lifelong, life-forming and self-reforming as a project for individuals, and potentially transforming as a communal project. The induction curriculum and new teachers' experiences of it can be adopted, then, in the terms set out by Stenhouse (1975) as a proposal whose principles and features, content and methods, are made publicly available, and deserve critical scrutiny. Since these curricula are likely to be devised and implemented in individual schools, albeit within broader guidelines or prescriptions, the pursuit of evidence related to those research questions will need to be part of the principles of procedure of induction programmes.

A constructivist view of educational knowledge has a long tradition. It is represented in a variety of forms, for example by Dewey (1912), Stenhouse

(1975), Rogers (1983), Schön (1983, 1987), Salmon (1988), Winter (1989), Elliott (1991) and others. In one representation, concerned with the role of the individual learner, Burgess (1979: 2) put the inquiry view of education in perspective when he asked with regard to learning in general, 'What takes place when a student learns and a teacher teaches?' After reviewing behaviourist, gestalt, romantic, and developmental learning theories, he concluded that whatever the differences in the range of learning theory,

> they all hold that learning takes place through the activity of the learner. Educational practice, however, implicitly assumes that learning takes place through the activity of the teacher . . . Unfortunately this almost universal practice among teachers flies in the face of what is almost universally agreed about learning.
>
> (Burgess 1979: 2)

This is a sentiment that can be applied to learning teaching and the work of professional tutors. So far as the individual learner is concerned, the theoretical basis of the position is reflected in the social psychology of Mead (1934) and other symbolic interactionists. Their contention is that human beings as social actors have a self that is built through interaction with others. The self renders us capable of interpreting, judging, analysing and evaluating circumstances, the expectations to which others ascribe us, and the meanings on which we place our experiences of the world (i.e. perceptions, interpretations, conceptions, knowledge). It also provides a mechanism of self-interaction, a capacity to address, respond to, and re-address ourselves and those perspectives – a reflective capability. It gives us the capacity to plan and organize action with regard to ourselves and our circumstances as we perceive them.

Through this process it is possible to engage with experience in ways that involve self-consciously forming and guiding conduct, towards ourselves, towards others, and towards situations. Action in this perspective is conduct constructed through reflective capability, as distinct from some behaviour which might be driven by instinct, or by instantaneous and overriding powers of emotion. In this scheme of things we:

- perceive and indicate to ourselves our circumstances;
- interpret those perceptions and situations;
- identify what we want to achieve;
- establish objectives;
- map a prospective line of behaviour;
- forge a course of action;
- note and interpret the actions and responses of others;
- size up the resulting situation and consequences;
- check our own responses and interpretations;
- spur ourselves on in discouraging circumstances.

In teaching this embraces the role of feelings, personal qualities and professional characteristics as well as what are often regarded as more rational and observable behaviours in practice. Both dimensions contribute their own qualities (Denzin 1984; Best 1985; Franks and McCarthy 1989; Fineman 1993; Goleman 1996) and their incorporation is included in ways of portraying the reflective process. Warnke's summary, for example, encompasses all events and experiences as contributory to the central principles of reconstruction:

> for Gadamer experienced people are those who have learned from events in their lives and have learned because they were aware of their fallibility. That is, they have learned because they were open to the possible refutation of their beliefs and prejudices and could therefore revise or supplement them in a productive way.
>
> (Warnke 1987: 157)

This particular portrayal focuses on the individual, and in that sense is much more about the social–psychological construction of knowledge. An enlarged, more encompassing view of knowledge acquisition is to be gained by considering how contributions can be made by individuals, or groups, to the accumulation of experience and communally held knowledge of, and perspectives on, education in general and teacher induction in particular. That is the continual reconstruction of educational knowledge in the public domain, which provides a mechanism whereby the individual learner and the knowledge generating community develop together. It was this more communal dimension of reflective practice that began Schön's (1971) articulation of existentialist and constructivist learning, based on his review of social programmes in the United States of America. He argued that social action projects are constantly displaced by other ideas, intentions, and activities, which gain their turn in being promoted and sponsored. By means of this displacement and consequent inattention to displaced projects, whatever might be learned from them tends to be lost.

If this thesis is applied to educational knowledge and especially to teacher induction, it can be related to the potential for the development of intelligent practice (Elliott 1989), or accumulated professional wisdom (Stenhouse 1975), or what Sergiovanni (1998) calls educational capital, and Bourdieu (1983) thinks of as social and cultural capital. The potential is just not being realized, it seems, when one considers some educational projects within which teachers gained expertise that are now redundant.

In teacher education, the introduction of all-graduate entry in Britain was accompanied by curriculum changes which were never systematically evaluated (Wilkin 1996). New pilot projects in induction for newly qualified teachers were not followed through (Bolam et al. 1975; Tickle 1994). The impact of competence-based assessment, coupled with school-based pre-service training, has not been independently monitored and evaluated. Despite generations of in-service training for teachers, anyone seeking evidence of its nature and effectiveness will have considerable difficulty locating that evidence. The educational community is not lacking in accumulated sources on the question of developing professional knowledge and competence after entry into teaching, however. The problem seems to be a failure to convert those sources into applied professional wisdom – or, in cases like induction in England, the problem is a tendency to reinvent an issue by giving it the appearance of a political initiative (DfEE 1998a; 1999b). Then, there is the likelihood that the accumulated sources will be overlooked in the scramble for action (Schön 1971).

As I said earlier, Eraut's (1994) comprehensive reviews of the literature on professional knowledge and competence unsurprisingly combine an attempt to classify their nature with matters concerning their acquisition. For the latter, he focuses extensively on the process category, and in particular on the deliberative process as it occurs in the context of practice:

> The key to reflection as a deliberative process lies in the phrases 'turning back', 'fixing thoughts', and 'deep and serious consideration'. The focus is on interpreting and understanding cases or situations by reflecting on what one knows about them. This knowledge may include both impressions which have hitherto not been reflected upon and any available personal and/or public knowledge deemed relevant.
>
> (Eraut 1994: 156)

By drawing on the work of Dewey (1933), as adopted by Schön (1983), I think we can see that what Eraut calls 'the revolution in thinking about professional expertise' is more the long, silent, social revolution than the dramatic upheaval. Or perhaps it is more a parallel paradigm, vying for space in the face of other powerful traditions and assumptions. It has many followers – including, probably, the vast majority of newly qualified teachers and their colleagues, who experience those processes but do not necessarily have the time, opportunity, or incentives to articulate them in the public domain. Herein lies one of the challenges of the long, quiet, professional revolution – to build the relationship between private and public educational knowledge.

Jarvis's (1983) 11 types of activity within the professional learning process distinguish between those that are educational and those that are not – the former measured by the criteria of openness, participation, humanism, dignity and respect for the learner. The nature and place of these values is obvious in the categories:

- self-direction;
- facilitation;
- being taught;
- being instructed;
- being trained;
- engaging in discussion;
- living;
- socialization;
- being influenced;
- conditioning;
- indoctrination.

This is a helpful distinction in so far as it reminds us that learning by, and/or from, experience does not necessarily mean becoming educated in the process. It is the latter, I believe, that sets the parallel paradigm of Eisner, Elliott, Eraut, Carr and Kemmis, Schön, and many others, apart from the dominant ideological position of the teaching standards and school effectiveness movement.

Research-based learning

These many sources have a lot to say that is applicable to the personal learning projects of individual professionals. Applied to the notion of new teachers studying themselves and their own practice, they all assume that knowledge is constructed actively within learning communities, not in isolation from the immediate environment, nor from the broader professional, educational, economic and political contexts of practice. This is possibly the major complication in getting to grips with professional learning. Personal and communal knowledge is available and used according to individual *and* shared interpretations of problems and situations. That necessarily involves a process of negotiated meanings, a dynamic discourse, argumentation in its best sense. Among those who favour this view of the acquisition of expertise, the resulting personally held or locally situated knowledge is seen as connected with the collective body of professional wisdom. In educational research terms, personal and 'grounded' theories of teaching interlock with propositional knowledge and concepts. The lack of such a communal approach to educational knowledge, which Lortie (1975) laments, can be rectified so that other practitioners and future generations of educators and their students can benefit. But even this assumes some method of sharing, passing on, or inducting newcomers into its substance, its methods, and the processes of its construction.

Common among notions about how professional educators might learn their trade are the premises of learning *by* experience. This implies individualistic and personal encounters with practice. That concept can be extended to include another common premise, of learning *from* experience. That implies a more analytical stance to experience and accommodates learning through reference to other sources in addition to direct encounters in practical events, as Eraut (1994) outlined. The procedures for engendering such an approach are not magical, though understanding precisely how they can be conducted to best effect is still rather elusive, and faces many fixed attitudes about the supposed separation of theory and practice. Transforming these attitudes and engendering induction methods into less hit-and-miss, and more systematic, procedures can be achieved through the development of a culture and process of inquiry. A knowing profession in these terms is one in which:

> teacher research is about how students and their teachers construct the
> curriculum, co-mingling their experiences, their cultural and linguistic

resources, and their interpretive frameworks. It is about how teachers' actions are infused with complex and multi-layered understandings of learners, culture, class, [race?], gender, literacy, social issues, institutions, communities, materials, texts, and curricula. It is about how teachers work together to develop and alter their questions and interpretive frameworks informed not only by thoughtful consideration of the immediate situation and the particular students they teach and have taught but also by the multiple contexts – social, political, historical, and cultural – within which they work.

(Cochran-Smith and Lytle 1998: 24)

In accord with many others who adopt a social–critical view of action research, these authors see the roles of teachers and professional tutors as including a process by which they engage in critical inquiry about practice and about the purposes, arrangements and consequences of schooling. They argue for the inquiry stance across the professional lifespan as distinct from discrete periods of inquiry within single projects, programmes, or places. Of course, it is possible to extend this notion to the development of a culture of inquiry across professional generations. That is a principle that could hold good in England with the Teacher Training Agency's flagship of teaching as a research-based profession. It would hold good so long as the concept of research based professionalism is adequate, so long as the idea is not displaced by competing ideologies or 'good ideas' before it takes root, so long as it becomes a key feature of what is expected of all teachers. Such a perspective would enable the construction of practical theory from within the profession as a whole (Carr and Kemmis 1986; Elliott 1991). That is less imaginable with regard to induction, in which participation by professional tutors is likely to be short-lived, dispersed, and fragile in the face of other responsibilities which they hold. The most that might be hoped for is that tutors will adopt an enquiring disposition in their relationships with new teachers.

A research-based approach to learning, incorporating grounded intra-professional theorizing, appears at first glance to be in some contrast to the presentation of theory devised by researchers, or quasi-theories propagated by policy makers, from which practice is intended in some way to improve. However, it is not contrary to the idea of the constructive consideration, criticism, or adoption/acquisition of theoretical ideas from research other than those derived from and grounded in experience. In the case of social theory of an extra-professional kind, for example within sociology, social psychology, linguistics, psychology, philosophy, or history, the questions are:

- what perspectives do they offer on education as a social process?
- how should these influence the dispositions and practices of professional educators and their tutors?
- how are those influences brought about?

Reading, and taking account of observations, descriptions, analyses, and theories from other teachers – or from professional tutors, educational researchers, biographers, historians, novelists, anthropologists, psychologists, or sociologists – is a lesser known pursuit within the professional culture of teaching. It is, though, part of the wider culture of professional education. While such sources appear to be distrusted by teachers as academic and non-practical, or else given little attention because of the time they demand, they are a large educational resource. Significant sums of public finance are spent on research. Policy decisions at institutional, local, and national levels of the service, as well as the practices of teacher educators, inspectors, curriculum policy makers, clinical psychologists, speech therapists, and so on, are premised on research and theoretical perspectives. Just whether or how these theoretical sources are reflected in the actions of newly qualified teachers in classrooms is a matter for induction programme planners and new teachers themselves.

What of the inquiring teacher in this pattern of new experience called induction? Having argued that the concept and process of research-based practice involves the active construction of knowledge, through action and reflection, and that action and reflection can apply to individuals, organizations, or communities, how do such grand visions relate to the actual sources and experiences of learning defined by new teachers themselves?

Sometimes action and reflection have been equated with experiential learning (Schön 1983, 1987; Kolb 1984; Winter 1989; Rasenen 1997). Rasenen summarizes one line of development, which draws on principles articulated in pragmatic philosophy, action research, developmental psychology, and activist education. He describes the reasons why experiential learning has remained a central focus in the professions (Rasenen 1997: 16). These are summarized as:

- an interest in valuing and accrediting experience gained in places other than formal education settings – *workplace learning*;
- a desire to bring about changes in practice through direct action – *applied research*;
- aiming to raise awareness of social issues and circumstances, and bringing about change within institutions – *school-based development*;
- valuing personal growth and development, individual agency, and diversity of experience and perspective – *self-appraisal*.

These interests, purposes, and sources of knowledge about the processes of teachers' learning have become so diverse that it is only possible here to steer a course into the literature which has grown apace in recent years. One interesting feature of it is that its equivalents in the study of children's learning might have much to offer, maybe providing a basis for an inquiry partnership between new teachers and their students about the quality of each other's learning – as suggested by Cochran-Smith and Lytle (1998). Costa (1991) for example, has brought together a compendium of research and promotional propositions on the development of learning processes. Once again, this is impossible to summarize here, and anyway represents only one source, but, for example, he distinguishes between kinds of thinking that can be invoked during the learning process, that seem applicable to teacher induction and experiential learning. For example, he includes:

- *Remembering*: Routine memory is invoked in response to information, or answers to simple enquiries. This kind of thinking is displayed when learning subject content or curriculum requirements, organizational procedures, the location of resources, the names of pupils and colleagues, tips suggested by mentors, information about pupils' progress, experiences of yesterday, and myriad other contextual references that are essential to the daily round of teaching.
- *Repeating*: Repeating involves the application of skilled practices, which might occur in, say the use of information and communications technology expertise, in modelling of practices demonstrated by experienced colleagues, reapplying procedures deemed to have succeeded in classroom management, developing routines for the efficient distribution of resources or use of teaching equipment.

    Judgements about what was worth repeating, and what was not, were often reported by new teachers in my research – accompanied by many stories of modification of tried strategies, or adaptations of suggestions made by others, as teaching strategies were honed towards optimum solutions to the problems of practice.
- *Reasoning*: Reasoning involves those kinds of judgements that weigh evidence and bring about modifications to practice, about the translation of subject knowledge into forms accessible by students, appreciation of the appropriate nature and place of ideas in the design of the curriculum, or the weighing of different potential solutions to the problems of group organization in the classroom. However, reasoning also might involve the explication of educational aims, or content, in the first place. It would include the capacity to listen to, or to generate and articulate educational arguments, to engage in critical discourse on education. One could presume that that in turn involves reasoning with students themselves about the values, purposes, practices and consequences of education, as well as with professional colleagues, managers, or ministers.
- *Reorganizing/relating*: Reorganizing and relating information and ideas is closely allied to, if not inherent in, creative thinking, which involves the recognition of the complexity of a problem, the imaginative construction of potential courses of action, and the novel application of, or adjustment to existing practical solutions. This is the kind of thinking that might be invoked in the use of clinical competence, as Zimpher and Howey (1987) define it. But it is also the bridging point into the realm of personal qualities, dispositions and values, since the imaginative search will depend upon those characteristics, and will relate closely to the combined realms of reasoning and emotion.
- *Reflecting*: Reflecting provides the capability to consider possibilities and consequences of ideas and actions. As my research with new teachers showed, this occurs by predicting, mentally planning for and hypothetically testing

out different scenarios that might be anticipated; or even allowing for the unanticipated intellectual or practical ambush, which is a known feature of educational territory.

The process of reflective thinking includes metacognition, that is the ways in which we think about our own thinking. This characteristic of professional knowledge is central to the notion of self-development, and to development through interaction with other professionals.

Costa takes us much further around the processes, recognizing the import-ance of:

- persistence;
- decreasing impulsivity;
- listening to others with empathy;
- cooperative thinking;
- flexibility;
- striving for accuracy and precision;
- questioning and problem-solving;
- drawing on past knowledge in new situations;
- taking risks;
- using ingenuity;
- maintaining inquisitiveness.

(adapted from Costa 1991: 100–16)

These qualities will hardly be a surprise to those interested in active learn-ing pedagogy, but I think they would be a surprise – a welcome one – if they appeared in the career entry profiles of newly qualified teachers. They would fit well as outcomes for teacher development within the broader concept of 'reflective thinking' or research-based teaching, and provide a basis for research about how such outcomes might be extended, amended, and more importantly, developed. So far, that debate has largely concentrated not just on reflective, but also on reflexive thinking (Carr and Kemmis 1986; Elliott 1991; Tickle 1994). This is the kind of thinking that takes us more deeply into the realm of self-scrutiny and the examination of the self, and of the values on which we depend for guiding our actions. It also affects our relationship with the values that surround us in the educational (and wider social and political) community, and the capacity of the community itself to engage in collective reflexivity. What that illustrates, though, is the import-ance of identifying topics of reflection/reflexivity/criticism, as well as the location of those processes in the social nexus of teaching. For example, one possibility is to reflect on the nature of one's behaviour in a classroom; another is to consider why a particular line of conduct was adopted; a third is try to establish the reasons for limits imposed on one's actions by social obligations or material conditions. All three are appropriate in a self-critical educational community. They could be engaged in introspectively, inter-personally, intraprofessionally, or inter-professionally.

As far as the individual teacher is concerned, Bruner's (1985) summary of models of the learner (see below) suggests ways that these kinds of thought processes might be incorporated into learning strategies, or into assumptions about how new teachers learn. Again, each of these displays implicit differences in perspective about the nature of knowledge and its acquisition. The analysis offers an eclectic view of the processes and the activity of learning, leading Bruner to assert that all learners have a host of learning strategies at their command, and that we should equip them with a menu of their possibilities as well as 'arm them with the procedures and sensibilities that make it possible for them to use the menu wisely' (Bruner 1985: 1).

The menu, which I have summarized, includes:

- *Tabula rasa*: the world is as it is. We should study it and understand how it is. Knowledge is external. The mind's need is to internalize. Success in learning is gained by experiencing the world as it is.
- *Hypothesis generator*: the learner selects intentionally what is to be learnt. Learning is shaped by hypotheses and active curiosity guided by self-directed projects. Success is to have a good theory and to test it out against observation and experience.
- *Nativism*: the mind is innately shaped by underlying structures for organizing experience. Opportunities to exercise innate powers of mind are the formula for success, providing an unfolding of the application of those powers as experience and response are accumulated.
- *Constructivism*: the world is made according to a set of structural rules that are imposed on the flow of experience. Mastery of structural rules at one level allows the learner to move to a higher set of rules.
- *Expert to novice modelling*: Define what is to be learnt, find an expert and determine how it is done; compare the novice's capabilities and simulate activities for them to perform, through stages of perfection. Success is achieved by being specific and explicit about performance.

Reflexive practice

Being armed with the procedures and sensibilities for the wise use of learning strategies would be an essential characteristic of the reflexive professional. It needs therefore to become the central characteristic for all newly qualified educators as they lead the way ahead into a transformed profession. This seems to be where the complexities faced by individual new teachers (the site of psychological struggles) converge with the social complexities (the site of professional struggles). That is where identities and social structures meet in the drama of education. It needs to be a participative drama – not a spectatorial theatre which the audience is constantly tempted to leave. It is here that the process of reflexive practice is key.

Beyond his 1971 study of social programmes, Schön (1983, 1987) elaborated his ideas about the relationship between practice and research – his theory of reflection-in-action and reflection-on-action. This is based on a seemingly simple notion: that when a professional person reflects in action they become a researcher in a specific and particular practical situation. What this means is that practice is research. The way Schön sees it, professional situations are complex and unstable because they combine so many variables. Which factors will be active in a situation cannot always be predicted or controlled. (Just take, for example, the emotional state of the people involved, the way concepts are grasped in different ways and at different rates by students, or the failure to convey information in what was predicted to be a straightforward lesson.) They are also difficult to act upon, because action needs to be judged according to how one reads each practice situation. The process of reflection and action involves the management of extensive information, which itself may be rapidly made redundant as new factors come into play. Such is the dynamic of classrooms and schools.

What is more, in teaching, the purpose is to bring about change among learners, to influence and manipulate events, to achieve a desired aim (Elliott 1991). In this respect research-based practice is said to be in the realm of artful inquiry, where further information will constantly be required, to judge the effects of actions and assess the next moves (Schön 1983: 268). Schön describes this constant activity as one of:

- appreciation of situations and their problems;
- action to change things;
- reappreciation of the effects of actions or other changes;
- further action.

Working through this process in a variety of situations, he says, leads to the development of a repertoire of experiences. That repertoire, derived from discerning information in the situation, formulating courses of action, and gathering evidence about the actions and their effects, is then available to refer to in new situations. The teacher draws upon experiences with the possibility of taking prudent courses of action in new circumstances. Experience in this view is used by combining the best of previous evidence, rather than as recipe knowledge, so that each new situation is dealt with through the same process, adding to the repertoire of practice. This process relates closely to the concept of self described by Gethin (1998) (pages 92–3) because in it resides a preparedness to generate and handle constant change, rather than search for certainties. It leaves us with that paradox again, of having the capacity to work in these ways during induction, when the proof of performance is at a premium.

The first year of teaching provides one answer to that conundrum. It can reasonably be regarded as a period when more practical experience is gained than at any other stage in a career, because of what is required in meeting the full responsibilities of teaching for the first time. That occurs in circumstances where a considerable range of new experiences is unavoidable; where the evidence needed to make sound judgements isn't always detectable; and where interpretation, inference and response are personal, drawing on semi-formed images of good teaching. It is also impossible always to judge the effects of action and to assess the nature of newly created situations, because of the rapid pace of decision making and volatile nature of circumstances in densely populated classrooms and schools.

The selection of information may be rapid and impressionistic; the likelihood of information being missed is considerable, and the potential for misjudgement enormous. In this view, as I have previously argued, the problem faced by new teachers in becoming effective teachers is that first and foremost they need to become effective researchers who are capable of:

- enquiry, from which problems can be adequately defined, posed, and understood;
- perceiving and planning possible courses of action as a basis for experiment;
- implementing appropriate strategic action to bring about change;
- monitoring the effects of their actions and responses to them.

Appropriate, effective action depends upon the quality of that research, and those capabilities need to be developed during the early phases of teaching. Their essence is the way judgements are made in practice. It is evident that the processes themselves need to be the focus of attention during tuition and self-managed appraisal so that new teachers can become more skilled in building the foundations of rapid, but sound judgements.

This is a process of scanning the circumstances of school life to decide what is relevant and valuable information in the day-to-day functioning of teaching, and in the longer-term interests of pupils and educational progress. It includes:

- understanding the social impact of dominant curriculum ideologies;
- challenging the base on which prescribed curricula are founded;
- appreciating the effects of the curriculum on individual pupils' lives;
- broadening the realm of student outcomes;
- asserting different models of teacher effectiveness;
- surveying and selecting from subject knowledge in ways that take account of new developments;
- reviewing and responding actively to changes in curriculum policies and prescriptions;
- extending knowledge of children's learning;
- drawing upon the latest studies of classroom assessment; etc.

All of these duties feed back in untold ways into well crafted judgements of curriculum design, lesson planning and instructional communication, in a constant orchestration of ideals, ideas, imagination, and information. Their application is the experience of teaching. That orchestration, that experience, hinges in part on the values that underpin and direct the making of certain judgements rather than others, and the disposition towards evidence that may confront as much as confirm the success of one's actions and achievement of desires.

Elliott (1991: 50) has argued that there are two kinds of practical reflection:

- that which is associated with realizing technical objectives in the curriculum, and which consists of technical reasoning about how to achieve pre-specified ends;
- that which is associated with process values and consists of ethical and philosophical considerations in the judgements made in trying to realize values.

The second kind of reflection helps to generate self-awareness and values clarification, and understanding of the theoretical frameworks that underlie teaching. It seems to me that the development of personal competence, engaging teachers in reflection which 'itself modifies conceptions of ends in ways which change one's understanding of what constitutes good data about practice' (Elliott 1991: 51) is the key to the broader, deeper and more rigorous use of reflective practice.

The realms of self, emotions, dispositions, values, and educational desires need to be taken into account as central elements that influence experience. Ways in which those qualities and characteristics are developed is through the process of reasoning, reflection, and reflexivity in supportive and supporting conditions which can help new teachers to handle aspects of self and the processes of self-construction. Our account of reflective practice then, needs to constitute more than a technicist conception of practical enquiry, because it could simply equate closely with the acquisition of 'mere skills' (Stenhouse 1975). What is clear from new teachers' induction is the need to achieve a mastery of practice in terms of such skills, together with the development of the capacity to handle experience in terms of the personal responses to situations. The prime feature of the induction situation is that it is unstable, destabilizing, and re-constructive. Learning how to learn is complemented and complicated by the place of self within the psychological and environmental conditions of induction.

Beyond the realm of the technical and clinical aspects of competence, reflective experience is conducted on the spot, triggered by practical problems, according to Schön. That is followed by less immediate self-managed appraisal of experience. Experiment and enquiry are conducted in each practice situation, with action, reappreciation of the newly created situation, and further action, eventually accumulating as a rich repertoire of practical knowledge. The learning cycle results in the creation of theories and understandings brought about by what Schön calls playful trial and error activity, but with a sense of purpose, rigour, and depth of attention. That depth of attention seems to be necessary to effect the development of theories and understandings.

In order to take account of conditions of change a number of key qualities are needed in this process that will guarantee continuity over the learning: recognition of the open-endedness of situations, accepting the inevitability of risk-taking, and realization or expectation that modifications in practice will be necessary (Schön 1971: 235). The experiences of new teachers illustrate and exemplify, in my view, how such a mode of research-based practice exists in their work as an essential ingredient of gaining experience (Tickle 1994). However, it can be displaced by the desire for proven practical strategies, especially if the messages given by those others who would construct teachers in a different image perceive the way forward for the profession as merely skills-based.

This is where the realm of personal competence, which incorporates the understanding and the articulation of the educational values on which practice depend, matters most. It is where confidence, self-respect, and the emotional aspects of teaching become crucial. The importance of the personal realm of competence, the clarification and development of values and of confidence, is suggested by Salmon (1988). She points out that the teacher's personal constructs of understanding are crucial to the kind of education on offer to the pupils. The implication is that knowledge of self (Nias 1989) as an element of professional knowledge, needs to be more substantially part of the agenda of learning teaching:

> Education, in this psychology, is the systematic interface between personal construct systems. This view of formal learning puts as much emphasis on teachers' personal meanings as on those of learners.
>
> (Salmon 1988: 22)

That psychology is as relevant to the professional tutor–inductee relationship as it is to teachers and pupils. Here meanings and the very core of selfhood are essentially provisional. The question is, how can they remain so and be esteemed for being so? Can we achieve situations where confident practice can be accepted as untrustworthy in this sense? Indeed, can we create situations in which untrustworthiness, provisionality, is a firm basis for confident practice? To do so means that the place of the emotions in learning teaching is central – but how about the acquisition and development of emotional qualities? It may be that the literature on beginning teachers is so replete with references to negative trauma simply because this connection has been overlooked in policy and provision. But if the links I have suggested above are unbreakable, then individual teachers' emotional constructs also need to become part of the agenda for building a repertoire of professional experience, and induction needs to be viewed as the building of a teacher's life.

Note

1 Some of the conversations of this group of teachers were reported in Tickle 1994 (pages 104–57). Additional data are reported here and at various places in the present book.

5 Developing an induction programme

Dreams unrealized

So by whom, in what forms, and how, should the development of professional expertise be supported (and assessed) during induction? Although,
as the previous chapter shows, much of the learning during the first year of
full time teaching occurs independently, it has been consistently acknowledged that the roles of employers and support staff are also crucial in the
furthering of professional development – in setting the conditions of appointments, in the design and management of induction programmes, in professional tutoring, and in supporting collaborative and self-directed learning.
Together they create and put into effect both the systems and conditions in
which the day-to-day practices of induction define the experiences of new
teachers. It is at these leadership levels of professional practice that induction is writ through with actual and potential fault points, as well as being
open to imaginative opportunity. What is wanted in broad terms from these
levels of leadership in induction practice is clear, wherever one looks in the
world. For example long-standing but unfulfilled promises of moderate work-
loads, systematic support, and provision of further development opportunities
for inductees recur in many places:

> there is no major profession to which a new entrant, however
> thorough his [sic] initial training, can be expected immediately to
> make a full contribution. Teachers in their first teaching posts need,
> and should be released part-time to profit from, a systematic pro-
> gramme of professional initiation and guidance, and further study where
> necessary.
>
> (DES 1983b: para. 84)

The imaginary (that is, the ideal) conditions of first appointments include lightened timetables, dedicated mentors, and a structured school-based induction programme. However, in England at least, inspectors report that few schools have a systematic approach to induction, and the desired conditions remain just that – conditions of desire (DES 1985a: para. 22; TTA 1998a). Employers have been consistently asked by policy makers to improve the quality of teaching through their responsibility to support and encourage professional development in the first and immediately subsequent years: 'A newly trained teacher needs structured support and guidance during probation and his early years in the profession' (DES 1985a: para. 178). The promise was repeated more recently:

> Our aim is to give every new teacher guided support during the first year... Schools will be expected to provide a planned induction programme for each newly qualified teacher... Mentor support would need to be provided.
>
> (DfEE 1997: paras 14 and 15)

These quotations are virtually the same words 12 years apart, and longer, for these contemporary concerns have persisted, but hardly progressed, for generations. Financial factors have undoubtedly played a major part in preventing induction from being reshaped. So far as one can foresee, that will continue, though recent promises in England do have a financial commitment attached to them (TTA 1998a). What is needed in these circumstances is a sense of economic realism, coupled with a reconceptualization of induction that recognizes that new teachers themselves can be placed in the forefront, playing a major part in leading their own learning, in cooperation with professional tutors. That is to recast the formal provision of support, in line with the sensitive school and staff development practices which exist in some schools, to cater specifically for new entrants. A dignified and respectful support system will be one conducted both proactively for school improvement, and responsively for individual teacher development. It will respect and facilitate the contributions that new teachers already have to offer to the communities that they join. It will also lead in new directions in the development of professional expertise, however. That will require more than simply confirming that standards of professional proficiency, as defined by external agencies, have been demonstrated by individual new teachers (or not) for purposes of certification.

This sounds like common sense, given the scale of professional knowledge to be mastered following entry to teaching, and its scope for improvement in the profession as a whole. However, if it was simply common sense, induction might have taken leaps ahead long ago, and might not have such a dire history (Evans 1978). The McNair Report (1944) for example proposed a probationary year with provisional recognition of qualified teacher status, with schools specially staffed for receiving and supervising new teachers. Nothing was done. The recommendations came only just before the post-war crisis in recruitment and the emergency teacher training scheme. Less than 20 years later a school population bulge resulted in a huge expansion of recruitment to teaching (NUT 1969, 1971; Plowden Report 1967). The first year was again seen as an opportunity for continued tutoring, as well as a time for the assessment of performance (DES 1968). Assessing practical proficiency at minimal competency levels in classroom skills, after offering help and guidance which was supposed to be provided within 'appropriate' conditions of work for new entrants, was the promise then too. The evidence of new teachers' experiences however provides a stark contrast to policy aspirations, with such support varying from little to none, and many teachers being abandoned to the isolation of the classroom (Collins 1969).

New teachers often did not have information about classes, syllabuses to be taught, or the induction support offered (if any), until close to or even after the date they began teaching (Taylor and Dale 1971). Taylor and Dale reported that new teachers saw the year as a period of assessment rather than one of professional growth. There was some prospect of shifting the emphasis towards encouraging professional growth when *Education: A Framework for Expansion* (DES 1972) proposed that the government should support induction in which new teachers would have at least 20 per cent of their time devoted to in-service training. Professional tutors were to be designated and trained, and a network of professional centres established to support induction arrangements. Pilot schemes were introduced as the forerunners to a national scheme of induction (Bolam 1973; Bolam *et al.* 1975; McCabe 1978; Davis 1979). The recommendations arising from the pilot schemes included:

- a call for systematic coordination of appointment and placement in schools;
- the provision of essential school information such as pupil lists, timetables, school handbooks;
- induction procedures to be made, and made known, well in advance of starting a new job;
- early contact with the employing school's personnel;
- orientation to the geography of the school and locality;
- provision of pastoral support through meetings with peers;
- guidance from colleagues upon taking up a post;
- alleviated working conditions, with reduced teaching loads;
- release from teaching for orientation and professional development meetings;
- opportunities to observe colleagues;
- a structured programme of induction within the school;
- identification of a named teacher tutor for the school-based support;
- a non-assessing mentor from outside the school;
- a climate of fairness towards, and trust by, new teachers.

Given these arrangements, it was argued, the first year would be characterized less as the crisis it was often represented to be. Induction was re-envisaged as a continuum of professional learning for all teachers, made effective through a focus on issues of practical classroom relevance, and the individualized problems and opportunities for learning of each of the teachers (Bolam 1973). The proposed national scheme coincided with, and was a victim of, the implementation of public spending cuts in England, which struck at the core of educational provision for 20 years of Conservative rule. Probation continued to imply that the aim of the first-year teacher is to become masterly in the constituent skills of teaching, or to be weeded out. Once achieved, continued skilled performance was what was required, overlaid by the rhetoric of continued learning:

> The notion of 'extended professionalism' . . . has not been fully and universally recognised. The expectation (for continued INSET) should be laid down during initial training, and the process should begin with induction.

> (DES 1987: 30)

Hoyle's (1969) distinction (adopted here by the DES) between teachers who maintain a learning stance in their teaching throughout a career, and 'restricted professionals' who do not seek to develop their practice, became virtually redundant as the impact of series-legislation and multiple and rapid changes hit the profession through the 1990s. Strategies for handling those changes, from flight out of teaching on the one hand, the embrace of prescription on another, with teacher industrial actions, and various responses in between, led to a much more complex professional picture. Coupled with Huberman's (1993) research, which shows that many teachers experience cynicism, disaffection, disillusionment, and so on, and extensive research that describes industrial ill-health (stress) among teachers, we are provided with a clear reminder that a great deal has to be achieved to improve the conditions of schooling for all members of the profession. In the meantime, in its most obvious sense, such people are a part of the profession into which new teachers will be inducted, and may even be directly instrumental in the induction arrangements. As confirmed by my own research (Tickle 1994) teachers in these categories can have a significant impact on the experiences of newcomers. They are among the colleagues who will attempt to transmit their attitudes and practices to new teachers. Indeed some have been found to be designated induction tutors, charged with the lead role in designing and coordinating support programmes. In such extreme cases, one might well ask: what forms does in-school induction take and how is it presented and received by new teachers? A detailed picture of the very personal and individualized experiences of a large number of teachers was presented in my previous book (Tickle 1994). Probably the most notable message from the evidence is that the intensity of experience and the specifics of circumstances make it difficult and somewhat purposeless to generalize beyond the individual case:

> SP: So I've got to be very careful . . . she came into my lesson – she didn't comment on it to me, which I thought was a bit off, she went behind my back and commented on it to my head of

department. And I thought, well, you know, I'm not a baby, I'm not a child – why don't you tell me? . . . I feel less attached to these kids. I just see them once a week and they go out and I see them the next time . . . On teaching practice I had less classes so I got to know more kids better, whereas here they just come in and they go out, it's rather like a conveyor belt system. And not having a registration class, again I just sort of get thrown in or go and see this class one day, this class another day. They just sort of come into the lesson and I give them the lesson, and then if they don't like it, they don't like it, if they do, they do. And I try hard to sort of get them involved in that one lesson a week. I am sort of there and I'm just sort of thrown in at the deep end; I'm not saying that nobody has made any special effort to say, 'Well, look out for this or look out for that' – I'm just there, and they haven't actually had [a newly qualified teacher] for a long time. I don't know – I'm not too taken up with the place. I don't feel that I belong at that school, I felt that I much preferred my teaching practice school, I think that is the main problem.

LC: Last Friday I really felt part of this school – it was netball, and the team won, and they were clapped in assembly. Some of the teachers had done something and they were all clapped by the children, and I felt, 'This is a nice, friendly school and I am happy to be here'. The children are saying 'hello' to me as I pass them now, and it makes such a difference, it really does.

SP: [I'd like] just interesting people to talk to – they are nice but they are superficially friendly – yes, they'll sort of say, 'How are you?' They haven't got time, they've got their own lives, they are not a very sociable staff amongst themselves, none of them socialize with each other, they just come in on a Monday morning, and go at 4 o'clock on a Friday afternoon. And that doesn't help my sense of belonging, I mean, everybody says how well I've settled in and everything, but it's a big strain on me to cope with this situation.

LT: You have a teacher tutor in the school?

SP: You see, I want a good reference when I leave there, and I don't want people to know how I really feel and if they think I'm doing fine, if they think I'm really happy – I don't want them to know how I feel, exactly, I don't want it to go down on my reference that maybe I haven't settled in . . . But you are being assessed, this is what annoys me, I know, not only am I being observed in lessons, but people are observing me in the staffroom and how I am interacting socially, it's been commented on to me, the woman who is in charge of me, she says, 'Oh, I've had my spies out, and we are really pleased with how you have settled in . . . I've been listening in the corridor to the comments of the kids, I've got my spies there'. Good grief, constantly under that sort of observation, that kind of pressure, so I can't relax and say, 'God, today I'm fed-up', because I know people are watching me and saying, 'She's fed-up today'.

LC: I don't think I'd want to admit that to my colleagues. [I'll tell] my friends. I phone up Pauline the whole time and tell her, and I am telling people here, but I couldn't . . . I wouldn't want to lay myself open.

We need to consider carefully who it might be that manages induction arrangements, as well as what they might include. The way they are defined and enacted depends on the quality of the existing workforce. As we know from controversies generated by the Inspectorate's desire to dismiss 'incompetent' teachers, this is a sensitive matter for the profession. What it means for induction is that the continuous commitment of experienced teachers to career-long professional growth and development, based on activities such as questioning the aims of practice, debating educational issues, analysing available evidence, arguing from informed perspectives, and becoming accustomed to examining assumptions, become prerequisites for them to play any part in induction – but that is a high ideal.

I present the extreme, minority, and unacceptable case set against the high ideal as an entry into consideration of the more complex picture of professionalism which awaits the inductee, because it is the whole professional body which, intentionally or not, defines the nature and quality of induction. The presence and quality of an instrumental support tutor is critical, and I will attend to that in due course, but first I want to take a more collective view. The way the profession collectively defines itself, or becomes defined, changes over time (Grace 1991; Lawn 1991). Hargreaves (1999), for example, proposed that there are four types of professionalism at large in teaching, each resulting from different phases in the social reconstruction of the profession. Actually, he asserts an initial age of 'pre-professionals' from when the 'technically simple [but] managerially demanding' job of teaching fostered a stereotypical, coercive, instructional role bent on high levels of social control and the efficient transmission of curriculum content.

Hargreaves recognizes that his use of this construct, as less than professional, might be culturally sensitive, that in some cultures notions of teacher authority differ, and that this form of authoritative teaching can be subject to refinement and reflection. That recognition is important because it leaves authoritative instruction available in the armoury of the educator, rather than either condemning it or asserting it as the only or preferred view of professionalism. Indeed, it might well be incorporated within Hargreaves' next identified age of the 'autonomous professional'. This concept is derived from a post-war period in western nations when the curriculum was decentralized, teacher-enacted innovation widespread, multiple teaching methods were used, and professional judgement was acknowledged as a prime feature of good teaching.

An age of 'professional collegiality' emerged, according to Hargreaves, as a feature of later twentieth-century schooling, at least in some circumstances, and in some locations. Characterized by a search for common purposes, mutual support, learning cultures, and collective responses to rapid changes that affected schools, this form of professionalism is easy to identify in recent educational literature, and in some schools.

In the 'new age' Hargreaves imagines the 'postmodern professional' will be born of the changes brought upon education by economic, social and technological developments, especially through communications technology – but only in some places:

> While some governments (especially in North America) have rolled with and embraced these uncertainties and complexities, valuing multiple intelligences, diverse learning (and teaching) styles, and a process-based rather than content-based curriculum, others have countered the spread of uncertainties with an emphatic assertion and imposition of false certainties.
>
> (Hargreaves 1999: 15)

The impact of these changes and contrasting reactions to them were discussed earlier, and Hargreaves adds his own slant on that discussion in a way that is pertinent to the kinds of induction policies, let alone induction tutors, we might expect to find in schools of the future, and thus the kinds of support programmes that might be created. Proactive, responsive professionals are unlikely to emerge from reactive and restrictive expectations of teachers. Yet the latter is what we appear to be witnessing in the dominant themes of the standards movement.

Of course stereotypes like these are merely indicative of professional characteristics, rather than definitive. Residual elements of pre- and autonomous professional are likely to have changed in the new era of centralized curricula, prescribed testing, imposed inspection targets, the surrender of professional judgement, insularity of schools, competitiveness between schools, and the dullness of uniform teaching standards. In lament, and paradoxically, Hargreaves dreams of the postmodern teacher as a reinvention of the autonomous and collegial types with added capacities for managing the profusion of information sources, handling moral issues and cultural diversity, vested with multiple intelligences, equipped with diverse and principled teaching strategies, and moving outwards into communities to 'face the danger' of working with parents.

An induction programme that will contribute to the self/social construction of this ideal type, across whole populations of new teachers, over a decade or more, will be very different from the one envisaged in England's Department for Education and Employment policy, elements of which are incorporated into the discussion in this book. If a programme also caters for the more expansive, more humane view of teaching that I have described earlier it will be even more challenging than Hargreaves' 'new professional' implies. In particular it will mean that a 'process curriculum' will need to be defined and understood for induction itself. It will mean that the nature of professional knowledge and expertise, with all its built-in complexity, and allowing for what is not known to be explored within the profession, will need to be understood by those who are inducted and those who provide for induction. In short, the goals and practices of induction will need to be defined and conducted in terms of the development of professional expertise in its broadest sense. Minimalist monitoring and assessment of performance will simply not serve either the individual new teacher or the communal and professional need to improve the quality of education.

In what follows I will incorporate some parts of the new policies in England as a minimum foundation for induction support. I will do so, however, wary that the unimaginative remedial baseline that dominates the mentality of what is a probation policy under the name of induction, should not block the vision of a more productive way ahead. There are now opportunities throughout the world to ensure system-wide induction provision which requires of policy makers, the profession's defining bodies such as the general teaching councils and the unions, employers and school managers, and induction tutors, to adopt, develop and display the same qualities and characteristics that are expected of new teachers themselves. There are some key factors that might contribute to a new future for induction, so as not to replicate past failures or to manufacture 'false certainties' based entirely on the supposedly efficient assessment of practice.

The following ideas are based on, and constructively extend, elements of the McNair Report (1944), the James Report (1972), Bolam (1973), Tickle (1994), the TTA (1999), and work in other parts of the world. They take account of the need to imagine, develop and implement a curriculum for induction – and to sustain attention to it, evaluate it, regularize its provisions, and institutionalize its practices throughout the profession in the years ahead. Most of all, they take account of the conceptions of professional knowledge and expertise that have been outlined, and recognize that its development by individuals, and collectively by the profession, is a joint venture in the accumulation and redistribution of professional capital. There are of course the day-to-day practicalities of induction also to attend to.

Administrative bodies

At both state and local levels administrators clearly have a major part in defining the induction experiences of new teachers, both in making policy, implementing it, and overseeing induction practices. Where the administrative body is also the employer, those responsibilities begin with employment legislation. Equally crucially, they lie in defining the non-legislative aspects of the conditions into which newly qualified teachers should be appointed – establishing the posts, duties and responsibilities that make reasonable demands on them, and which provide for continuing professional growth. Those conditions of desire, as I called them earlier, have again emerged in the most recent induction policy in England. They have re-emerged in a way that reflects the realities of the postmodern labour market, bowing to the growth of temporary employment, short-term contracts, and career instability that is now endemic in the educational marketplace. There is a restated intention that teachers should serve their induction period in circumstances that provide for professional development, but little to ensure that all the conditions of desire identified since 1944 will emerge. The new arrangements, amended here by me to include desirable factors of job security, portray the responsibility of policy makers and employers to appoint new teachers in circumstances that:

- ensure security and stability of employment for the induction year as a minimum;
- provide clear job descriptions and expectations;
- involve teaching only within the age range and subject(s) for which they have been trained;
- present the teacher with unexceptional management and discipline problems;
- are based on regular teaching of the same class(es);
- require normal planning, teaching and assessment;
- include no more than 90 per cent of teachers' usual timetable;[1]
- allow sufficient preparatory time before commencement of the job;
- ensure that orientation visits and essential information are provided;
- offer a professional development programme, starting as early as possible after appointment;
- bring about regular contact with a designated, trained, and committed professional tutor;
- make assessment procedures for induction explicit and part of professional growth;
- commit new teachers to view their work as subject to continuing professional development through practical enquiry.

(adapted from various sources)

The conditions of employment and formal procedures for the assessment of induction are persistent problems. At its worst, short-term contracts, the accumulation of induction time in variable circumstances, possibly in a 'special measures' school or one under inspection, and a spread of periods of service that can contribute to the 'induction year', over up to five years, maybe in more than one school, can each reduce any hope of achieving what has just been described as the desirable conditions of appointment. The paradox here is that those circumstances of instability of postmodern schooling have hit induction itself particularly hard. For some teachers entering the workforce, this increases the likelihood of personal destabilization and uncertainty, on top of the usual intensity of taking up a new career.

It has usually been argued that new teachers need more stable conditions for their own growth and development, and the details of policy aspire to that in most respects. It is ironic that they might need a less chaotic personal environment in order to learn how to cope more adequately with the more chaotic, wider educational events. In what would be considered appropriate circumstances, with stability, guaranteed allocations of reduced teaching time for professional development use, a shared image of inquiry-based learning, and a systematic induction programme led by a trained tutor, the way is open towards a profession peopled with members who are active in the development of their own practice, who have a major contribution to make in the construction of educational knowledge, and who could be equipped to lead the way ahead for a research-based profession. It is that image and that mission that needs to be established first and foremost in the policies, the conditions, and the enactment of support programmes.

Then the attention given to the procedures for implementing and sustaining induction provision might establish, in practice, renewed responsibilities for support and assessment roles. Most of all within those roles, the tension between probation/provisional teacher registration on the one hand, and maximizing the professional contributions of new teachers on the other, needs to be explicit, explored, and eroded. The orientation adopted towards career entry profiles and 'induction standards' will be crucial in that process. If it is presumed that the main parties involved – new teachers, colleagues, professional tutors and headteachers – will simply adopt and apply the definitions of teaching that these profiles convey, aspirations of professionalism are lost, and so is the hope of quality in educational practice.

Both of these will depend on adaptations that take the more expansive view of professional knowledge already described. The real success of induction will rest on the capacity to incorporate a professional, critical-inquiry stance towards the career entry profile and induction standards in England, and their equivalents in other countries. It is a stance that can be adapted to any administration's attempt to define teaching competence, and take account of the provisionality and contestability of these matters. That applies, too, to the procedures and practices of induction itself, where the way has been left open for new teachers to raise concerns about the induction programme, and headteachers are charged (by policy) with ensuring that these concerns are addressed satisfactorily. In what follows, the practical procedures that can be invoked from authoritative sources have been adapted to incorporate the principles that underpin the notion of a learning professional community. It is that combination of principles and procedures – better called principles *of* procedure (Stenhouse 1975), which keep the hope alive of a way forward for professionalism and educational quality, by adopting a research stance to the induction curriculum.

That is unlikely to happen when the administration's duties are narrowly and unimaginatively defined. In England they are required to:

- identify a named contact for newly qualified teachers (NQTs) on induction matters;
- assure itself that schools and governing bodies are aware of, and are capable of meeting, their responsibilities for monitoring, support and guidance and for undertaking a rigorous and equitable assessment of the NQT;

- keep a record of the names and term of induction of the NQTs for which it is responsible, based upon information from headteachers;
- liaise with other administrations as appropriate in relation to NQTs employed in more than one school;
- decide, in the light of the headteacher's recommendation, whether an NQT has satisfactorily completed the induction period;
- inform the NQT about whether or not it has accepted the headteacher's recommendation on completion of the induction period;
- keep the NQT informed about next steps following this decision;
- follow up any forms that have not been signed to ensure that it is fully aware of the circumstances;
- communicate its decision to the General Teaching Council (GTC) and to the Secretary of State;
- retain the assessment reports until the GTC has confirmed full registration or has removed the NQT from the register.

(adapted from DfEE 1999b,c)

Dull, bureaucratic, expedient, monitorial, systems-maintaining – and all arguably necessary, but hardly flowing with educational imagination. Governing bodies are simply charged with the job of overseeing the establishment of induction arrangements within their schools. Perhaps these obligations could be redrawn to include at least a leadership role in defining the induction curriculum. To take just one simple idea towards that end, in a recent analysis of the outcomes of in-service teacher education, Harland and Kinder (1997) identified a range of factors that were deemed to be the professional development benefits (outcomes) of in-service courses, which could be adopted as principal aims for induction programmes. They included:

- materials and resources gained by teachers;
- information acquired;
- new insights and awareness;
- development of values;
- affective outcomes;
- motivations and attitudinal outcomes;
- knowledge, understanding and skills;
- impact on/changes in practice;
- institutional benefits.

(based on Harland and Kinder 1997)

The list is not claimed to be definitive or exhaustive, but suppose such an approach were adopted in setting out the broad aims (intended outcomes) of a programme of induction, rather than first and foremost specifying discrete skills and the procedures for assessing, recording, and reporting on them. Coupled with the setting of appropriate learning conditions, and accompanied by principles of procedure for the pursuit of professional improvement in the personal and the communal senses, there would be a considerable reorientation to the way ahead for induction. I believe there would be a different kind of experience for new teachers, in becoming part of learning communities. The specification of induction standards by ministerial or administrative staff (DfEE 1999b) in these terms would reorientate induction, and would imply the adoption of a range of means of learning, including research-based practice and collective approaches to school improvement in which new teachers might begin to take a leading role.

Headteachers/principals

Research leaves little doubt that the headteacher, or principal, of a school is a crucial figure in ensuring the effectiveness (or failure) of the induction process. The precise role and day-to-day functions of the headteacher, between acting as a managerial facilitator of employment arrangements, guaranteeing the availability of support programmes, and acting in direct relation to the assessment and registration of teachers, is complex. Yet it is a very minor, and possibly very occasional, responsibility within the principal's role. For the new teacher, though, it probably represents the most important part of headship. Some of the difficulties associated with it were considered in detail by Tickle (1994) and the Association of Teachers and Lecturers (1999), demonstrating the need for careful and consistent development and monitoring of those who adopt these responsibilites.

To some extent the specific functions that headteachers undertake in relation to new recruits are conditioned by the size and type of school, and the delegation of duties to other staff. It is therefore difficult for policy makers to be prescriptive, or for researchers to generalize, about how a principal's participation might, or actually does, work. Those variations and the uniqueness of contexts and personnel mean that it is even more necessary for headteachers themselves to adopt an enquiring stance towards the conduct of their induction responsibilities. Allowing for those variations in context, and presuming a reflexive approach, it is supposed that headteachers will be responsible for ensuring that:

- an appropriate designated member of staff takes responsibility for each NQT;
- key people in the induction process are prepared for their roles;
- a programme of monitoring, support and assessment is in place for each new teacher;
- timetables representing no more than 90 per cent of normal teaching and preparation time are allocated to new teachers;[2]
- assessment of performance is rigorous, fair, and conducted according to established procedures;
- any new teacher whose registration is deemed to be at risk should be observed teaching by the headteacher;
- completed assessment reports are submitted to the local administrators;
- recommendations regarding teacher registration are made to the administration;

- the NQT has the means of raising concerns about the induction programme, and ensuring that these concerns are addressed satisfactorily;
- the administration is kept informed about the employment status of each new teacher;
- liaison is conducted with others in relation to employment and induction progress;
- the governing body is kept informed about arrangements for induction.

(adapted from DfEE 1999b,c and Tickle 1994)

Once again, this checklisting of duties represents the day-to-day functioning of essential systems maintenance. It remains subject to interpretation and translation into the interactive encounters that become the life-experiences of new teachers. That is, much of it might be routine and bureaucratic; some of it might be seen as surveillance; or it might provide an educational challenge to devise not just a programme, but a principled induction curriculum. The designation of non-teaching time might be protected from the routines of planning and marking, and used for educational enquiry and goal-oriented professional development. It is here, in the detail, that the way ahead might be missed and a way back to the past be taken instead.

Induction tutors

Some of the conditions of induction are likely to be made possible only if funding is allocated for a designated person, who is able to coordinate and directly offer professional support to each new teacher. Trustworthy and trusted monitoring of progress and professional development, and providing well-founded feedback on practical performance, is a required, major part of that role throughout the first year of teaching. It is clear from evidence that new teachers seek confirmation of their professional standing in terms of classroom proficiency as the prime concern. They also need support in negotiating opportunities to pursue their own innovations and projects. Even where other responsibilities allow it, headteachers are not appropriate designated persons for this purpose, though they may play a significant and supportive background part. Nor are line managers necessarily best placed, because of their roles in formally assessing inductees (see below), though once again, they are likely to play a crucial supporting role in the induction partnership.

In practice the direct contact, provision of many elements of support, the creation of opportunities, and gathering of evidence of performance, might be undertaken by more than one person, except in very small schools. The arrangements, relationships and interactions will be unique to each circumstance, which makes the role of an experienced colleague acting as induction coordinator the pivot of success. At the most significant points for a new teacher, a professional tutor who is neither the principal nor line manager is more likely to emphasize and provide a fair balance between support and development in the interests of the employee, and the quality control interests of the managers.

At an equally important level for the way ahead in personal and professional development, informed by principles of research-based practice, it is a designated tutor who is more likely than a headteacher to be fully engaged in his or her own teaching and thus, closer to the pupils' learning. It is also possible that a professional tutor will develop and deploy tutorial expertise more consistently over longer periods than line managers. In schools with departmental structures, for example, the latter might variously, and occasionally, find themselves with induction responsibilities. The availability of a professional tutor, with accumulated expertise, and working in partnership with departmental staff, is likely to enhance the work of line managers, as well as provide safeguards for new teachers.

KM: If somebody just says that everything is all right, it's not helpful at all, is it? Saying, 'Everything is fine' could mean, 'Well, it's not really but I don't want to go into it', or, 'You're just average and just coping', or, 'You're doing fantastically'.

LC: I had I suppose constructive comments made after —— came in because he assessed the lesson, he's the maths specialist and he assessed the maths lesson, investigating, which didn't work out too well, and so he felt able to give me advice and I suppose at the time I found it quite difficult – I mean, nobody likes being criticized and everybody would rather be told beforehand and then helped over the problem than having to do it and fail and be seen to fail and then get help, which is what happened. I obviously didn't do too well and he went and talked to the head about it and after that I was given a whole lot of support in maths. I went to visit classrooms and the head came into my class and took over and had a special group going out to another teacher and the teacher – you know, a lot of support this way, that he did care about me. But I couldn't help thinking at the time that it was a lot of stress and bother when it would have been nice to have had a chance to talk about it beforehand, and sorted that out . . . worried about my maths, and I'd like a bit of help before I actually had to fail.

LT: Were you conscious of your worry about this before it happened?

LC: Yes, and I'd talked to the deputy head about it, but again I wasn't given the right opportunity, I mean, you answer, you speak to people and give them what you think they might be wanting to hear. I mean, the conversation I had with the deputy head wasn't, 'What are the problems you are having at the moment? Tell me how I can help you?' More very general – 'How are things going?' It wasn't that, 'I want to get into a deep discussion about this' – it's 'I want to know generally how things are going' So, I wasn't really specific about it – I hadn't been given the right question really, I hadn't been fed the right vibes to answer it. I mean, I know this in class, children have to fail before you can help them – they have to work through the card and get it wrong before you see the problem. You don't teach a topic to the class, explaining the possible problems and then letting them get on with it.

LT: Are there other examples in your work apart from maths where you've anticipated difficulties in the same way and had wanted to talk with people about them beforehand, but hadn't had the chance?

LC: I suppose the Jason problem, with his dad coming in was another example of that, and we had those problems with Jason and through lack of experience didn't know the right way of going about sorting it out before it became a big problem, and his dad phoned the school, and was worried. So that would be another example. But all these things are so long ago now – that first term – that things have got so much better since then.

In small primary schools intermediate line managers don't usually exist, highlighting the need for professional tutors to work with headteachers on behalf of new entrants. In all cases, the nature of these relationships is a key factor for unlocking the potential of collaborative enquiry between new and experienced teachers. There are established, directly shared interests between them. But the key unlocks rather more than mutual classroom inquiry and interests in personal qualities and professional characteristics of new teachers. It raises the hope that through appropriate preparation in the tutor role, and via coordination and leadership of other teachers involved with induction, the principles of procedure for a critical stance towards teaching standards will be developed. That would require the development of understanding of professional knowledge and expertise, and knowledge of how it is acquired, to be shared more widely.

However, induction tutors and other teachers concerned with induction carry out their functions in the midst of many responsibilities. Tutor funding needs to be allocated to ensure that training in the role is undertaken, and that commitments to it are developed over time. The likelihood of temporary occupancy of the role of tutor, especially in primary schools, means that commitments, as well as the practicalities of finding time, could be largely overcome through specific funding. Of course the role need not be (and in many schools is not) ring-fenced. The designation of a professional tutor would enable collaborative enquiry and pedagogical leadership approaches (see Sergiovanni 1998, Chapter 6) to be adopted, and to focus on the development of quality teaching or leadership by the tutor and other colleagues, and by inductees when appointed. That would go some way to ensuring that new teachers were inducted directly into a climate of collaborative enquiry, and a milieu of the school as a learning community.

The personal and professional qualities needed of professional tutors, especially in relation to induction, are therefore manifold, and cannot be simply assumed to exist or to be deployed on an occasional basis by line managers.

The key characteristics of good tutoring identified in a research project by new teachers and tutors (Tickle 1994) include the following:

- accessibility;
- reliability;
- professional credibility and respect;
- experience;
- honesty and humility;
- approachability and calmness of manner;
- supportive, constructive and encouraging style;
- being a good listener, sensitive, and sympathetic;
- showing empathy, and handling matters with humour.

(adapted from Tickle 1994: 179)

To these we need to add a clear and comprehensive understanding of professional knowledge and expertise. In the way ahead, it will be necessary also to add to these qualities the professional dispositions and expertise in research-based teaching, and the capacity of pedagogical leadership that would be in place in a school that is a learning community. These do not simply grow unnurtured and unfunded. Nor do they arise in the solitariness of tutor duties, but in the busyness of school life and interactiveness of school inquiry. So while the principles of research are fostered, the day-to-day functional knowledge remains intact. For the latter, it would be better if the delegation of specific actions to named individuals became a requirement within each individualized programme, to ensure that each new teacher knows what to expect from whom. For example, the induction tutor should be expected to carry the broad responsibilities that follow:

- undertake preparation for the role;
- be fully aware of the requirements of the induction period;
- ensure that the new teacher is fully informed about the induction programme;
- organize, implement and coordinate day-to-day support and assessment in consultation with each new teacher;
- ensure rigorous and fair judgements about the new teacher's performance;
- keep records of support and formal assessment activities undertaken, and their outcomes;
- make any necessary arrangements for additional support and experience.

(adapted from TTA 1998a: para. 86; 1999b)

Collegial support

The induction tutor is also likely to carry out some specific tasks as part of the range of people upon whom a new teacher may depend for particular help. The identification and delegation of specific tasks that can ease the start of a new teacher's working life has been carefully worked out and detailed in some schools. In others, the routines, policies, and expectations may be so taken for granted that they are hard to detect for newcomers. It may be difficult to know exactly what will serve newcomers best, especially as they begin to penetrate the interpersonal dimensions of a community. There is both the formal and the informal world of school cultures to attend to, and the ways in which initiations occur are the shared responsibility of all members of a community. The professional qualities of the induction tutor are just as important in the working relationships between other colleagues and new teachers. There are also specific, identifiable pieces of information, advice, and support that may be appropriately provided at different stages in the induction year by these colleagues, both formally and informally. One part of the tutorial role is to ensure that the points of contact and timing of formal events are documented. Tasks include three main types:

- specific actions to be taken in promoting context-specific and wider professional knowledge;
- general support and care towards the development of personal qualities and professional characteristics;
- guiding research-based teaching and school inquiry.

The critical moments when the first two will be needed are often unpredictable, and might be more than one moment – in short, much of this knowledge is accumulative. Some, albeit relatively arbitrary, stages and checkpoints can be located however, and named staff allocated to ensure that a list of common needs are met.

Soon after appointment:
- clarify employment contract procedures;
- provide welcome and introductions;
- arrange tour/orientations;
- plan times to meet teaching colleagues;
- meet induction personnel and describe roles;
- ensure school dates and prior meetings are known;
- outline teaching responsibilities;
- arrange receipt of information essential for teaching;
- survey resources;
- fix further preparatory visits/contact numbers;
- offer assistance with residence;
- invite requests for other advice and information.

Well before the start of the job:
- discuss teaching timetable;
- provide and explain information of direct importance to teaching programmes – duties, room plans, resources;
- provide pupil lists and records;
- discuss quality assurance and accountability mechanisms;
- go over school routines, introduce school handbook;
- discuss core values, policies, development plans;
- explain staffing structure, organization of the curriculum;

- go over assessment/examination arrangements;
- introduce support staff;
- explain rules and routines of the school;
- provide calendar of events;
- discuss programmes of study for allotted class(es) and timetable allocation;
- help with planning/lesson forecasts;
- orientate to classrooms/facilities;
- allow time for preparation of lessons and resources;
- instruct in use of school equipment;
- arrange meetings with children where possible;
- tour locality and provide information about it;
- outline the induction programme and responsibilities;
- provide informal contacts and observations;
- plan use of induction time;
- negotiate professional development portfolio;
- explain in-service arrangements;
- advise on professional contacts outside school;
- discuss achievements/concerns in teaching quality.

At the beginning of the first term:
- ensure the teacher gets to know the school layout;
- help with classroom arrangements;
- make sure routine duties are clear;
- advise on timetable and lesson plans;
- confirm resources are available/explain arrangements for access to resources, including locations and purchasing;
- advise on pupils' records;
- provide contact points/times with key personnel;
- arrange meetings with staff and discuss their roles, responsibilities, and duties as they affect induction and the teacher's own work;
- discuss pastoral system/discipline policy;
- advise on parent–teacher contacts;
- start support programme;
- monitor workload/time management;
- invite requests for other support.

Into the first term:
- ensure regular informal contact;
- guarantee at least weekly dialogue on teaching and learning, and the gathering of evidence from it;
- move fully into the support programme, with additional contextual information and policy matters;
- set conditions that allow professional development needs to be identified, and agree upon personal goals that relate to them;
- establish principles for professional development, including a professional development portfolio, starting with a research-based project of interest to the new teacher;

- take account of aspects of the career entry profile and induction standards, based on evidence-gathering and analysis as reflected in a negotiated project;
- agree on an observation of classroom learning and teaching schedule, agreeing provision of feedback coordinated by the induction tutor;
- agree on a schedule of observation of experienced teachers, by the new teacher, based on the research portfolio agenda;
- advise on special needs pupils and support services;
- give encouragement and consider successes;
- begin review of research, incorporating progress of the personal project;
- introduce expectations for self-appraisal, within the context of research-based practice;
- listen and respond with advice when appropriate;
- support trying out of personal teaching strategies, within the conditions for risk taking and research of practical experimentation;
- encourage contributions to staff meetings.

Towards the end of the first term:
- discuss induction assessment arrangements and match with self-appraisal and collaborative enquiry activities;
- confirm knowledge of legal, administrative and professional framework of rights and responsibilities;
- explain duties of administrators, responsibilities of governors and the headteacher;
- conduct review of professional development portfolio and introduce new area of professional knowledge and expertise;
- review progress of initiatives and school contributions.

During the second term:
- confirm that the minimal knowledge, skills and achievements in the career entry profile are recognized and achieved;
- confirm that all minimally specified induction standards have been met and continue to be taken into account/maintained in the personal development programme;
- move into an agreed research and development programme;
- involve formative assessment as part of regular reviews of progress based on the development of research capability and the improvement of professional qualities and characteristics;
- discuss formally the teacher registration procedures.

During the third term:
- spend time with the school's special educational needs (SEN) coordinator in order to address specific and general SEN issues;
- extend understanding of professional knowledge and maintain oversight of national, local, and school policy developments;
- provide further support for personal initiatives, or a programme of contributions from personal strengths, to the school as a learning community;

- plan personal development for the following year based on professional knowledge and expertise, and the research portfolio;
- review school policies on issues of gender, race, social justice, exclusion and inclusion, and consider these in the light of experience, observation, and personal practices;
- process the formalities of assessment for induction and teacher registration.

The newly qualified teacher

In this sequence of events, the new teacher will become familiar with the realms of professional knowledge and expertise that they are expected to develop. If reflexivity and metacognition is to function effectively, a growing sophistication in that understanding, and in the gathering of evidence from practice to compare with the chosen conceptual frameworks, will be an essential and intrinsic part of that development. In which case, each new teacher will need to:

- engage from the beginning in professional development;
- be familiar with induction standards (as defined by others);
- be able to move the professional development programme ahead of those standards;
- attend support meetings and events that are relevant to identified needs;
- be actively involved in the programme of monitoring, support and assessment in ways that are agreed with the induction tutor, and based on an understanding of professional knowledge;
- be fully engaged in their professional development in ways that demonstrate the capacity to contribute to professional knowledge;
- make use of the school's internal procedures for raising professional concerns, including the need to acknowledge and support open, collaborative inquiry;
- engage in a professional review of personal progress, and institutional factors concerning educational quality, in discussion with the induction tutor throughout the period.

Assessment

The formalities of assessment and the conduct of meetings between new teachers and induction tutors or headteachers can be seen as a major stumbling block for professional development and educational progress if they are not set in place as an intrinsic part of the professional development portfolio. Devastation is not too strong a word for the potential effects of bad handling (Tickle 1994). On the other hand, like any assessment-led curriculum, they can be a major determinant of change and a catalyst for advancement of both individuals and the profession. The differences lie in the criteria adopted, the forms of assessment used, and the conduct of the participants in the process, illustrated in the following conversation among new teachers:

LT: [Have you had] visits from other teachers or the head?

KM: [The inspector] wanted to see me doing things in the classroom, but it was quite good for him to see how I controlled the swimming because it's quite dangerous doing that . . . he watched and then we went back to the classroom, and he asked me what sort of atmosphere I was trying to create in the classroom, to explain things. We talked about reading, and he said everything was fine, that he probably wouldn't come in again.

LT: Did you get a written report?

KM: No. I've got a written half-yearly report by my headmaster, but I don't know if [the inspector] did one after he'd seen me, I suppose he did, is he supposed to? The headmaster comes into the classroom quite a lot because my classroom is a sort of passage to other parts of the school.

LT: [LC], what have your experiences been?

LC: At the beginning of the term the head used to walk in and that was quite off-putting because he wouldn't comment, he'd just walk in and look around at things and then walk out again. Never commented afterwards either, so it's very difficult to get an impression of what he's thinking, you guess what it would be, if it is noisy that that's what he's been concentrating on most – probably he wasn't – you don't know. I've not had any written report or anything, have you? From anyone.

SP: I've had just written reports on one lesson that was done by the senior mistress who is in charge of me, and that's just one lesson that she observed and she wrote her part of it – and that was all. Got some verbal comments from my head of department . . . and that's it, really. It becomes a tense situation because they are not sure what he's doing there. And so it's never a typical lesson, I don't think it ever can be. And the thing I worry about most is that because I've been left on my own so frequently and only now is this intense activity, because the report's got to be written, the head of department and the senior mistress feel that they ought to come into my lessons pretty quickly so that they can cover themselves and write something fairly accurate about me, that that is undermining my position because the children will think, 'Here we are, we've got people coming in all the time, is this a reflection on her, or is it a reflection on us?' And I feel very uneasy about that, but there's no way that I can stop that, and I have mentioned it. I've said to my head of department, 'Look, you do realize that this might be undermining my authority?' At the same time I realize that by saying that he could start thinking – because you never know, do you, what they are thinking – very strange vibes, you get, but he might think, 'Oh, she doesn't want me in on that lesson, not because she's got a good relationship with them, but because maybe she can't control them, maybe there's some difficulty in that class – preventing her from letting me come in'. I am playing to them – it's as much me establishing myself with them rather than with the children. So, I think it's a very unfair situation, but there's nothing you can do about it, you've just got to accept it – it's just for one year.

DD: Nobody's come in to actually watch a lesson. From that point of view I am in a fortunate position that my classroom is attached to another classroom, it does mean that virtually all day my classroom is open and there's also free flow. I think my report has been written very much on what the head of year knows, but nobody has deliberately come in and . . .

LT: Your school report, have you seen that?

DD: I have, yes.

LC: I haven't seen mine.

DD: Yes, the head showed it to me . . . anything to comment, and I said, 'No. Thank you very much, I couldn't have written a better one myself, thank you.'

LC: I haven't seen any reports and it is unsettling because you assume it's going all right and you assume people would have talked to you about it if it was going badly, but there's always that little niggle, you know, it might just be the position I'm in that makes me think that, or it might be, I don't know, perhaps lack of self-confidence on my own part, but nevertheless I do have that little doubt, you know, I would like to see it and know, be sure and be told.

KM: I've seen my written report so I know that there's nothing wildly wrong. But I assume that if there was something wrong that they would do something about it before – they can't just turn round at the end of the term – 'sorry, you've failed' – can they? Can they?!

LC: I don't know.

SP: They were meant to let you know before Christmas whether you were at risk.

I have already declared the inspectorial/monitorial approach to be inappropriate except in extreme cases, and backed a constructivist approach. This is detectable, just, in the formal induction requirements in England. The prescription provides at least one meeting every half term to review progress, plus three formal assessment meetings:

- first meeting to focus on the extent to which the NQT is already meeting the requirements for certification;
- second meeting to deal with the teacher's further progress towards meeting the requirements;

• final meeting used to determine whether all the requirements for the satisfactory completion of the induction period have been met.

The evidence to support assessment, and to be used during meetings, is expected to draw on:

• written reports from school staff who have observed the new teacher as part of the monitoring and support programme;
• evidence of the progress of pupils;
• notes of any review discussions;
• lesson plans, records and evaluations;
• self-assessments and records of professional development;
• liaison activities with colleagues and parents.

The reporting procedures that follow these assessment meetings are to include:

• brief and simple summaries from the first two assessment meetings of the NQT's progress in relation to the requirements for satisfactory completion of the induction period;
• a simple statement from the third meeting, signed by the headteacher, recommending the satisfactory completion of induction.

Copies of the completed reports are expected to be signed by the headteacher, the induction tutor where this is not the headteacher, and the new teacher, and sent within 15 working days of the assessment meeting to the administrators (full details can be found in DfEE 1999b,c).

The prominence given to others' assessments of performance will need to be matched by strengthening the acknowledgement of self-evaluation, and requiring induction tutors to work with new teachers on developing their capabilities in research-based teaching and self-development. That would add both rigour and fairness to the process of assessment by enabling NQTs to become more proficient in the evaluation of teaching and learning, and by ensuring that induction tutors' expertise is also being developed. By giving NQTs a central part in the process of collecting evidence of their practice, and using criteria against which it might be judged, there would be some hope of advancing the profession in the direction of a profoundly different and substantially enhanced practical knowledge base. Again, these aspirations need to be combined with the processing of experience:

> LT: Well, yes, let's move on to talk about how things feel now – halfway through the year.
>
> LC: I think the Christmas term really does seem such a long time ago – all those problems and hassles – I remember that all happened in a week – Jason's dad phoning up and the inspector coming in – it was such a horrible week, and having to get through it, whereas now things seem so much more stable and secure. I went to the university last week and was with a group of PGCE students and realized just how far I have come. How nervous and anxious they

were about things and, you know, how you've got over all of that, and coping with it – it seems a world away, but it was only last year.

LT: Sue, how about your experience?

SP: Halfway through the year. Well, it feels very established, I suppose, feel very confident, but I always did feel very confident, and I'm still not sure whether [teaching] is the right thing for me. Still have these pangs when I get up in the morning, I think, 'Oh dear, I've got . . .' well, not that I've got to go to school, it's when I get to school, look around and I think is this what life is come to? Get fairly disillusioned at times. But that's just when I think about it. Once I get in the classroom with the children and I do the teaching – it's fine – I'm fairly happy, and sometimes confident about it – and they can lift me up. But it's sometimes going through the door, passing the sixth formers, and thinking I wish I was one of those, and I wish I hadn't made myself in a state that I'm in right now – teaching – I wish I had my time again; I'd do things differently. All the time I'm looking through the possibilities and they are so changeable, nothing is definite, but that's, I mean, at school I do give a totally different impression – committed. The woman who is in charge of me said that [I had] 'potential to become head of department' – that's a very nice thing to say, a very positive comment, but quite frankly I don't think I want to be a teacher that long to be in that position. I feel very similar to the way that I felt at the beginning, you know, confident, fairly happy in the teaching, but not sure if it is the right thing to do.

DD: I'm not so sure because I just feel at the moment, I just feel inside when I'm there, unconfident, believe it or not, I just feel it's a bit of a battle at the moment. It probably doesn't come over like that but I feel quite tense inside, which is something that I hadn't come across last term, and maybe it doesn't show to anybody else, it probably doesn't show, this is almost a battle between me and them. Just this thing about being quiet and working quietly and not getting as much done as I'd like them to do, and not working, or their attitude is not the attitude that I want them to have. Some days it's better than others, but at the moment I'm just feeling this is my sticky patch. We've all got to go through them, and as a result I don't know whether it's my lessons that are causing the problem, or is it just their attitude, which it could be. I know that a lot of them are growing up so fast and they are getting, 'Oh, I'm bored'. Because I'm the sort of person I am, they will actually tell me they are bored, and you think, 'Oh, good grief'. That's the last thing you want to hear, that this is boring.

LT: Has that happened just this week?

DD: Er, no, it's something that has been building up, just a feeling that I've been getting. I've got to face it when I get back and I'm thinking, am I going to be on edge and therefore is that going to reflect to the children, and therefore am I going to make the situation worse – how can I relax so I'm not so on edge with them, and niggly with them? I mean, it could be just a symptom of being tired and all the things that have been happening.

SP: I think in that kind of situation you often want some positive reinforcements, some positive encouragement, often from your superiors.

DD: Yet I saw that report.

SP: Sure, didn't that lift you up a bit – give you some confidence?

DD: No, not internally, it was great to see it, but no.

SP: Why not?

DD: I don't know, probably just because of my state of mind.

LT: Is it something to do with your very high aspirations for your own teaching and a sense that things aren't quite matching up to that?

DD: Possibly, but it's also with regard to my control, whether I'm actually keeping control. For example, yesterday afternoon they were so noisy, just messing around and not getting their work done and I said, 'Gosh, my lot were noisy this afternoon', and Andrew said, 'Were they? I thought they were ever so quiet'. I didn't think they were quiet at all, I thought they were awful.

LC: A lot of it is to do with state of mind – you can be in a really good mood and nothing matters – they can be chatty but you see it as really constructive work that's going on, and you don't mind.

KM: I think it's halfway through the year – feel like that . . . it just seems to be that sort of time . . .

DD: I don't feel fed-up, I just feel internally panicking sometimes, not even the word panic – that's too strong, just anxious inside. But it doesn't come – it probably does come out – I'm not sure whether it does or not, you can't tell what you look like from inside – you can't tell how you are reacting.

LT: Do you talk about it with anyone?

DD: No, I haven't, maybe it's taken me to sort of now-ish to actually admit it to anybody [laughs].

LT: You mean like tonight?

DD: Like tonight. I mean, I've been thinking it, but it's just a case of actually admitting it, which is a quite hard thing to do.

LT: Yes. But that's not unlike the sort of anxieties that Liz described – wanting to find a solution to a problem but not being able to talk about it, not being able to ask the right questions. You said, when you talked with the deputy head he didn't ask the right questions, to unlock your anxiety?

LC: That's right. It is that you want somebody to ask it, it's so difficult to start spilling it out because it will come out wrong, it will sound a lot more than – they'll probably think, 'Oh, Deb's got a real problem', because it isn't that, you just need somebody to be

     sensitive and to ask the right question, to be supportive in the
     right way.

DD: I think it's just that I'm very conscious that if I don't overcome this
     particular problem at the moment, what are they going to be like
     in the summer term when they are getting ready to leave? I think
     I've got a very good relationship with them on an individual level.

In England the induction standards' specific selection of elements of professional practice constitute nothing more than a minor supplement to the
career entry profile (TTA 1999a). It is an insufficient selection of teaching elements, as the review of professional knowledge and the analysis of education's
future needs has shown. Other personal qualities and professional characteristics that have an impact on the quality of teaching and learning need
to be accommodated in these standards, and these should be specified – for
example, commitment to professional standards, respect for learners, patience,
interpersonal sensitivity, reliability, capacity for self-critical and collaborative reflexiveness, making significant contributions to the development of a
department or school, contributing to the knowledge base of educational
effectiveness. A place would have to be created for local/individualized specifications, to be negotiated by induction tutors and new teachers, so that the
relationship between personal knowledge and the wider professional knowledge base is understood, and actively built. The full implications of the earlier
chapters of this book, in other words, suggest a radical departure from the
bureaucratic minimalism of the English system, towards a professionally
defined way ahead.

In practical terms, for example, the final assessment meeting of the induction year will be expected to provide the basis for target setting and professional development planning for the second year of teaching, when the
normal teacher appraisal arrangements will begin to apply. Well, what will
that mean? What targets? Who will define them? From what range of possibilities will they be drawn? Professional practitioners' fullest sense of 'work'
and the full scope of 'working knowledge' will need imaginative leaps to be
made by members of the profession. This is a curious anomaly in the formal
induction requirements. After all, should it not be possible for new teachers
to put themselves at risk of deregistration on the basis of failure to develop
characteristics other than those that can be observed during classroom performance? That may be a debate that needs to be had among induction
tutors, new teachers, and the wider profession. It certainly needs to be an
explicit debate, since it is likely that such 'non-classroom' criteria will be
enforced informally, which could lead to disputes, appeals, or injustices (see
Tickle 1994).

Extensions to the period of induction, appeals against negative assessment, and the termination of employment are all built into formal provisions. They are each problematic, even in relation to those new teachers in
permanent jobs, because the timetable that is placed on those responsible
for induction constrains what can be achieved in the way of diagnoses,

support, and review. A third assessment meeting at the end of the third term is not practicable for 'at risk' cases. What is worse, there is also a possibility of a wider consequence, in the extended use of temporary contracts to cope with the perceived problem of provisional teacher registration, that there will be deleterious effects on the professional development of new teachers.

Let us not fall again into the negative equity trap, however. While some form of minimalism is intrinsic to standards setting, I believe we have a duty to define the higher order of professionalism, and hence of professional. That definition, in terms of the knowledge base that I have described earlier, is both a longer term goal, and a complex and dynamic process in which new teachers will be caught up. As I have shown, the 'outcomes' remain debatable, internationally, though I have declared my preferred reading of what will constitute the professional practitioner along the way ahead. If the foundation for that preferred professional can be established during the first year of teaching, within the framework of professional knowledge described, then it might be possible to envisage a more complete sense of induction in the immediately subsequent period of development. That will need to incorporate the development of the most effective tutorial practices too, however, so that the processes of the induction and the conduct of professional learning is also actively constructed (Tickle 1992). The potential for that is evident, I believe, in discussion among new teachers towards the end of their first year:

DD: Yes, it's definitely a balancing act, and it's one that I have tried and tried and tried over the year to work and I've learnt from – 'That didn't really work, let's try a different one'. Next time a similar system, a similar circumstance crops up, but it's something that you desperately need to work at.

DM: People have said my lessons are better now than they used to be, I think, because of things I've learnt; they are worse because I know I now can see the mistakes I was making and the mistakes I am making. You know, the little things, maybe, the question that wasn't phrased clearly enough, I thought I'd just put it out and see the loads of blank faces and thought, 'They are thick, aren't they?' or something like that, you know, you just, you won't have seen the problem. I'm now beginning to see the problem, so instead of me appreciating that there has been an improvement, it's almost as if my self-evaluation is beyond my improvement, so I can turn round and say, 'Well, they could be better', whereas I think sometimes you are in a position when you are first starting off of 'I don't know how anybody can do this better' almost the sort of confidence of ignorance.

DD: I think also because we are no longer dealing with the basics of standing in front of the children and actually taking lessons, now we are thinking in more detail, more carefully about the details and about how things are phrased, ways you can present it, a better way of tackling the subject, and you can see, I've been thinking, 'Well, I did it that way, now that worked reasonably well, but I certainly won't do it that way again and I would certainly change the way that I approached that for various reasons'. Make it more clear to the children, make it more interesting for the children, and again that's only come with reflection [on] the way something did or didn't work.

LT: Is that also true of other aspects of the job. You mentioned report writing, for instance.

LC: It's one of the worst things I've done all year, one of the hardest.

LT: You mentioned parents' evenings, cycling proficiency, netball, sex education for the first time –

DD: Report writing was horrendous. It's got better, but I literally spent about seven hours doing one section. I could not believe the length of time it took, trying to be concise but trying to be accurate, and trying to cover all the things that the children had done to be positive in everything, but also to be critical, and that was very difficult and in the end I feel like I've come out with stock phrases, which I don't feel is very satisfactory, but . . .

LC: You spend hours trying to avoid the clichés, and then find that you have to write them.

DD: Because they are the succinct ways of putting things.

LC: Oh, it's so frustrating. But it is very, very hard to put a whole child's year into four inches.

DM: I also think there is the pressure, having read other people's reports and knowing the child – will the parents be able to actually understand the English that had been used. It's almost – that is something else on top of this. It's very easy to sort of write down that, 'Your child shows considerable aptitude in following the philosophical . . .' Whatever, it's easy to put that and it may say exactly what you want it to say, but it might be a lot of gibberish to the parent trying to read it. They will look at the mark and find an A for effort and an E for achievement and want to know what on earth you're going on about.

DD: And at the same time you are also writing for the staff, for the staff that you are handing your children on to. It's got to be dual-purpose really. I spend ages trying to find the word and I thought of this great word, and I thought, 'Well, will the parents understand it?' And then because I felt that they possibly wouldn't, I had to spend another quarter of an hour thinking of another suitable word that really said what I wanted to say, but in not such a long-winded way.

DM: I think you have to make a compromise between a succinct way of saying something, and the understandable way of saying something.

DD: And you also don't want to be incorrect in what you say; you could make a statement, but then I always felt in a lot of cases I had to qualify what I had said, and therefore that took a long time to do that. Oh, it's horrendous.

DM: One hundred and twenty-five reports to write in about a week and a half. And I said how on earth am I going to do this, and —— said, 'Well, don't write too much'. By the last lot I did, the fortieth, don't know whether I've become better at writing reports but I've certainly become quicker. It becomes in the end, just to get the work done, you don't look as closely as what . . . the way you are putting it down, you end up with certain stock phrases – 'This child worked with a consistency that is pleasing'. That sort of thing, you begin to make more general umbrella statements – 'This child shows great aptitude in observing experimental occurrences, but really needs to strengthen their objectivity when coming to conclusions' – you don't become that specific. You end up with an umbrella which covers most things, and then you put a qualifier on it that it would be pleasing if they could improve their ability to draw conclusions or improve their ability to use their knowledge to discuss something. You know, these sort of things but if it ends up as if you make generalizations, then there's the child-related thing, you know. You get one report and you say, 'Who's this? I don't teach this person', it turned out that I did. It's not that I don't go round talking to the children, but the child is so quiet you go around saying hello but the name just hasn't stuck, and they've been away quite often, and how on earth do I write a report on this person?

LT: Tell me about the competent side of things, the way things look at this stage in the year compared with the beginning of the year?

LC: A lot more confident in class – that's a big improvement because I don't get in a flap so easily and I can deal with things happening that are unexpected, and I can change things around when I want to and that helps the children because that means that I have a lot more confidence introducing new topics and new ways of working.

LT: Is that just an inner feeling or do you think that also shows outwardly?

LC: Well, it's definitely an inner feeling and I'm sure it's showing itself in the fact that I enjoy being in the classroom a lot more now and the children know that I smile a lot more, talk to them, I can let certain children chat during certain lessons if I feel they need, you know. I don't have to keep drawing in the reins, having one rule and that's it. And that must be better for the children 'cos I treat them much more like individuals now instead of worrying and thinking, 'I've got to do this'. I don't have to worry about that so much. So, that's a big improvement.

LT: So that that feeling of confidence, more security, a greater sense that you are competent in certain things in classroom management actually leads to better quality of experience in the pupils because you – those other things like you being flexible and adaptable actually hinge on that?

LC: Yes, the thing is you can have a joke with them, all those sorts of things. Just them knowing where they stand with me and that they can come up and talk to me, you know, lots of things like that. And also in the school I feel a lot more confident, that I can tell a child not to run down the corridor and feel quite confident about it – the kind of feeling I'm a bit of a fogey, and they won't believe me anyway, that sort of thing, and definitely I am much more part of the school then.

LT: So that's giving you a sense that you are making a contribution to the rest of the school [yes] not just in the classroom?

LC: Yes, that's right, being respected as a proper teacher.

LT: How do you feel on that?

DD: I certainly feel more confident with the other members of staff and particularly as they are so much older and I'm definitely the baby of the school. I feel more confident now by just generally being with them and chatting with them. I feel a lot more confident.

LT: How does that show itself?

DD: They talk to me, I talk to them [laughs]. They ask me about things . . . [inaudible]. We were talking about things for next year, and I'm supposed to be in charge of RE and staff were saying, 'How do you want us to teach next year?' Well, we discussed it then and I made some suggestions and we bandied some ideas around.

LT: Now, that's an aspect of your role that we've not talked about, I mean, that responsibility.

DD: I have to do all the budgeting for RE, as I am RE coordinator. I had to put the order in for some things; I had to put a bid in for the amount we wanted, and that didn't really help me, I was the first one to have to put my bid in and then I had to leave. It is a big problem. Next year I'm totally rewriting the curriculum guidelines for RE, so I've had lots of thoughts on that, talked to various people, but that will be a big responsibility next year. So I shall have to see how that goes. Other than that I can't think of any-where else where I'm confident [laughs].

LT: That's that modest self-evaluation that Dave was talking about.

LC: We had some people come for interview, the girl who has got it will be a probationer next year, and she spent a few days at school and the head put her under my wing and sent her off to my class and things and we talked lots and lots about the school – I just realized how that was me – she was asking exactly the same ques-tions, and worried about the same things and panicking, trying to write down everything, and I've just come on so much, I mean, all the things that she was worrying about, I realized now how out of proportion they were in my mind. How I have learnt and developed, and she will, as well.

LT: And all of that presumably is general knowledge about the school, about the routine?

LC: Yes, all the things that took so long to work out in the first half-term and yet I couldn't begin to put into words to Susannah to help her; they are just things she is going to have to go through and find out for herself. Where you go if you want an extension lead. What happens on the morning before you break up for Christmas, all these silly little things that – the way you sit your class in assembly. There are so many – hundreds of things that I've learnt that I just take for granted now – do them so naturally now, and yet were really problems last year.

LT: All of those things are specific to the institution that you are working in, not things which you can bring with you to a job.

LC: Nobody can teach you them, or help you out on PGCE course.

DD: Yes, it was interesting I must say doing the talk last week to the postgrad students. C'est moi, yes. It was me. Really I only brought out all the things that we've talked about, parents' evenings, reports, making space. I must say that although that's out of school, that is an area where I must be more confident because school things are taking up less time outside of school. I don't know what that says about anything really, but things aren't taking as long and therefore I have actually got more time for myself, or I am making more time for myself, or I am not allowing it to take longer, and I am getting now a social life and I am getting involved in other things, non-school things, which I think is important.

LT: Is that true for you, Liz?

LC: Yes, definitely. I don't feel that quality is suffering either, which of course is important. I am preparing it just as much as working out ideas, but I don't spend hours and hours working it out and writing out notes for them.

DD: And you do it in your head, you know, you find yourself mulling over ideas for a long time, and mulling over the way that it is then going to be put into action, so a lot more is done up here rather than writing copious notes of everything and how things are going to be done.

LC: When I look back to my first week at school, it had every minute mapped out, from 8.55–9.10 we will do this, and from 9.10 – I mean, I don't need to worry about that now. I know basically in the first part of the morning we will do, you know . . .

LT: Tell me how that works, how has that come about?

LC: What?

LT: That you can plan in your head.

LC: Well, I spent just as long sorting it out – all I need to do now is jot down notes in my diary, perhaps a word, and I will know enough, probably what it is is that – if I were to get my diary for the first week it would have every single little thing written down. It would have – everything is written down, all the people I've got to talk to, when I've got to take the register back, what we are doing in the library, where they put the library tickets, first thing I've got to tell Sarah something, all little notes for, every little detail is written down. Now I don't need to write down that they've got to put the library ticket back in the book before they take out another one – I don't need to write things like that now. So, all the little details that used to – I used to have so many things going on in my head that I had to do before I could get through a lesson, I don't need that now – most things are in control or ticking over or working to a routine, so now all I have to concentrate on is the lesson. All I need if I've thought about it a lot, like . . . mull things over in my head, all you need is the one word, you know, sliding experiments, and that sends it back to me, 'Oh yes, that's the particular experiment that we are doing and the way that we are going to set it out when we start it up to get the equipment'. That's all I need now, I don't need a whole page of equipment to get out.

LT: Yes, that's the sort of things I mean, the introductions to it, the way in which you convey questioning, instructions and so on, the whole development of a lesson.

DD: And it has to be thought out. I find myself thinking over things at odd times in the middle of the night, driving somewhere, when I'm doing other things, and just thoughts come into my head about something that I may well be doing later on in the week, or the following week, or tomorrow, whenever it may be, and thinking, oh yes, what have I got to do during the day – I've got that lesson now, I'm doing that so that needs to be . . . and I'll think about it, or if there's a lesson that I've got to really start thinking about how I've got approach that – a lot of thinking, it's almost subconscious in one sense because you are not concentrating on a thing, these ideas are just mulling around and ticking around and you are doing lots of other things. And then when it comes to actually then formally thinking, right, what's happening, all these things have already been mulled over and so it's very quick just to make either a mental note . . . or just a quick jot down somewhere.

LT: So, it's mental designing?

DD: Unless, of course, it's a subject I know absolutely nothing about and I need to actually do some background reading myself to actually feel confident with the subject before then I can ask the children to go and research it because when they ask me something and I know nothing about it, it doesn't make me feel very confident.

LC: The other thing is I think I'm teaching much more real lessons now. On teaching practice at the beginning they were very much one-off lessons; they might even have been following the scheme but even so, I'd done a particular introduction, a particular middle bit and a particular end for each lesson, whereas now I know what I did last week and I know the natural development from last week's lesson to this week's. It's much more realistic than think-ing, 'Week 2 of this particular scheme is so and so, now I've got to go and teach so and so'. I might well be teaching it, but I'll be teaching it in a much more natural way, I think, so much follows on . . .

DD: And you link in with things that I try to link back to what we've done in the week before or the term before, 'If you remember when we were doing such and such we talked about this'. Whether their long term memory can actually remember it is a sore point, but at least they are getting to know that I do hark back to some-thing we did in the autumn term and so I try to develop things and link things in, even if it's not quite the same. So they know that I'm going to link across the subject, and I'm going to link back to stuff we've done, just so they are getting the idea of a whole.

LT: It's not just mental designing for the instant or for the specific, it's actually fitting the parts of the whole design together, backwards and forwards.

DD: Yes, well, now I'm thinking about what I'm doing next term and linking back to how I did it, what resources I used, what resources I'm going to need for the next term to complete these particular subjects. I did that in the first term last year, but that didn't work particularly well, so I'll reorganize that and rethink that. So, yes, I'm doing mental gymnastics at the moment from last September to this coming September, so I've already got some ideas in my head about what I'm going to do about it.

Notes

1 DfEE consultation figure 1998c. Previous reports recommended 80 per cent.
2 DfEE 1999c.

6 Beyond the first year

Advancing professionally

The induction year itself can be better understood, planned, and provided for if there is a clear sense of where teachers might go next in the development of their practice and their careers. The combination of contributions that new teachers bring to a school, and further investment in their development, means that the first year itself is, at least, a time of consolidating technical expertise, and a time for more intensively improving their problem-solving capabilities. If the way ahead that I have outlined so far is achievable, it will also be a time when personal qualities and professional characteristics are developed, and when they more clearly define their identities in, and relationship with, the profession. The capacity to handle and to initiate change is also likely to become more established by this time, with the potential to focus on strategic projects for self-improvement and the improvement of the circumstances in which they work. Commonly, that will include a move towards professional leadership, either informally because of their up-to-date knowledge and expertise, or their desire to see changes. Or perhaps it will be more formal, through individual career aspirations, or through the nature of primary school staffing, which requires most teachers to act as subject leaders for their colleagues. These situations require a focus on the management of change, of one's own practice, that of colleagues, or of the educational environment.

Formally, it is the point when teacher appraisal comes into play in ways that are different from the assessment of induction. It is when confirmation or disconfirmation occurs in one's identity as a teacher, even among the majority for whom registration and professional respect are assured. What employers describe as the problem of retention, new teachers experience as decisions about remaining in the job. Zehm (1999: 49) offers a North American perspective on this:

> Approximately 20 percent of beginning teachers leave the teaching profession after their first two years of teaching. Some are weeded out during their probationary status as beginning teachers. We do not know how many of these beginning teachers, who have voluntarily or involuntarily left their classrooms, have done so because they lacked the personal–professional esteem and understanding of self necessary to build effective relationships with students, parents, and teachers.

As Huberman (1993) reminded us, fluctuations in response to being a teacher, and about one's teaching, occur at different times for different people. But the postinduction period, which is (or perhaps I should say ought to be) regarded as one of professional and personal affirmation, is also one that couples with experimentation, or with frustration, maybe, where there is lack of opportunity to use available capabilities and to pursue professional idealism. Some of the fluctuations and variations in new teachers' lives, ranging from crisis and change of career, to promotion and higher status in teaching, are recorded in my earlier work (Tickle 1994, 1999). Whatever the responses of individuals are, they vary according to different kinds of teaching activity. Competence, confidence and control in some areas of professional life create the foundations for handling new uncertainties, taking risks, initiating change, working collegially and communally, researching circumstances, developing deeper understanding, being critical. These can be complex and confusing forces, and the paradoxes and dilemmas do not necessarily diminish with the passage of the induction year. Indeed, the changes that occur can bring new issues, new types of challenge, which makes the immediate postinduction period a crucial one. Assuming that confirmation of qualified teacher status, or registration, represents a cut-off point in the need for support and development is a seriously dangerous assumption to make.

That is especially evident from the point of view of the retention problem in teaching, but we can take a more constructive view than that. To see the first year as a cut-off point is also potentially another missed opportunity, because it is at that meeting point between consolidation and experimentation that the building of a research-based, collaborative professional life can be properly laid down. Beyond the first year, teachers enter more fully into the realm of professional appraisal. Creating and collectively participating in change, rather than simply reacting to imposed requirements, provides a more imperative sense of the need for teacher appraisal to be built around principles of research-based professional practice. However, there is a potential problem in taking this view of induction and postinduction. If the skills of teaching are so extensive that they cannot all be mastered by the end of the first year, then adding the development of personal qualities and professional characteristics to the induction programme itself might be regarded as asking for the impossible.

To add to that the mastery of research dispositions and expertise could be seen as contemptible. So these qualities and realms of professional expertise need to be seen as accumulative. If the acquisition of professional leadership skills is added to the early career stage, the demands placed on teachers become, seemingly, even worse. Yet each of these features figure in some way in the practical realities of becoming a teacher, from the earliest stages of learning to teach. The crisis that induction often is, and the problem of retention, may well be the result of these matters not being attended to satisfactorily in support programmes. From that perspective, and from the more constructive standpoint of developing professionalism, what is needed is a longer-term view of how each of these aspects of practice might be developed, so that induction can be accurately envisaged as a foundation phase in which all elements of professional practice are engaged, rather than simply as a confirmatory and certificatory one focused on classroom skills.

In that view of things, self-appraisal needs to be extended from classroom performance to personal development, into collegial and community research partnerships, and on to the development of educational leadership by teachers. This combination of skilled teaching, personal development, and curriculum leadership is the basis of professional life from which pupils, their parents, teacher colleagues, and local communities will benefit most. Is this a grand vision? I hope so, but not grandiose. As I have said, the practical demonstrations of involvement in activities beyond the classroom, in personal development and in communal leadership, are part of the daily experiences of most recently qualified teachers and their more experienced colleagues. They are part of the realm of responsibilities of teachers, and require accommodation in induction programmes, where the growth can begin, and postinduction support, to take that growth forward.

It would certainly be true that the practicable would become impossible, and the impossible contemptible, if the attitude to these matters is to view them as further extensions to checklists of expectations, demands, and isolated competencies. They do not need to be seen that way, and indeed should not be. Even if the agenda for professional learning during induction is primarily focused on functional know-how and instructional expertise, practical experience will not avoid some involvement in and consideration of personal, school-wide and community-based educational involvement. As confident management of expertise develops, these matters need to be attended to more fully, with learning structured around different aspects of practice. The scope can be identified as follows:

- personal development agendas;
- classroom practices;
- collegial/department issues;
- school policy matters;
- community concerns.

The range of elements within each of these areas could be as extensive as the induction standards are for classroom practice, if the checklist approach were to be used. That would look like a terrifying taxonomy of mastery to be achieved. It is unnecessary and would be unhelpful, I believe. It is potentially more fruitful to find a principled way for professionals to identify their own agenda for learning, rather than prescribe one that is fragmented and unachievable. Providing principled, structured, systematic support during and immediately beyond their first year, related directly to personal development and professional expertise in these areas, is presented in this chapter. It is intended to consider how this period in teachers' careers, and the new roles and responsibilities in leadership, can be introduced in ways that develop those dispositions towards life-long learning through educational research, with the pursuit of qualities of excellence built into the processes of that learning. Locating the studies in the context of 'expert teacher' aspirations, this offers an imaginative outlook that suggests that induction itself is necessarily rather more than a one-year process.

The normalization of a career framework by Dreyfus and Dreyfus (1986) and Ingvarson (1998) have already been criticized as too simply chronological and failing to recognize that older teachers and new ones have much in common in situations of change. The more complex notion of new teachers being expert in some respects can readily be extended to areas of activity in personal and school-wide development. Acting as exemplars to other teachers in their capacity for imaginative problem-solving, in dealing with personal development needs, as mentors to student teachers and inductees, as innovators in taking on the responsibilities of curriculum coordination and leadership, are all within the experience of teachers at the supposed beginner or stabilization stages. Even the more sophisticated models of careers from Huberman's (1993) studies do not address career profiles in relation to the nature and acquisition of teachers' working practices and responsibilities. The question is, how to both deepen and extend these aspects of professional expertise, on a communal basis.

That question is particularly poignant because the demands of the 1990s for the adoption of greater responsibility acknowledge that mastery, expertise, and notions of leading teachers lie in the personal dimensions of professionalism. The identification of advanced career paths has formally confirmed perspectives on career entry and progress which bring these matters to the fore. Policies that identify an élite core as master teachers or teacher leaders, however, especially with some making rapid career leaps, have limited scope. We need educational provision for all teachers to become extended professionals (Hoyle 1969). Extendedness needs to begin as early as possible in a career, since it is not just about taking additional responsibilities, but more about broadening the concept of professionalism. The case for profiling across the teaching forces of the world to include aspects of professional characteristics and personal qualities, as well the capacity to research practice and bring about change through leadership, is a clear implication of the concept of the new professional.

Self-appraisal

The central principles of this book are intended to promote reflective practice and action research, informed by notions of the professional empowerment of individual teachers, their supported, professional self-development,
and the enhancement of their leadership capabilities. This approach is intended to balance the prevailing move towards simplistic ways of cataloguing
competency as it reins in, regiments, depersonalizes, and deprofessionalizes
teaching through curriculum legislation, assessment, and the prescription of
narrow career entry and induction standards. In it the idea of self-appraisal is
a central feature, involving teachers in personal responsibility for engendering reviews of their practice and bringing about improvements in it. This is
a basis of professional community and self-development, confidence, and
respect – ideas which, mainly through the activities of the organized professional associations, contributed to the formally constituted, legislated framework of appraisal that has formed part of teachers' conditions of service in
England since 1989 (Elliott 1991).

A comprehensive image of self-appraisal – not only as appraisal of practice
by one's self, but of appraisal of aspects of one's self as professional – offers
a more tolerant, humane, and person-centred view of the education of new
teachers, in my view. It is a more inclusive notion of teacher development,
which presumes the adoption of professional responsibilities, and acknowledges both the communal and the personal investments in the professional
capital of new teachers. The idea of self-appraisal for professional growth
promotes inquiry as part of a celebration of the notion of persistent personal
growth and constant development of identity within teaching. Programmes
of this kind can include teachers of all subjects, across pupil age-ranges,
and types of schools and colleges. They can explore through practitioner
research the problem of opening up dimensions of the self as teacher. With
support from professional tutors and peers in defining and refining realizable research, and methods of inquiry, teachers can extend the boundaries
of participation in, and contribution to, professional development in the
direction of personal competence, coupled with the growth of contributions
to the public knowledge base of teaching. That can include aspects of leadership, where personal qualities and characteristics are paramount, and where
the capacity for critique and radical action can often be best placed (Zimpher
and Howey 1987).

In that realm of capability, the conception of the teacher is one who has
an understanding of self, has a sense of self-actualization, and 'uses the self
as an effective and humane instrument' (Zimpher and Howey 1987: 104),
both in their own, their students', their colleagues', and their situation's
development. Certain conditions are necessary to help in the process of self-
exploration, such as maintaining trust, asking critical questions in supportive, non-threatening ways, and negotiating partnerships to establish conditions
that encourage risk-taking. The aims of such work are to develop the capacity to make sound professional judgements in practice – including capable

leadership. It is in these realms where strategic leadership requires political capabilities. The presumption is that the search for prudence, or practical wisdom, that is 'the ability to discern the most suitable, politic, or profitable course of action' (Stenhouse, cited in Ruddock and Hopkins 1985: 52) must encompass a search for evidence within professional situations, which will form a basis for judgement and guide actions. Questions that can be used by teachers for judging the quality of inquiry and effectiveness in their work are:

- Does the work demonstrate a capacity for generating and gathering information and evidence upon which to make judgements in teaching, in personal development, or in leadership?
- Does it display effective ways of analysing the evidence found in practice?
- Are justifiable practical actions based upon the analyses?
- Is there an explicit process for evaluating the effects and effectiveness of the actions?

The pursuit of sound professional judgements and the use of these questions presume that there is room for action in the development of teaching, self, and leadership, as well as a willingness to act to change situations. Initially the question is: which research issue/problem is most worth thinking about, and which evidence related to it should be looked for? What constitutes the most suitable, politic and profitable subject for potential development, the sources of evidence available, and the methods that might be used for collecting, recording and analysing that evidence, are crucial decisions. This kind of work is designed to:

- provide a better awareness and understanding of teaching as a personal commitment and professional activity;
- activate collaborative enquiry that can handle self-appraisal, competence and growth;
- offer opportunities to develop and use research methods appropriate to self-appraisal, which may be more autobiographical, reflective, and introspective than methods used in other in-service activities;
- develop perceptions of self – the good points, biases, blind spots, dreamer spots, and untapped reservoirs of unknown potential – as legitimate matters for study;
- focus on practice and the aims, values and beliefs on which it is based;
- analyse working environments, because if teachers are to modify their practice or aspects of their self effectively, then they must understand and manage the environment in which they work.

Through tentative proposals for avenues of research and consideration of research methods and evidence that attend personally significant issues, individualized research plans and strategies for carrying them out can be devised. The sites of research may sometimes be within the classroom or school, but often also outside them, where critical friendship agreements may be used to elicit and record evidence of a personal kind. Or in the case of leadership activities, a set of conditions and working procedures might need to be negotiated with colleagues. These are likely to include:

- the establishment of conditions necessary to explore aspects of self in teaching, through negotiated principles of procedure;
- exposure to theoretical matter on the self, competencies, and appraisal, in order to provide a metaperspective on personal and professional development;
- the identification and negotiation of substantive topics of personal research that have significant meaning to individuals;
- taking of risks in the teacher-research methods, and the data sought, in pursuit of self-understanding and self-development.

This kind of focus can be expected to culminate in a dual level of the experience of self-appraisal – on the substantive aspects of self chosen by a teacher, and on the processes involved in undertaking an appraisal of self. The latter equates, in research terms, with a methodological critique and is intended to help each person to improve the means by which aspects of self are appraised. The following guidelines can be used to help to create a worthwhile project:

- define an aspect of teaching for self-appraisal;
- devise appropriate methods to examine it;
- use these methods to identify strengths and/or weaknesses in the defined area;
- set realistic aspirations for development in the light of available evidence;
- plan appropriate courses of action to meet these aspirations;
- evaluate the process and effectiveness of the research undertaken.

Teachers may express surprise at having an opportunity to deal with matters that seemed unreachable in initial training and in their schools' agenda for induction and further professional development. However, it is widely believed that work of this kind undertaken by teachers brings the role of the reflexive self to bear upon issues of personal and professional importance in ways that have significant potential for enhancing development.

Topics chosen among teachers I have worked with personally over many years have included the following, for example:

- a seemingly self-confident woman teacher whose public presentation of confidence deliberately masked deep insecurity, leading to identity conflicts, and the self-closing of avenues to advice and support that she wanted;
- teachers whose practices were steered by an overriding desire to be personally popular with students, sometimes to the detriment of other goals, who sought to understand the origins of this desire and its impact on their practice;
- a self-elected introvert teacher in adult company who was under pressure, especially from the principal, to talk more among colleagues;

- a teacher who sought to acknowledge individuality and personal rights among adolescents, and who was at odds with a school regime of retribution towards students;
- teachers who experienced low self-worth, because of comments from colleagues, students, or parents, or from their own self-doubt about the efficacy of their practice;
- a secretly gay male teacher fearful in his staffroom relationships and conversation, so that he did not regard himself as functioning effectively as a professional colleague or as a person with integrity and courage;
- a teacher of religion whose moral code excluded conventional punishments and social control, and who wished to set a different example to students;
- a young female teacher who experienced sexual harassment from male students and male colleagues, and who sought to develop constructive strategies that would help both her and them;
- a short-tempered and irritable teacher who wanted to change her fractious responses to pupils' questions and persistent requests for help;
- a teacher intent on treating boys and girls equally in every respect who became conscious of a tendency in her practice to treat them very differently;
- a teacher who suffered severe self-deprecations, and who sought to devise mechanisms for managing her self-esteem.

Initial discussions on such personal aspects of teaching include the reasons why the topics chosen are significant. Sometimes this might mean adopting autobiographical methods to uncover key or even core values (Nias 1989), and perhaps the reasons for attachment to them. It means generating trustworthy methods for identifying and recording evidence. In some instances it involves monitoring the teacher's own responses to situations, and to the actions of other people. The risks are several-fold. Opening up to others the nature of the research, by looking for necessary evidence, and exposing the vulnerabilities that it is intended to overcome, makes sensitivity a prime need. Risks might be sustained, as in the case of a gay teacher's relations with colleagues. Like Sparkes' (1994) lesbian subject, Jessica, the inquiries were helpful in developing a deeper understanding of the situation and personal responses to it, though the course of action chosen left the circumstances unchanged and the problem unresolved. Another risk is that of shaking the foundations on which professional action and conduct has formerly depended, of displacing what were deemed sound values and judgements, without yet formulating replacements. The possibility is that residual loyalties to beliefs and values cohabit with newly forming ones, as deeply-held values are confronted by new experiences and changes in perception. Equally, a teacher wrestling with a deep conflict between career ambition, which needed confidence to be noticed by others, and inner acknowledgement of novicehood, needs sensitive support and mechanisms for reconciling conflicts.

These few examples indicate that, like the individual cases reported by Dadds (1996), Nias (1989), Sparkes (1994) and others, the presentation of the subtleties and details of life experiences deserve space that is not usually available in formally designated appraisal. In the conduct of self-appraisal of this kind, the need for professional esteem and self-approbation is evident. I recognize that perpetual self-growth intrinsically involves self-challenge and disapprobation of the self in some respects. That tension itself deserves careful attention. There can be little doubt that 'self-confrontation in the explication and clarification of values' (Zimpher and Howey 1987: 104) and aspects of personal commitment and interpersonal involvement in leadership, carry potential costs as well as benefits. The balance of investments and returns on capital, to follow Sergiovanni's (1998) analogy, needs careful management. If the personalities, perceptions and predispositions of individual teachers are somehow to be nourished without seeing them detrimentally as deficient in some respects, however, then a developmental and constructivist approach to postinduction which is capable of handling such matters is essential.

Approaching leadership

The view of career and extended professional that I raised earlier offers us the chance to rethink radically the premise of an élite core of teacher leaders, and instead to consider the potential of what Sergiovanni (1998) calls pedagogical leadership. He sees this as an alternative to traditional ways of thinking about school leadership, from which he selects images of the bureaucratic, the visionary, and the entrepreneurial leader. His argument is that despite their widespread use, these traditional models of leadership have not improved schools as learning communities. Pedagogical leadership offers different strategies for school improvement, by investing in schools as 'caring, focused and inquiring communities within which teachers work together as members of a community of practice' (Sergiovanni 1998: 38). The investment that Sergiovanni imagines is in building a learning community, within which the capital assets are social, academic, intellectual and professional. The investment of these human assets is seen as the key factor in bringing about educational benefits to students.

Although Sergiovanni is primarily concerned with the role of school principals, the sense of leadership and the perceived position of the 'investors' can be read as quite different from the conventional relationships associated with headteachers, experienced teachers and newly qualified teachers. Those conventions are about to be perpetuated in proposals for teacher induction and the establishment of advanced skills teacher categories in many parts of the world. The alternative offers a better way forward:

> In communities, leadership and learning go together. So does leadership and sense-making. Leaders and followers reflect together, learn

together and inquire together as they care together and construct a reality that helps them navigate through a complex world. The process of reciprocal influence is guided by shared purposes and involves accepting roles that are connected to moral obligations.

(Sergiovanni 1998: 41)

What this implies is that although different members of a school community might hold differentiated formal roles and statuses, the contributions to each other and to the educational community will have the same (mutual) esteem and capital value. In fact, teachers are seen as practising at the forefront of pedagogical leadership because they are the closest to the students, providing the academic, social, and spiritual guidance. The school principal is seen by Sergiovanni as the 'head follower' of the school community's purposes. Through this transformation of the relationships, schools are able to generate leadership capital, which is not characterized by bureaucratic procedure or personality, or by the hunt for finance, but by the authority of ideas, values, and commitments to the education of students. That is not to say that these other institutional and personal dimensions of professional life will disappear. It is to reassert the primacy of purpose. Membership of school communities that adopt this stance are empowered by their responsibilities and leadership, it is claimed. By these means:

As leadership capital expands, leadership density in the school increases. Leadership density increases the likelihood that social, academic, intellectual and professional capital will expand.

(Sergiovanni 1998: 43)

If concepts of professionality and the range of roles and responsibilities with which teachers are now charged creates a need to identify and develop both personal and leadership qualities, then these must begin within, but take new entrants beyond, the first year of teaching. Those qualities come into play within a classroom, where pedagogical leadership has its main stage. Even in the induction year they extend into responsibilities of collegiality and partnership in the wider community, where the purpose of leadership is to affect the experiences of students, but the focus of action is indirect. In which case, in-service work among teachers at the postinduction stage needs to include the possibilities of provision based on:

- the development of professional judgements in pedagogical leadership practices;
- aspects of self-appraisal for leadership growth;
- involvement in collegial activities and leadership ventures within schools.

Actions and activities of this kind are common among newly qualified teachers. The range of their contributions to schools identified in Tickle (1994) shows a simple picture of where they bring about change because of their particular talents and their desire and willingness to take a lead. Stories of exemplary conduct influencing colleagues, of gentle persuasions to adopt new ideas, and of heroic achievements in transforming outdated classrooms can be identified in many places. I recently worked with a new (woman) graduate mathematician, appointed to a high school department of four long-serving men teachers, who were not using computers in their teaching. In a campaigning spirit to change the situation in her own classroom and across the department, the task of getting others to accept the need for change, negotiating a strategy for it, and developing the confidence and technical knowledge of these senior colleagues, provided initial research (into their attitudes and school finance) followed by a year-long development strategy of equipment acquisition and in-service tutoring.

A modern foreign languages graduate, specializing in French and German, who introduced a range of classroom methods using activity-based, participatory learning, became seen as exemplary by established colleagues and the senior management of a high school. The methods were used as models for the development of departmental policy, and the transformation of classroom environments, including the use of information and communications technology. A woman primary school teacher with an interest and expertise in design and technology, who coordinated a Strengths, Weaknesses, Opportunities and Threats (SWOT) analysis throughout the school, devised and negotiated a strategy for supporting staff development and changes in classroom facilities and practices.

Other examples can be found in schools throughout the world. They arise, it appears, by chance of circumstance. They depend on a coincidental meeting of new teachers with energy and professional capital, the perception of opportunities to capitalize on it, and the sensitivity to invest further in it by supporting innovation. What is more, they are subject to being fragile, ad hoc, and idiosyncratic. A principled professional approach would ensure that such innovations and change, whether in the realm of self, in individual practice, or in leadership, is placed on a sound footing with research-based practice at its centre. That will need systematic participation in the development of research capabilities, taking the profession beyond loose notions of being reflective practitioners.

Introducing prudence

Approaches to professional and school development that actively encourage teachers to research their own and their institutions' practices, and work out their own strategies for change, are usually associated with experienced teachers. The initial emphasis in these activities is on the identification of personal and practical professional concerns. For some, the emphasis is on problems arising from leadership practices, or issues that pertain to bringing about change through such practices. Whatever the professional context, an assumption is that evidence plays a central part in understanding events, or in clarifying the nature of problems, and monitoring the effects of actions. This presumes that understanding situations and problems by way of research will lead to more intelligent identification of needs, and more intelligent courses of action.

This relationship between evidence and practice is a critical relationship not only for professional action, but also for effective professional development. 'Growth' in this sense hangs on developing the capacity for generating better interpretations of evidence, in order to improve one's own and/or colleagues' understanding of what is happening in professional practice situations. Expertise in the analysis of evidence of practice, to arrive at more informed conduct that is based soundly in that capacity for handling evidence, is the goal. I have previously called this the development of professional judgement in practice. Stenhouse (1975) called it prudence, or practical wisdom, and defined it as the capacity to judge the most profitable courses of action.

There are many possible starting points towards the development of prudence. A lot of what happens in professional practice is based on the evidence that is immediately (and impressionistically) available in the circumstances where we take action. Often the circumstances prevent the best use of evidence, or even cause the evidence to go unnoticed. In professional work the demand for action can lead us to adopt attitudes whereby evidence is deflected, ignored, or not sought. Schön (1983: 68) described this phenomenon among professionals as 'becoming skillful at techniques of selective in-attention, junk categories, and situational control'. He argued that the preservation of constancy in our knowledge, and the removal of uncertainty, were characteristic of such non-reflective practitioners.

The kind of research imagined to counteract this tendency has the capacity to aid personal understanding and help self-realization. It is a form of practical philosophy (Elliott 1991). This is referred to often as reflexive – to distinguish it from merely reflective – research. The difference signals the need to engage simultaneously in research of problem situations, of action, of values, and of one's own learning and development that accrues from that research. These tasks are complex indeed – and a clear measure of professionality. The values and perspectives that drive professional practice in particular directions – the personal beliefs and constructs that guide one's thinking and actions – are difficult sometimes to identify, or to articulate. Their acquisition will be embedded in personal biography. They may be embedded in professional cultures into which one has been inducted, and to which one fully subscribes. In seeking to meet professional needs it is also possible to unfold values to reveal aspects of self, which I have called personal qualities, that have a different kind of bearing on professional practice. It means that what is often thought of as legitimate empirical research is complemented by or even merges with aspects of self, and self-exploration. Collegial support can guide decisions about the focus of inquiry, its subsequent methods and conduct, and the creation of records of the learning that occurs.

Topics

Where appropriate then, the growth of prudence may be sought by a teacher in order to develop curriculum coordination and leadership. These do not preclude the possibility that an individual curriculum coordinator might seek to enhance his or her own personal (perhaps subject) expertise – to engage with the world as an historian, as a geographer, as an artist; as a caring person, as someone lacking confidence, as a subject of sexism, racism or homophobia, or as someone who has observed victims of injustice and wants to take professional action to create a more educative climate. Or a person might want to develop their understanding of key ideas that influence professional practice – what it is to be professional, the nature of self, equality, service, differentiation, curriculum, learning, relations with parents, learning processes, evaluation of the curriculum, historical research, or policy analysis. Each one requires insights to be developed for a professional picture of practice to be achieved.

Let me pursue the discussion from the point of view of curriculum leaders. Issues of coordination, collegiality, and leadership arise when contemplating practical action for staff development. The development of strategies for effecting change may depend upon the receptiveness of colleagues, and it is important to understand the conditions and processes that affect such receptiveness. Understanding the ways in which ideas are adapted and accommodated as relevant to particular learners or working contexts is also important for effecting change, and for understanding the nature of the changes that come about. Such matters involve negotiation, and raise issues of autonomy, the delegation of responsibility, and matters of self-esteem, self-respect, and valuing of individuals within negotiations for staff development. All of these avenues of action might be effected more successfully on the basis of practitioner research.

These are matters that are likely to arise as practical action is contemplated, and strategies worked out for identifying staff development needs, undertaking staff development planning, negotiating provision to meet individual staff needs, providing subject knowledge and teaching expertise for the transmission of that knowledge to pupils, and engaging in curriculum planning for a subject within the context of school development planning. It is possible, then, to think of a research project as one that begins by seeking data in order to understand a situation better, and thus to be in position to make more informed judgements about how to proceed in staff development activities – an evaluation of an existing situation, leading to action.

The researcher

It will be evident by now that action research places the researcher at the centre of the research evidence: as one of the sources and providers of evidence, and as the gatherer and interpreter of it. It is often argued that research should be objective, and that for it to be so the researcher must purge any biases. Clearly in action research, where a professional is engaged in trying to change situations, that is not feasible. I prefer an alternative possibility, drawn from the work of Gadamer (1975). He argued that the attempt to purge bias from enquiry is a misleading and impossible trail, that being necessarily involves presuppositions and prejudices, brought to situations as foresight and preconceptions, and that it is these ideas that make understanding possible. Rather than seeing investigators' prejudices as an intrusion to be prevented, Gadamer argued that, as an unavoidable attribute of human existence, they might better be seen as constituting a condition for understanding rather than a hindrance to it. That is made possible by approaching evidence with an openness to alternative possibilities of interpretation and understanding than our preconceptions would allow if they were not controlled by the discipline of openness.

Openness means revealing preconceptions, making them available for criticism, discovering distorting perspectives, and engaging in revision. Revision may be enhanced and objectivity arrived at by making available the presuppositions, the objects of interpretation, and the interpretations. Understanding becomes self-understanding, as interpretation and self-reflection combine.

Doing research

The purpose of any investigation is to provide a closer look at a chosen aspect of practice, personal characteristics, or leadership qualities. Deciding the topic, judging the scope of the project, devising principles for the conduct of the research, deciding what data to select and collect, and from whom, and working out how to record it, all exercise the mind during research. Decisions about how to make sense of – or analyse – data, what it means in relation to the topic and one's practice, and how best to compare the sense that one makes of it with other evidence that might be available, and with what other people make of it, also occupy the researcher. The implications for one's practice will be part of the 'making sense' stage of the research, and decisions about any changes in practice that may be appropriate will follow – as will decisions about how best to record the research, and the evidence of professional learning that arises from it, either for oneself or for others for whom it might be significant and helpful.

However, doing research is not so neatly sequential as that. It is not uncommon, for example, for data that begins to emerge to cause a rethink on the way the problem was defined. Or evidence might arise that is so convincing that some immediate changes in practice are justified or essential, thus changing the situation and the focus. It is well worth recording decisions about these factors in the research process, perhaps in diary format, so that they can provide a systematic or disciplined framework for the project. If amendments to the procedures are made, they would be made on justifiable bases, in response, say, to experience in implementing the research methods adopted, or preliminary analysis of data.

Opening up practice

Sometimes the most teasing of all steps in the research process can be the first one, deciding what aspect of practice to select for special attention – what to research more fully than normal practice allows. It may be teasing because one has only a vague sense of an issue, an uneasy feeling about events, or a sense of evidence that is hard to pin down. It may mean opening up and questioning what one thought were certainties, examining what one has 'always known', as well as exploring doubts and dilemmas that were already inherently uncomfortable. There are many potential topics, out of which it is necessary to decide what is most relevant and worthwhile for developing understanding, as well as what is feasible (in terms of having access to data, for instance where others are involved, and in terms of time and available resources).

Selecting the purpose and focus of research is a necessary but sometimes lengthy process. It is easy to imagine grand projects among the complex events of professional life, less easy to select a focus that is manageable within a given timescale, or in the amount of time available to attend to it. The topic might stem from a general concern to monitor events in a situation, with the intention to develop insights into one's own ideas and practices, or in order to improve insights, understanding, and practice within a professional group. A desire, perhaps, to understand events in school situations, or to scrutinize policy to understand the origins and locus of curriculum ideas, especially where there is an apparent conflict of viewpoints and beliefs affecting policy and practices, might be more important. Deciding on a topic may be helped by considering the questions:

- What, ideally, do I most want to know or investigate?
- Why is the topic significant for me?

A record of evidence can be kept using the steps shown in the boxes on the following pages (Boxes 1–9). Recording these initial ideas and being prepared to review and amend them as one proceeds with the research is a worthwhile discipline for refining ideas, and for judging if a project is feasible. In the case of planned actions this will include wanting to know if events turn out as one intended them to, or to know what will happen as a consequence of (or despite) one's actions. Such research questions, hypotheses, problems, or issues take one's thoughts into the world of predictions, speculations, anticipations, and enquiry. This is a professional world of puzzlement and uncertainty, and needs fluidity in thinking, and initially a willingness not to 'know' too much, but rather to want to know. However, we usually know some things based on evidence gained from experience of a situation,

---

Box 1

Write a brief note of what you see as a professional need, or what you
want to investigate.
  Say why it has priority and significance. Try to make the topic clear,
realizable (i.e. what you can reasonably hope to achieve) and manageable (in the time available).

Box 2

Describe the situation, briefly and impressionistically, in writing. Provide whatever evidence is available. Consider how trustworthy the
evidence is (is it convincing?). Record and file the description to provide
a comparison against later evidence.

---

and have reasonably well-informed judgements about our professional needs.
It is worth recording these at the initial stage of research.

  In fact, the topic of enquiry and the reason why it is significant often
stem from informed judgements about what may happen or may be happening in practice, something one suspects is happening, or not. From such
impressions or aspirations a wish to know more about a situation or problem in practice arises, and provides the impetus for the research. Describing
a situation or problem as it appears to be, that is as one thinks it is, and its
personal, institutional or social context, provides a way to clarify ideas about
the problem itself and one's awareness of evidence related to it. This can
begin by considering the questions:

• What is the situation or background to the need/issue like now?
• What do you think you know about it?

Principles

Identifying needs and carrying out research, especially of the reflexive
kind, can be threatening, particularly if one comes to it with a 'deficiency'
attitude, and where one is working with colleagues. On the other hand it
can be celebratory. I have sometimes called this the celebration of ignorance
– because without ignorance there would not be space to become better
educated, or to change the way one sees the world. Gethin's (1998) representation of the Buddhist view of the changing self offers a nicer way,
without the connotation of ignorance.

The process involves questioning deeply-held values, opening up one's practice to scrutiny, changing one's perceptions of the world. It means starting from scratch, accepting not knowing, and taking risks associated with learning new knowledge, testing new professional strategies, and learning how to carry out research. It almost invariably involves other people, their thoughts, ideas, perspectives, values and actions. It is important to follow principles in the conduct of the research that will ensure, so far as possible, that it is effective, worthwhile, and at the same time ethical.

The principle of openness (to oneself and others) can be a sound basis for the conduct of observations, research discussions, interviews, or reports, to ensure a supportive climate and collaboration with those involved. This principle should guide the research process wherever possible, that is one should be open about the subject, purposes and uses of the research with everyone concerned with it.

Listening to other people's ideas with an open mind also appears to help focus upon one's own concerns in a receptive manner. The principle of open-mindedness to one's own misgivings, misapprehensions and misdemeanours is also a valuable asset to have. Sharing and scrutinizing ideas and evidence appears to be mutually beneficial, in the sense of opening up more information for the researcher, and helping others to think about their part in the matters being researched. This involves, however, making one's own ideas explicit and acknowledging that they may be based on very different values from those of others involved.

A process of constant negotiation and interaction is needed, and this can be rather destabilizing. It should be destabilizing, in the sense of self-conscious questioning of practice – but to be constructive, the conduct of learning should also seek to enhance confidence, knowledge and skills within the focus of study, and enable participants to evaluate events in a supportive, sharing atmosphere. A principle of sensitivity is needed. The following aims and practices can enhance openness, open-mindedness, and sensitivity, and provide a supportive environment, if they are adopted as principles of procedure during research:

- identifying and sharing the aims of the research, one's own needs in carrying it out, and helping others to understand what the work is about and the problems it entails;
- listening to others' reports of events in professional practice and helping them to find ways of sharing them;
- asking questions about the topic and others' work related to it in ways that will help to focus on it without threat to the self-confidence of others or oneself;
- applying constructively critical questions to one's own work, and sharing those thoughts with others.

Where evidence is being recorded, a principle of anonymity may help to achieve openness, by ensuring that where it seems appropriate names of people and places are changed to protect individuals from possible consequences of sensitive data being communicated to others. If the people involved know that they will be protected in this way, access to such data might be gained more easily. If young children are involved, or others where negotiation of the use of data is not feasible, anonymity can provide a general safeguard. It is a safeguard principle, and in many instances will be quite unnecessary. The researcher must judge each research situation, and raise the question of the right of those involved to control the disclosure of real names.

The promise that information will be treated in confidence can also, sometimes, help one to gain evidence that would not otherwise be available. However, the principle of confidentiality may also compromise the principle of openness, and make it impossible to use data. On the other hand one may feel able to open up one's own work and ideas only in confidence. It is worth considering this principle, but generally speaking it reflects, and represents, a rather negating stance towards the development of professional practice within a community. It may be more appropriate to more personalized professional needs.

Whichever of these principles is adopted will affect the decisions and negotiations that will need to be carried for the research to take place, especially if others are in any way involved. Declaring the principles on which one wants to proceed will ensure that individuals know what is happening, and what their rights are, including a right not to participate, the right to scrutinize any data they provide, to amend or correct what they say, or to restrict the circulation of evidence they provide. They will also ensure that the conduct of the research will be open to review as it proceeds, and that the outcome of the research, where possible, will be shared and open for discussion among interested people.

Evidence

What is data? Put simply, a sense datum is an immediate experience of the physical world – sound, colour, feel, movement, etc. More usually in the social research sense a datum is a single piece of information, sometimes heard, sometimes seen, or maybe written and read. Data are a series of such information about people's ideas, actions or interactions, which can take many forms:

- policy documents, or documents produced in planning curricula;
- visual aids or worksheets, which often communicate instructions that are part of an interaction between teacher and student;
- discussions between colleagues, or with learners, and learner interactions within day-to-day activities;
- professional environments and resourcing, which convey important information about the physical construction of practice spaces, as do the timing and phasing of activities;

- interventions in supporting (or prompting) learning (e.g. physical movement, eye contacts, or helping with students' work);
- learners' thoughts about their work or themselves in relation to it, and
  teachers' thoughts about learners and their work;
- written texts such as syllabuses, tasks, and responses to tasks.

The list could be endless.

It is important to remain sensitive to data's potential. However, social
settings like professional arenas are so full of data that it is also important
to ensure that a particular research interest is allowed to steer attention
towards the most significant data for that topic, and to guide its collection.
The relationship between the topic and the question of what data are significant is one that will perhaps perpetually pose a problem in carrying out
research. There will usually be far more data in a situation than one can
handle; they might have to be recorded urgently if they are not to be lost.
Until the data have been recorded and thought about it is often not evident
whether they will be useful or not. One solution to the dilemmas this can
pose is to constantly check the data against the identified need, or research
topic, and the aims or questions that are priorities within the topic.

In the first place, data may be evident in a situation, for example through
observation of events in a practice context under normal conditions, or in
the responses one makes to new demands or unfamiliar tasks. On other
occasions data might be less evident, and have to be solicited, as in the case
of requesting an interview with a colleague to hear about why they practice
in a particular way. Data might even have to be engendered, in the sense
that professional situations can be devised or managed in order to generate
new kinds of responses from other people. That kind of circumstance would
be common in testing new materials or teaching methods.

Gathering evidence

It will usually be necessary to negotiate access to and the use of evidence
among others involved in research. Sometimes that will be followed immediately by recording data – for example, asking if a colleague will agree to be
interviewed, agreeing future use of the interview responses, and proceeding
to tape the interview, or asking for a questionnaire to be completed, or if
photographs can be taken, and establishing how they may be used later.
The different forms in which data occur are likely to need different ways of
acquiring them and collecting them together, or recording them. Some of
these seem to be self-evident, as in the case of students' work, photographs,
video film, or tape-recorded interviews. In each case, however, other ways
of describing events might be possible, such as descriptive observation notes
in place of photographs or film, or interview notes in place of audiotape.

In all cases records need to be kept of locations, occasions, sources and
respondents, so that the places, times and people can be identified and fitted

---

Box 3

Where action is to be invoked, describe the proposed professional action that will take place, so far as it can be predicted.

Box 4

Consider and make a record of responses to the following questions:

- What evidence do I need?
- Where can it be found?
- What techniques should I use for collecting, recording, storing it?

---

into the larger picture of the research at the stage of collating and analysing the whole of the data. Simple methods such as a box file or ring binder system, self-adhesive labels, or stick-on memo notes, can prove invaluable in the organization of data so that sections of them can be retrieved or referred to easily when they are needed. Several techniques of data collection from the tradition of quantitative research are available. They include:

- testing;
- surveys;
- questionnaires;
- experimental programmes;
- clinical interviews;
- systematic observation;
- analysis of documentary evidence.

The traditions of qualitative research include:

- the analysis of documentary evidence;
- the use of written accounts of events, or statements;
- interviews (structured by pre-set questions, or unstructured and free-flowing);
- observation of situations and actions;
- participation in and concurrent observation of activities and events;
- group discussion;
- reflective dialogue;
- autobiography.

As always in professional life, research will mean managing time differently to allow for more sustained collection of evidence, rather than finding additional time. That will be so whether one works alone or with the help

---

Box 5

Consider the question:

• What should be the time-scale and time-use strategy for the project?

Box 6

Consider the question:

• What would be the most appropriate equipment and resources for the project?

Box 7

Consider the question:

• Who should be invited to participate in the research?

---

of students or colleagues. Consideration of time is important in terms of the total time-scale of the project, as well as the amount of time given day-to-day for negotiating the research, gathering data, organizing and analysing it, writing, and reading. This will be a main consideration in deciding what to research, since any research needs to be manageable and realizable within the time-scale available and within the day-to-day time of a busy professional role.

In addition, the resources to consider include suitable means of recording and storing data which will help to provide a picture of events: notebook or diary, files to store records, tape-recorder and audiotapes, still camera and film, video recorder and tapes, materials for pupils' work, a word processor or computer with a database facility, etc.

Perhaps the most significant resource of all is the availability of persons who can provide the data needed, and who are therefore crucial to the project. Deciding which individuals to invite to participate, and how many, is another judgement that can be made only in relation to the topic, timescale, and so on. The group and the choice of setting that are relevant to the area under investigation needs careful consideration.

There is a risk in doing research with personal value that it will be done without reference to other relevant research and records of practice. Relevant work from other enquiries can be a valuable resource, to provide broader reference points, or to use concepts that help in making sense of a situation. With this in mind, reading should be undertaken as an enquiry in itself, with the prospect of treating written material as evidence, as printed impressions of people's ideas, information and events. Reading does not provide a straightforward source of understanding, there for borrowing. It provides a range of sources, and alternative viewpoints, to which the reader will bring their own. The interface between the reader and those sources is one arena for intellectual struggle, with its attendant confusions, demands of information handling, and the coming to terms with new ways of thinking.

It is worth recording an outline of the research and inviting colleagues to consider it, to ensure nothing has been forgotten, or to have a second view of what is being proposed. This can be used as a personal checklist, and can act as a public account of the thinking behind the research. It also provides a useful exercise in the concise presentation of ideas. The plan can later be used to help to organize notes. The following outline guidance can be used for reference:

Outline of research

1 Topic

This might be stated as the focus, a problem from practice, an issue that concerns you, an interesting puzzle or dilemma you face, a feature of experience you have noticed and would like to investigate, a question you would like answered by using evidence, an evaluation task you have been asked to carry out, a research theme from literature you want to investigate further yourself.

2 Aim

This is stated as what it is you hope to find out about, or to learn from the gathering of evidence. If it is action research, it will include a statement of what you intend to change or improve, the action you plan to take, and what you want to find out about its consequences.

3 Significance

This is stated in terms of why it is important to do the research, for yourself, for your institution, for educational policy, for the sake of community knowledge, or for learners with whom you work, what the potential benefits are, who will gain from it, and how.

4 Evidence

This ensures that the research relates closely to the topic, to identify the most informative kinds of evidence, such as behaviour that is observed, comments that are invited, ideas that students produce.

5 Methods

These include techniques such as observation fieldnotes, camera, completion of questionnaires, interviews, diaries, gathering of documents, work created by learners.

6 Record

This includes how dates will be noted, individuals identified, records filed, documents related to each other, literature sources remembered.

7 Sources

You must select the most central informants or potentially key documents, so far as these can be predicted.

8 Place

This includes how many sites will be used, how widespread are the people, and how narrow or broad is the sample involved.

9 Reading

This includes time allocations for library searches, for reading, and for selecting and summarizing in relation to new research evidence.

10 Resources

These include special equipment such as cameras, computers and audiotape, or a simple notebook, or printed questionnaire.

11 Ethics

Consider ethics in deciding what to research, what agreements to reach with those involved, how evidence might be used, and who should have access to it.

12 Timetable

This includes plannes time, negotiating responses from people, deadlines for evidence gathering, time for analysis, and dates for writing up a final assignment report.

13 Interpretations

This includes the ways in which you will approach the interpretation and analysis of data and evidence, including how you will handle your own biases, how you will ensure all possible interpretations are considered, and how you will create categories and build theories.

14 Products

You must consider the likely content, length, and form of any reports.

15 Dissemination

How will the research be made public and by whom it will potentially be utilized?

Analysing evidence

Research simultaneously involves generating and collecting data, interpreting and organizing them. It is difficult in practice to separate these actions, but some initial analysis is likely to occur during the gathering and storing of data, whether that is in the memory or in a record. A mass of data is not difficult to collect, but in order to make any sort of contribution in an investigation it will have to be analysed and classified in some way. For example: by categorizing the data in relation to the questions posed, by looking at possible relationships between the data collected about needs and actions, and the data collected about events that stem from actions.

Box 8

Consider the questions:

- To what extent do your ideas match what you thought might happen or was happening before the investigation?
- To what extent did any of your inquiry generate illuminative experiences?
- Has something come to light of which you were unaware?
- Have you been alerted to any assumptions that were being made?

Making sense of data can be based on a search for patterns in the responses of informants or the actions observed. These might well be subsets of information within the research questions being asked. To use a simple example, the question, 'What educational strategies did I use?' might generate data on a range of categories, such as giving instructions, inviting ideas, setting written tasks, dictating notes, asking questions.

Within the category 'asking questions' there might be subsections depicting types of questions: those requiring factual knowledge, those setting problems, those inviting opinions, and so on. As patterns, issues and sets of data begin to be recognized they are translated from tape recordings, responses to tasks, notes, transcripts, documents, and such, into evidence.

Interpreting data also requires systematic ordering, but this process of analysis can be devised as a simple discipline that begins with the labelling of documents, transcripts, etc. (date of diary entry, occasion of a discussion, discovery of new ideas, name of person interviewed or observed, date and place of an action or an event).

Using card dividers, plastic wallets, and numbering pages, paragraphs and any other obvious subunit of a file or document can also begin as data are gathered. These can be indexed, or colour-coded, so that if one wants to locate evidence of (to use the earlier example) particular kinds of questioning, or gender issues, or particular attitudes, etc. it is possible to do so systematically.

Sorting out the data will lead to a process of selecting from them. This is a time of making more sense of those first impressions, of confirming the evidence first uncovered, by adding to it from the data. Distortions can also occur in this process, through the selection of data that one wants to find. At this stage it is possible to begin to summarize one's ideas that result from thinking about the evidence.

Deciding what to include as most significant in reporting to other people involved in collaborative research is a crucial phase. It will also mean deciding appropriate formats for sharing information and ideas – tables, charts, extracts of interview transcripts or fieldnotes, photographs, reading lists, etc. Decisions about selection and format will be influenced by interpretations,

> **Box 9**
>
> List the main categories of evidence that the research provides.

and they will also influence the way the presented data are discussed. Preparation of a draft portfolio based on the data, but adopting a critical perspective on what has been done so far, and what has been learnt, is a worthwhile step towards making the research presentable.

Action

The major purpose of research is likely to be to inform one's own understanding, to help to develop professional practice in some way. To recap, it is assumed that prudent action requires a basis of evidence that is as substantial as it can be – to achieve better-informed action than otherwise would occur. Changes in the detail of existing ways of doing things can result from the initial analysis of data. Replacing existing ways of doing things with different ways in a wholesale manner is also possible. Within an innovation, though, the process is about testing new ways of doing things, and problems arising in the execution of a professional plan can also be solved as evidence begins to accumulate.

Proposals for action that are based on the research evidence can include statements of the aims of the changes or adjustments, and the reasons for them. These would be in the form of implications derived from the evidence, or recommendations for continuing and reinforcing particular actions, or for implementing changes. Like all proposals for professional action, these will take account of the evidence in the context of the situation, and will include immediate, short-term, and future long-term possible actions. Action plans, or principles of procedure that will be adopted to inform actions, may become the final part of a research portfolio. (They could include further proposed research if it is felt that more evidence is needed.) They will be based on the construction of sound argument derived from the research evidence, and justified on that basis.

Quality

Judgement about the quality of research and the learning that accrues from it can be made in terms of its value for improving professional practice, or for developing one's understanding of a situation. As I have noted earlier, the relationship between quality of research and quality of practice is not easy to pin down. Does research help prudence to grow? When? How? I guess we are not quite sure. I can only lay claim to a belief that professional needs can best be met by the conduct of research that is rigorously conducted, relevant to the practices of the participants, and reflexive in terms of open self-criticism of the ideas behind it, and the learning gained from it. Such research can sometimes be supported in group activities among colleagues in the workplace, in order to bring rigour, test relevance, and stimulate further reflexivity. Some criteria can be used as a guide to judging quality within a portfolio record, which stands as a testament to professional development. Seeking to define quality in the whole of a research project, the following list of criteria was created by professional practitioners to suggest what credible and creditable research would need to include to meet their approval (Tickle 1995):

- the voice of the researcher being made public;
- the inclusion of the researcher's values, beliefs and assumptions;
- the identifying of a need, a theme for professional development, an issue that they seek to resolve, a research question that they wish to pursue;
- the clarity of the research question or issue, the purpose of the research, and its process;
- the demonstration of the importance of the research as justification for doing it;
- the addressing of an issue that is of interest to others in the educational community;
- the devising of a means of addressing it in relation to the researcher's professional context;
- the providing of assurance that practical action strives to achieve educational aims;
- the presenting of arguments and ideas that help to address the needs identified;
- the making of explicit connections between the research and the learners to whom educational aims were directed;
- the incorporation of revisions in the direction of the research and changes in practice resulting from it;
- the demonstration of a self-critical stance towards practice and research;
- the bringing of multiple perspectives to the data, and ensuring accuracy in its handling through self-checking;
- the showing of the grounds on which sense has been made and understanding gained from the analysis of evidence and/or experience;
- the discussing and reflecting upon their professional learning, in ways that go beyond unsubstantiated opinion;
- the developed awareness of the conceptual and theoretical background and literature relevant to the topic;
- the presentation of sufficient and convincing evidence to support assertions and claims made or new practices developed;
- the conclusions following directly from evidence;
- the assumption that something similar should be capable of being done by others;

- the characterizing of the work as unfinished, a continuing venture with the inclusion of new questions that arise from the research;
- the provocation through the setting of challenges to others and oneself in the ideas presented.

(adapted from Tickle 1995)

This list does not define the internal standards of each criterion, that is, it does not declare that complete assurance, total clarity, fully inclusive, masterly demonstration, of the appropriate rules of rigour is required. That is also true of criteria gleaned from the international literature on educational action research, which I have used to compare with that other list (Tickle 1995). However, their essence is of the reflective practitioner, determined to do the best possible for students, seeking continuous self-improvement, and working for the communal improvement of their professional service. The test is whether they lead in professional practice to qualities of:

- prudence – practical wisdom and the capacity to judge the most profitable courses of action;
- openness – representations of action and of underlying values;
- open-mindedness – reviews of evidence and responsiveness to it;
- communal self-reflection – engaging in collective examination of prejudices and practices;
- courage – in exposing curriculum proposals and practice; and in exposing research endeavours;
- growth – a willingness to change and acknowledge change;
- contemplation – living with the fermentation of understanding, especially of the theory–practice relationship, while seeking maturation.

The tenth and final element of the DfEE/TTA 'induction standards' requires that every newly qualified teacher

should demonstrate that he or she takes responsibility for their own professional development, setting objectives for improvements, and taking action to keep up to date with research and developments in pedagogy and in the subject(s) they teach.

(TTA 1999a)

These principles of practitioner research provide a basis for the kind of learning community called for by Cochran-Smith and Lytle (see p. 121), and for the accumulation of educational capital (Sergiovanni, see p. 171), coupled with the extended focus on professional characteristics and personal qualities, they represent a necessary supplement to those core essentials of professional credibility – the technical requirements of planning, teaching, class management and assessment. Taken at face value, the focus on those core skills leaves a sense of disappointment, in the limits of the imagination of policy makers, administrators, and assessors, that is strengthened. These are unimaginative and shallow expectations, given the scope and the scale of the educational problems to be solved, and the combined intelligences of the new generations of professional educators that are available to communities for solving them. In those broader and deeper criteria of quality – as gleaned from professionals and from the action research literature, and listed above – the task is not just keeping up to date with research, but keeping apace *in* it as a basis for continuing improvement in professional practice and in the communal improvement of education. They seem to me to offer a considerably more demanding way ahead, and a vitally more creative one that might not only attract, but also retain, those powers of regeneration that new teachers represent.

Bibliography

Adler, M. (1982) *The Paedeia Proposal*. New York: Collier Macmillan.

Agne, K. (1999) Caring: the way of the master teacher, in R.P. Lipka and T.M. Brinthaupt (eds) *The Role of Self in Teacher Development*. Albany, NY: State University of New York Press.

Alexander, R. (1995) *Versions of Primary Education*. London: Routledge.

Alexander, R.J., Craft, M. and Lynch, J. (eds) (1984) *Change in Teacher Education: Context and Provision Since Robbins*. London: Holt, Rinehart and Winston.

Altrichter, H., Posch, P. and Somekh, B. (1993) *Teachers Investigate Their Work*. London: Routledge.

Andrews, I. (1987) Induction programmes: staff development opportunities for beginning and experienced teachers, in M.F. Wideen, and I. Andrews (eds) *Staff Development for School Improvement*. London: Falmer Press.

Applegate, J.H. (1989) Readiness for teaching, in M.L. Holly and C.S. McLoughlin (eds) *Perspectives on Teacher Professional Development*. London: Falmer Press.

Argyris, C. and Schön, D. (1974) *Theory in Practice: Increasing Professional Effectiveness*. San Francisco, CA: Jossey-Bass.

Atweh, B., Kemmis, S. and Weeks, P. (eds) (1996) *Action Research in Practice: Partnerships for Social Justice in Education*. London: Routledge.

Australian Teaching Council (1996) *National Competency Framework for Beginning Teaching*. Sydney, NSW: Australian Teaching Council.

Baldassarre, V.A. (1998) Comparative study of the induction programmes for beginning teachers in Europe. Paper presented to the European Education Research Association Conference (ECER), Ljubljana, Slovenia, 17–20 September.

Barber, M. (1997) *The Learning Game: Arguments for an Education Revolution*. London: Indigo.

Barry, K. and King, L. (1998) *Beginning Teaching and Beyond*. Australia: Social Science Press.

Bennett, N. (1976) *Teaching Styles and Pupil Progress*. London: Open Books.

Berger, P.L. and Luckmann, T. (1967) *The Social Construction of Reality*. London: Allen Lane.

Berlak, H. and Berlak, A. (1981) *Dilemmas of Schooling*. London: Routledge and Kegan Paul.

Berliner, D.C. and Tikunoff, W.J. (1976) The California Beginning Teacher Evaluation Study: overview of the ethnographic study. *Journal of Teacher Education*, 27(1): 24–30.

Bernstein, B. (1971) On the classification and framing of educational knowledge codes, in M.F.D. Young (ed.) *Knowledge and Control*. London: Collier Macmillan.

Bernstein, B. (1977) *Class Codes and Control, Vol. 3: Towards a Theory of Educational Transmissions*. London: Routledge and Kegan Paul.

Bernstein, B. (1990) *Class Codes and Control, Vol. 4: The Structures of Pedagogic Discourse*. London: Routledge.

Bernstein, B. (1996) *Pedagogy, Symbolic Control and Identity: Theory, Research, Critique*. London: Taylor & Francis.

Best, D. (1985) *Feeling and Reason in the Arts*. London: George Allen & Unwin.

Beynon, J. (1987) Ms Floral mends her ways, in L. Tickle (ed.) *The Arts in Education: Some Research Studies*. London: Croom Helm.

Bloom, B.S. (1956) *Taxonomy of Educational Objectives*. London: Longman.

Blumer, H. (1962) Society as symbolic interactionism, in A.M. Rose (ed.) *Human Behaviour and Social Processes: An Interactionist Perspective*. London: Routledge and Kegan Paul.

Blyth, A. (1965) *English Primary Education*. London: Routledge and Kegan Paul.

Bolam, R. (1973) Induction programmes for probationary teachers: a report of an action research project funded by the DES and carried out at Bristol University 1968–72. Bristol University School of Education.

Bolam, R., Baker, K. and McMahon, A. (1975) The Teacher Induction Pilot Schemes (TIPS) Project: a national evaluation report. Bristol University School of Education.

Bond, D., Keogh, R. and Walker, D. (1985) *Reflection: Turning Experience into Learning*. London: Kogan Page.

Booth, M.B., Furlong, J., Hargreaves, D.H., Reiss, M.J. and Ruthven, K. (1989) *Teacher Supply and Teacher Quality: Solving the Coming Crisis*. Cambridge: University of Cambridge Department of Education.

Bourdien, P. (1983) Cultural reproduction and social reproduction, in R. Brown (ed.) *Knowledge, Education and Cultural Change*. London: Tavistock.

Boyer, E. (1983) *High School*. New York: Harper and Row.

Brinthaupt, T.M. and Lipka, R.P. (eds) (1992) *The Self: Definitional and Methodological Issues*. Albany, NY: State University of New York Press.

Brinthaupt, T.M. and Lipka, R.P. (eds) (1994) *Changing the Self: Philosophies, Techniques, and Experiences*. Albany, NY: State University of New York Press.

Britzman, D.P. (1991) *Practice Makes Perfect: A Critical Study of Learning to Teach*. Albany, NY: State University of New York Press.

Brophy, J. (1992) Probing the subtleties of subject-matter teaching. *Educational Leadership*, 49: 4–8.

Broudy, H.S., Smith, B.O. and Burnett, J. (1964) *Democracy and Excellence in American Secondary Education*. Chicago: Rand McNally.

Brown, A. and Dowling, P. (1997) *Doing Research, Reading Research*. London: Falmer Press.

Brown, G. (1975) *Microteaching: A Programme of Teaching Skills*. London: Methuen.

Brown, S. and McIntyre, D. (1986) The qualities of teachers: building on professional craft knowledge. Mimeo, Scottish Council for Research in Education and University of Oxford.

Brown, S. and McIntyre, D. (1993) *Making Sense of Teaching*. Buckingham: Open University Press.

Brown, S., McAlpine, A., McIntyre, D. and Hagger, H. (1988) Gaining access to experienced teachers' professional craft knowledge. Paper presented to the annual conference of the British Educational Research Association, University of East Anglia, 9–12 September.

Bruner, J. (1977) *The Process of Education*. Cambridge, MA: Harvard University Press.

Bruner, J. (1985) Models of the learner. *Educational Researcher*, June/July: 5–8.

Bruner, J. (1986) *Actual Minds, Possible Worlds*. Cambridge, MA: Harvard University Press.

Bullough, R.V. (1989) *First Year Teacher: A Case Study*. New York: Teachers College Press.

Bullough, R.V. (1992) Beginning teacher curriculum decision making, personal teaching metaphors, and teacher education. *Teaching and Teacher Education*, 8(3): 239–52.

Bullough, R.V., Knowles, J.G. and Crow, N. (1991) *Emerging as a Teacher*. London: Routledge.

Burgess, T. (1979) Educating for capability. *Journal of the Royal Society of Arts*, February: 1.

Bush, T. and West-Burnham, J. (eds) (1995) *The Principles of Educational Management*. London: Longman.

Busher, H., Clark, S. and Taggart, L. (1988) Beginning teachers' learning, in J. Calderhead (ed.) *Teachers' Professional Learning*. London: Falmer Press.

Butt, R., Townsend, D. and Raymond, D. (1990) Bringing reform to life: teachers' stories and professional development. *Cambridge Journal of Education*, 20(3): 255–68.

Calderhead, J. (ed.) (1987) *Exploring Teachers' Thinking*. London: Cassell.

Calderhead, J. (ed.) (1988) *Teachers' Professional Learning*. London: Falmer Press.

Calderhead, J. (1989) Reflective teaching and teacher education. *Teaching and Teacher Education*, 5(1): 43–51.

Calderhead, J. (1992) Induction: a research perspective on the professional growth of the newly qualified teacher, in General Teaching Council, *The Induction of Newly Appointed Teachers*. London: General Teaching Council Initiative for England and Wales.

Calderhead, J. and Shorrock, S.B. (1997) *Understanding Teacher Education*. London: Falmer Press.

Carr, W. (ed.) (1989) *Quality in Teaching: Arguments for a Reflective Profession*. London: Falmer Press.

Carr, W. (1995) *For Education: Towards Critical Educational Inquiry*. Buckingham: Open University Press.

Carr, W. and Kemmis, S. (1986) *Becoming Critical: Knowing Through Action Research*. London: Falmer Press.

Carvel, J. (1998) Woodhead under fire, *Guardian Education*, 15 December: 16–17.

Clandinin, D.J. (1986) *Classroom Practice: Teacher Images in Action*. London: Falmer Press.

Clandinin, D.J. and Connelly, F.M. (1990) Narrative, experience and the study of curriculum. *Cambridge Journal of Education*, 20(3): 241–54.

Clandinin, D.J. and Connelly, F.M. (1995) *Teachers' Professional Knowledge Landscapes*. New York: Teachers College Press.

Clark, M.S. (ed.) (1992) *Emotion*. London: Sage.

Cochran-Smith, M. and Lytle, S.L. (1998) Teacher research: the question that persists. *International Journal of Leadership in Education*, 1(1): 19–36.

Collarbone, P. and Farrar, M. (1993) Induction revisited – a life time in the profession? *British Journal of In-service Education*, 19(1): 23–8.

Collins, M. (1969) *Students into Teachers*. London: Routledge and Kegan Paul.

Connell, R. (1989) The labour process and the division of labour, in B. Cosin, M. Flude, and M. Hales (eds) *School, Work and Equality*. London: Hodder and Stoughton.

Connelly, M. and Clandinin, J. (1988) *Teachers as Curriculum Planners. Narratives of Experience*. New York: Teachers College Press.

Cooley, C. (1902) *Human Nature and the Social Order*, 1983 edn. New Brunswick, NJ: Transaction Books.

Cooper, P. (1993) *Effective Schools for Disaffected Students: Integration and Segregation*. London: Routledge.

Corcoran, E. (1981) Transition shock: the beginning teacher's paradox. *Journal of Teacher Education*, 32(3): 19–23.

Cordingley, P. (1998) *Constructing and Critiquing Reflective Practice*. London: Teacher Training Agency.

Costa, A.L. (1991a) The search for intelligent life, in A.L. Costa (ed.) *Developing Minds: A Resource Book for Teaching Thinking*. Alexandria, VA: Association for Supervision and Curriculum Development.

Costa, A.L. (ed.) (1991b) *Developing Minds: A Resource Book for Teaching Thinking*. Alexandria, VA: Association for Supervision and Curriculum Development.

Cox, C.B. and Dyson, A.E. (eds) (1969) *Fight For Education: A Black Paper*. London: The Critical Quarterly Society.

Cox, C.B. and Dyson, A.E. (eds) (1970) *Black Paper Two*. London: The Critical Quarterly Society.

Dadds, M. (1996) *Passionate Enquiry and School Development: A Story About Teacher Action Research*. London: Falmer Press.

Davis, D.J. (1979) *The Liverpool Induction Pilot Scheme: Summative Report*. School of Education, University of Liverpool.

Day, C. (1993) Reflection: a necessary but not sufficient condition for professional development. *British Educational Research Journal*, 19: 83–93.

Day, C. (1996) Professional learning and school development in action: a personal development planning project, in R. McBride (ed.) *Teacher Education Policy*. London: Falmer Press.

Day, C., Pope, M. and Denicolo, P. (eds) (1990) *Insights Into Teachers' Thinking and Practice*. London: Falmer Press.

Delors, J. (1996) *Learning the Treasures Within: Report to UNESCO of the International Commission on Education for the Twenty First Century*. Paris: UNESCO.

Dent, H.C. (1977) *The Training of Teachers in England and Wales 1800–1975*. London: Hodder and Stoughton.

Denzin, N. (1984) *On Understanding Emotion*. San Francisco, CA: Jossey-Bass.

Denzin, N. (1989) *Interpretive Interactionism*. London: Sage.

Denzin, N. (1992) *Symbolic Interactionism and Cultural Studies*. Oxford: Blackwell.

Department of Education and Science (DES) (1968) *Probation of Qualified Teachers: Administrative Memorandum 10/68*. London: DES.

Department of Education and Science (DES) (1972) *Education: A Framework for Expansion*. London: HMSO.

Department of Education and Science (DES) (1976) *Helping New Teachers: The Induction Year*. London: DES.

Department of Education and Science (DES) (1977) *Teacher Induction: Pilot Scheme's Progress*. London: DES.

Department of Education and Science (DES) (1982) *The New Teacher in School*. London: HMSO.

Department of Education and Science (DES) (1983a) *The Treatment and Assessment of Probationary Teachers: Administrative Memorandum 1/83*. London: DES.

Department of Education and Science (DES) (1983b) *Teaching in Schools: The Content of Initial Training*. London: HMSO.

Department of Education and Science (DES) (1984) *Initial Teacher Training: Approval of Courses, Circular 3/84*. London: DES.

Department of Education and Science (DES) (1985a) *Quality in Schools: The Initial Training of Teachers*. London: HMSO.

Department of Education and Science (DES) (1985b) *Quality in Schools: Evaluation and Appraisal*. London: HMSO.

Department of Education and Science (DES) (1985c) *Better Schools*. London: HMSO.

Department of Education and Science (DES) (1987) *Quality in Schools: The Initial Training of Teachers: An HMI Survey*. London: HMSO.

Department of Education and Science (DES) (1988a) *The New Teacher in School*. London: HMSO.

Department of Education and Science (DES) (1988b) *Qualified Teacher Status: Consultation Document*. London: DES.

Department of Education and Science (DES) (1989) *Initial Teacher Training: Approval of Courses, Circular 24/89*. London: DES.

Department of Education and Science (DES) (1990) *The Treatment and Assessment of Probationary Teachers, Administrative Memorandum 1/90*. London: DES.

Department of Education and Science (DES) (1991) *School Teacher Appraisal: Circular 12/91*. London: DES.

Department of Education and Science (DES) (1992a) *Reform of Initial Teacher Training: A Consultation Document*. London: DES.

Department of Education and Science (DES) (1992b) *School Teacher Probation: Circular Letter*. London: DES.

Department of Education and Science (DES) (1992c) *The Induction and Probation of New Teachers 1988–1991*. London: DES.

Department for Education (DfE) (1992a) *Administrative Memorandum 2/92: Induction of Newly Qualified Teachers*. London: DfE.

Department for Education (DfE) (1992b) *Circular 9/92: Initial Teacher Training: Secondary Phase*. London: DfE.

Department for Education (DfE) (1993) *Circular 14/93: Initial Teacher Training: Primary Phase*. London: DfE.

Department for Education and Employment (DfEE) (1996) *Circular Letter 1/96: Teacher Training*. London: DfEE.

Department for Education and Employment (DfEE) (1997) *Excellence in Schools*. London: DfEE.

Department for Education and Employment (DfEE) (1998a) *Consultation on Proposals for the Induction Year*. London: DfEE.

Department for Education and Employment (DfEE) (1998b) *Teachers – Meeting the Challenge of Change*. London: DfEE.

Department for Education and Employment (DfEE) (1998c) *Teaching: High Status, High Standards – the Compostion of the General Teaching Council*. London: DfEE.

Department for Education and Employment (DfEE) (1999a) *Teachers – Consultation on Pay and Performance Management*. London: DfEE.

Department for Education and Employment (DfEE) (1999b) *The Education (Induction Arrangements for School Teachers) Regulations 1999*. London: DfEE.

Department for Education and Employment (DfEE) (1999c) *Circular 5/99: The Induction Period for Newly Qualified Teachers*. London: DfEE.

Dewey, J. (1933) *How We Think – A Restatement of the Relation of Reflective Thinking to the Educative Process*, Boston, MA: Heath.

Downie, R.S. (1990) Professions and professionalism. *Journal of Philosophy of Education*, 24(2): 147–59.

Doyle, W. (1985) Learning to teach: an emerging direction in research on preservice teacher education. *Journal of Teacher Education*, 36(1): 31–2.

Draper, J., Fraser, H., Smith, D. and Taylor, W. (1991) The induction of probationer teachers: implications of an industrial model. *Scottish Educational Review*, 23(1): 23–31.

Draper, J., Fraser, H., Smith, D., and Taylor, W. (1992) *A Study of Probationers*. Edinburgh: Scottish Office Education Department.

Dreyfus, H. and Dreyfus, M. (1986) *Mind Over Machine: The Power of Human Intuition and Expertise in the Era of the Computer*. New York: The Free Press.

Earley, P. (1992) *Beyond Initial Teacher Training: Induction and The Role of the LEA*. Slough: National Foundation for Educational Research.

Earley, P. (1993) Initiation rights? beginning teachers' professional developments and the objectives of induction. *British Journal of In-service Education*, 19(1): 5–11.

Edwards, T. (1998) Reynolds trivializes the complexity of both the means and the ends of effective learning, *Research Intelligence: Newsletter of the British Educational Research Association*, 66: 29–30.

Eisner, E. (1979) *The Educational Imagination*. London: Macmillan.

Eisner, E. (1996) *Cognition and Curriculum Reconsidered*. London: Paul Chapman.

Elbaz, F. (1983) *Teacher Thinking: A Study of Practical Knowledge*. London: Croom Helm.

Elliott, J. (1978) How do teachers learn? in J. Porter (ed.) *The Contribution of Adult Learning Theories to the In-service Education and Training of Teachers*. Paris: OECD.

Elliott, J. (1980) Implications of classroom research for professional development, in E. Hoyle, and J. Megarry (eds) *Professional Development of Teachers, World Year Book of Education*. New York: Kogan Page.

Elliott, J. (1989) Educational theory and the professional learning of teachers: an overview. *Cambridge Journal of Education*, 19(1): 81–101.

Elliott, J. (1991a) *Action Research for Educational Change*. Buckingham: Open University Press.

Elliott, J. (ed.) (1992) *Reconstructing Teacher Education*. London: Falmer Press.

Elliott, J. (1998) *The Curriculum Experiment*. Buckingham: Open University Press.

Ellis, C. and Flaherty, M. (eds) (1992) *Investigating Subjectivity: Research on Lived Experience*. London: Sage.

Eraut, M. (1994) *Developing Professional Knowledge and Competence*. London: Falmer Press.

Erben, M. (ed.) (1998) *Biography and Education*. London: Falmer Press.

Evans, N. (1978) *Beginning Teaching in Professional Partnership*. London: Hodder and Stoughton.

Fineman, S. (ed.) (1993) *Emotion in Organizations*. London: Sage.

Forster, K. (1996) Outcomes-based education: lessons from the United States. *Unicorn*, 22(2): 88–100.

Franks, D.D. and McCarthy, E.D. (eds) (1989) *The Sociology of Emotions*. Greenwich, CT: JAI Press.

Friere, P. (1972) *Pegagogy of the Oppressed*. London: Penguin.

Gadamer, H.G. (1975) *Truth and Method*. London: Sheed and Ward.

Gadamer, H.G. (1976) *Philosophical Hermeneutics*. London: University of California Press.

Gaede, O.F. (1978) Reality shock: a problem among first year teachers, ERIC database. Unpublished manuscript.

General Teaching Council (GTC) (1992) *The Induction of Newly Appointed Teachers*. London: General Teaching Council Initiative for England and Wales.

General Teaching Council For Scotland (GTCS) (1990a) *Assessment of Probationary Teachers: Guidance for Headteachers*. Edinburgh: GTCS.

General Teaching Council for Scotland (GTCS) (1990b) *The Management of Probation*. Edinburgh: GTCS.

General Teaching Council for Scotland (GTCS) (1991) *What About Probation?* Edinburgh: GTCS.

Gethin, R. (1998) *The Foundations of Buddhism*. Oxford: Oxford University Press.

Giddens, A. (1996) *Modernity and Self Identity*. Cambridge: Polity Press.

Gilroy, P. (1989) Professional knowledge and the beginning teacher, in W. Carr (ed.) *Quality in Teaching: Arguments for a Reflective Profession*. London: Falmer Press.

Golby, M. (1989) Teachers and their research, in W. Carr, (ed.) *Quality in Teaching: Arguments for a Reflective Profession*. London: Falmer Press.

Goleman, D. (1996) *Emotional Intelligence*. New York: Bantam Books.

Good, T.L. and Brophy, J.E. (1994) *Looking in Classrooms*, 6th edn. New York: Harper Collins.

Goodlad, J.I. (1984) *A Place Called School*. New York: McGraw Hill.

Goodlad, J.I. (1994) *Educational Renewal: Better Teachers, Better Schools*. San Francisco, CA: Jossey Bass.

Goodson, I. (1983) *The Making of Curriculum*. London: Croom Helm.

Goodson, I. (ed.) (1992) *Studying Teachers' Lives*. London: Routledge.

Goodson, I. (1993) Forms of knowledge in teacher education, in P. Gilroy, and M. Smith (eds) *International Analysis of Teacher Education*. London: Carfax.

Goodson, I. and Walker, R. (eds) (1991) *Biography, Identity and Schooling: Episodes in Educational Research*. London: Falmer Press.

Gore, J.M. (1995) *Emerging Issues in Teacher Education, report from the Innovative Links Project*. Canberra: National Professional Development Project.

Grace, G. (1991) The state and the teachers: problems in teacher supply, retention and morale, in G. Grace and M. Lawn (eds) *Teacher Supply and Teacher Quality*. Clevedon: Multilingual Matters.

Grant, C. and Zeichner, K. (1981) Inservice support for first year teachers: the state of the scene. *Journal of Research and Development in Education*, 14(2): 99–111.

Greenwood, D.M. and Levin, M. (1998) *Introduction to Action Research*. London: Sage.

Griffin, G.A. (1985) Teacher induction: research issues. *Journal of Teacher Education*, 36(1): 42–6.

Grossman, P.L. (1992) *The Making of a Teacher: Teacher Knowledge and Teacher Education*. New York: Teachers College Press.

Habermas, J. (1968) *Knowledge and Human Interests* (English translation 1971). Boston, MA: Beacon Press.

Hall, G.E. (ed.) (1982) Induction: the missing link. *Journal of Teacher Education*, 33(3): 53–5.

Hamachek, D. (1992) *Encounters with the Self*, 4th edn. Fort Worth, TX: Harcourt Brace Jovanovich.

Hamachek, D. (1999) Effective teachers: what they do, how they do it, and the importance of self-knowledge, in R.P. Lipka and T.M. Brinthaupt (eds) *The Role of Self in Teacher Development*. Albany, NY: State University of New York Press.

Hammersley, M. (1977) *Teacher Perspectives: Units 9 and 10, Schooling and Society Course E202 Educational Studies*. Milton Keynes: Open University Press.

Hammersley, M. and Hargreaves, A. (eds) (1983) *Curriculum Practice: Some Sociological Case Studies*. London: Falmer Press.

Hammond, K.R. (1980) *Human Judgement and Decision Making*. New York: Hemisphere.

Hannam, C., Smyth, P. and Stephenson, N. (1976) *The First Year of Teaching*. Harmondsworth: Penguin.

Hannam, C., Smyth, P., and Stephenson, N. (1988) The whole experience: Diane Elliot's first year, in R. Dale, R. Ferguson, and A. Robinson (eds) *Framework For Teaching*. London: Hodder and Stoughton.

Hanson, D. and Herrington, M. (1976) *From College to Classroom: The Probationary Year*. London: Routledge and Kegan Paul.

Hargreaves, A. (1978) The significance of classroom coping strategies. Paper presented at the Westhill Conference, Westhill College, Birmingham, 5–7 January.

Hargreaves, A. (1985) *Two Cultures of Schooling: The Case of Middle Schools*. London: Falmer Press.

Hargreaves, A. (1988) Teaching quality: a sociological analysis. *Journal of Curriculum Studies*, 20(2): 211–31.

Hargreaves, A. (1994) *Changing Teachers, Changing Times: Teachers' Work and Culture in a Postmodern Age*. London: Cassell.

Hargreaves, A. (1996) *Developing Teachers Professionally*. London: Cassell.

Hargreaves, A. (1999) Reinventing professionalism, presentation to the International Conference on Teacher Education, Hong Kong, 22–24 January.

Hargreaves, A. and Fullan, M.G. (eds) (1992) *Understanding Teacher Development*. London: Cassell.

Harland, J. and Kinder, K. (1997) Teachers' continuing professional development: framing a model of outcomes. *British Journal of In-service Education*, 23(1): 71–84.

Harrison, G.N. and Sacks, S.R. (1984) Student to teacher: novel strategies for achieving the transition. *Journal of Education For Teaching*, 10(2): 154–63.

Hayon, L.K. (1990) Reflection and professional knowledge, in C. Day M. Pope and P. Demicolo (eds) *Insights into Teachers' Thinking and Practice*. London: Falmer Press.

Henry, M.A. (1988) Multiple support: a successful model for inducting first-year teachers. *Teacher Educator*, 24(2): 7–12.

Hill, C. (ed.) (1976) *The Levellers and The English Revolution*. Nottingham: Spokesman Press.

Hillgate Group (1989) *Learning to Teach*. London: The Claridge Press.

Hollingsworth, S. (ed.) (1997) *International Action Research: A Casebook for Educational Reform*. London: Falmer Press.

Holly, M.L. and McLoughlan, C. (eds) (1989) *Perspectives on Teacher Professional Development*. London: Falmer Press.

Holly, M.L. and MacLure, M. (1990) Editorial. *Cambridge Journal of Education*, 20(3): 203–6.

Holt, J. (1964) *How Children Fail*. London: Penguin.

Holt, J. (1967) *How Children Learn*. London: Penguin.

Holub, R. (1991) *Jurgen Habermas*. London: Routledge.

Hopkins, D. (1985) *A Teachers' Guide to Classroom Research*. Milton Keynes: Open University Press.

Hoyle, E. (1969) *The Role of the Teacher*. London: Routledge and Kegan Paul.

Hoyle, E. and John, P.D. (1997) *Professional Knowledge and Professional Practice*. London: Cassell.

Huberman, M. (1993) *The Lives of Teachers*. London: Cassell.

Huling-Austin, L. (1990) Teacher induction programmes and internships, in W.R. Houston (ed.) *Handbook of Research on Teacher Education*. New York: Macmillan.

Ingvarson, L. (1998) Professional development as the pursuit of professional standards. Paper presented at the Professional Standards and Status of Teaching Conference, Edith Cowan University, Perth, Western Australia, 24–6 February.

Ingvarson, L. (1999) Assessing teachers for advanced certification and professional recognition: recent research and developments. International Conference on Teacher Education, Hong Kong, 21–4 February.

Inner London Education Authority (ILEA) (1980) *The ILEA Induction Scheme: A Survey of Probationers' Experiences and View of The First Year of the Scheme*. London: Research and Statistics Division, ILEA.

Inner London Education Authority (ILEA) (1985) *ILEA Induction Scheme: Five Years On*. London: Research and Statistics Division, ILEA.

International Study Association on Teachers and Teaching (ISATT) (1998) Invitation to the Fifteenth International Conference in Dublin, Ireland. ISATT.

Jackson, P. (1968) *Life in Classrooms*. Eastbourne: Holt, Rinehart and Winston.

James Report (1972) *Teacher Education and Training*. London: HMSO.

Jarvis, P. (1983) *Professional Education*. London: Croom Helm.

Johnston, J.E. and Ryan, K. (1983) Research on the beginning teacher: implications for teacher education, in K. Howey (ed.) *The Education of Teachers: A Look Ahead*. New York: Longman.

Jones, D. (1990) The genealogy of the urban schoolteacher, in S. Ball (ed.) *Foucault on Education*. London: Routledge.

Jones, L. and Moore, R. (1993) Education, competence and the control of expertise. *British Journal of Sociology of Education*, 14(3): 85–97.

Kagan, D.M. (1992) Professional growth among preservice and beginning teachers. *Review of Educational Research*, 62: 129–69.

Kelly, A.V. (1977) *The Curriculum: Theory and Practice*. London: Harper and Row.

Kerry, T. (1982) *The New Teacher*. London: Macmillan.

Kinchloe, J.L. (1990) *Teachers as Researchers: Qualitative Inquiry as a Path to Empowerment*. London: Falmer Press.

Kinder, K. and Earley, P. (1993) Key issues emerging from an NFER study of NQTs: models of induction support. Universities Council for The Education of Teachers annual conference, Oxford, 12–14 November.

King, M. (1994) Locking ourselves in: national standards for the teaching profession. *Teaching and Teacher Education*, 10(1): 95–108.

Knowles, G. and Cole, A.L. (1994) *Through Preservice Teachers' Eyes: Exploring Field Experiences Through Narrative and Inquiry*. New York: Merrill.

Kohut, H. (1971) The psychoanalytic treatment of narcissistic personality disorders: outline of a systematic approach. *Psychoanalytic Study of the Child*, 23: 86–113.

Kolb, D. (1984) *Experiential Learning: Experience as the Source of Learning and Development*. New York: Prentice Hall.

Kyriacou, C. (1993) Research on the development of expertise in classroom teaching during initial training and the first year of teaching. *Educational Review*, 45(1): 79–87.

Lacey, C. (1977) *The Socialization of Teachers*. London: Methuen.

Lamber, J. (1992) Induction of newly trained and appointed teachers, in General Teaching Council, *The Induction of Newly Appointed Teachers*. London: General Teaching Council Initiative for England and Wales.

Lawlor, S. (1990) *Teachers Mistaught*. London: Claridge Press.

Lawn, M. (1991) Social constructions of quality in teaching, in G. Grace and M. Lawn (eds) *Teacher Supply and Teacher Quality*. Clevedon: Multilingual Matters.

Leat, B. (1991) Competence, teaching, thinking, feeling. *Oxford Review of Education*, 19(4): 499–510.

Leinhart, G. (1992) What research on learning tells us about teaching. *Educational Leadership*, 49: 20–5.

Lipka, R.P. and Brinthaupt, T.M. (eds) (1992) *Self-Perspectives: Across the Lifespan*. Albany, NY: State University of New York Press.

Lipka, R.P. and Brinthaupt, T.M. (1999a) Balancing the personal and professional development of teachers, in R.P. Lipka and T.M. Brinthaupt (eds) *The Role of Self in Teacher Development*. Albany, NY: State University of New York Press.

Lipka, R.P. and Brinthaupt, T.M. (eds) (1999b) *The Role of Self in Teacher Development*. Albany, NY: State University of New York Press.

Lo, L. (1999) Teacher development and teacher education in Hong Kong and the Chinese mainland. International Conference on Teacher Education and Teacher Development in a Changing World, Chinese University of Hong Kong, 15–17 January.

Lortie, D. (1975) *Schoolteacher*. Chicago, IL: University of Chicago Press.

McBride, R. (ed.) (1996) *Teacher Education Policy*. London: Falmer Press.

McCabe, C. (1978) *Induction in Northumberland: An evaluation*. Mimeo, School of Education, University of Newcastle upon Tyne.

McCulloch, M. (1994) Improving initial teacher training? Policy in action 1984–94, in M. McCulloch and B. Fidler (eds) *Improving Initial Teacher Training?: New Roles for Teachers, Schools, and Higher Education*. Harlow: Longman.

McClure, S. (1988) *Education Re-formed*. London: Hodder and Stoughton.

McFadden, M.G. (1996) Second chance education: accessing opportunity or recycling disadvantage. Unpublished PhD thesis, Charles Stuart University, NSW, Australia.

McIntyre, D. (1980) The contribution of research to quality in teacher education, in E. Hoyle and J. Megarry (eds) *Professional Development of Teachers, World Year Book of Education*. New York: Kogan Page.

McIntyre, D. (1988) Designing a teacher education curriculum from research and theory on teacher knowledge, in J. Calderhead (ed.) *Teachers' Professional Learning*. London: Falmer Press.

McKernan, J. (1991) *Curriculum Action Research*. London: Kogan Page.

McLean, S.V. (1999) Becoming a teacher: the person in the process, in R.P. Lipka and T.M. Brinthaupt (eds) *The Role of Self in Teacher Development*. Albany, NY: State University of New York Press.

MacLure, M. (1993) Arguing for your self: identity as an organizing principle in teachers' jobs and lives. *British Educational Research Journal*, 19(4): 311–21.

McNair Report (1944) *Teachers and Youth Leaders*. London: HMSO.

McNiff, J., Lomax, P. and Whitehead, J. (1996) *You and Your Action Research Project*. London: Routledge.

Mahony, P. (1998) The rise and fall of standards in teaching. Paper presented to the Professional Standards and Status of Teaching Conference, Edith Cowan University, Perth, Western Australia, 24–6 February.

Marrin, M. (1999) Standards of practice for the teaching profession. International Conference on Teacher Education and Teacher Development in a Changing World, Chinese University of Hong Kong, 15–17 January.

Maslow, A. (1954) *Motivation and Personality*. New York: Harper and Row.

Maslow, A. (1973) What is a Taoistic teacher? in L.J. Rubin (ed.) *Facts and Feelings in the Classroom*. London: Ward Lock.

Mead, G.H. (1934) *Mind, Self and Society*. Chicago, IL: University of Chicago Press.

Miller, A.I. (1997) Three wise men, two worlds, and one idea. *The Independent on Sunday*, 23 February: 40–41.

Moses, P. (1996) Meeting the needs of newly qualified teachers. Mimeo, University of Central England in Birmingham.

Moyles, J., Suschitsky, W. and Chapman, L. (1998) *Teaching Fledglings to Fly? Mentoring and Support Systems in Primary Schools*. London: Association of Teachers and Lecturers.

Munro, R. (1989) A case study of school-based innovation in secondary teacher training. Unpublished PhD thesis, University of Auckland, New Zealand.

National Board for Professional Teaching Standards (NBPTS) (1989) *Towards High and Rigorous Standards for the Teaching Profession*. Detroit: NBPTS.

National Centre for Research on Teacher Learning (1993) *An Annotated Bibliography: Findings on Learning to Teach*. College of Education: Michigan State University.

National Commission on Education (1993) *Learning to Succeed: Report of the Paul Hamlyn Foundation*. London: Heinemann.

National Project on the Quality of Teaching and Learning (1996) *National Competency Framework for Beginning Teachers*. Leichardt, NSW, Australia: Australian Teachers Council.

National Union of Teachers (NUT) (1969) *The Future of Teacher Education*. London: NUT.

National Union of Teachers (NUT) (1971) *The Reform of Teacher Education: A Policy Statement*. London: NUT.

National Union of Teachers (NUT) (1992) *Induction Arrangements for Newly Qualified Teachers*, Circular 275/92. London: NUT.

Neville, B. (1992) *Educating Psyche: Emotion, Imagination and the Unconscious in Learning*. North Blackburn: Collins Dove.

New South Wales Department of Education and Training (NSWDET) (1997) *Beginning Teacher Induction Programme*. Sydney: NSWDET.

New South Wales Department of Education and Training (NSWDET) (1998a) *Towards Identifying Professional Teaching Standards for New South Wales Schools*. Sydney: NSWDET.

New South Wales Department of Education and Training (NSWDET) (1998b) *Towards Greater Professionalism: Teacher Educators, Teaching and the Curriculum*. Sydney: NSWDET.

New South Wales Ministerial Advisory Committee on Teacher Education and Quality Teaching (1994) *Desirable Attributes of Beginning Teachers*. Sydney: NSW Ministry of Education and Youth Affairs.

New Zealand Ministry of Education (1997) *Quality Teachers for Quality Learning: A Review of Teacher Education*. Wellington: New Zealand Government.

New Zealand Ministry of Education (1998) *Interim Professional Standards: Primary School Deputy/Assistant Principals, Primary School Teachers*. Wellington: New Zealand Government.

Nias, J. (1987) Teaching and the self. *Cambridge Journal of Education*, 15(1): 17–24.

Nias, J. (1989) *Primary Teachers Talking*. London: Routledge.

Nias, J. (1996) Thinking about feeling: the emotions in teaching. *Cambridge Journal of Education*, 26(3): 292–306.

Nixon, J. (1981) *A Teacher's Guide to Action Research: Evaluation, Enquiry and Development in the Classroom*. London: Grant McIntyre.

Office for Standards in Education (Ofsted) (1993) *The New Teacher in School: A Survey by HM Inspectors in England and Wales (1992)*. London: HMSO.

Organization for Economic Cooperation and Development (OECD) Centre for Educational Research and Innovation (1994) *Quality in Teaching*. Paris: OECD.

O'Rourke, B. (1983) Lion tamers and baby sitters. *English Education*, 15(1): 17–24.

Parliamentary Select Committee on Education and Employment (1997) *The Professional Status, Recruitment and Training of Teachers*. London: DfEE.

Perkins, R. (1989) *The Rise of Professional Society: England since 1880*. London: Routledge.

Peters, R.S. (1972) The education of the emotions, in R.F. Deardon, P. Hirst and R.S. Peters (eds) *Education and the Development of Reason*. London: Routledge and Kegan Paul.

Phillips, D.C. (1987) *Philosophy, Science, and Social Enquiry*. London: Pergamon.

Plowden Report (1967) *Children and Their Primary Schools: Report of the Central Advisory Council for England*. London: HMSO.

Pollard, A. (1985) *The Social World of the Primary School*. London: Holt, Rinehart and Winston.

Pollard, A. and Tann, S. (1987) *Reflective Teaching in the Primary School*. London: Cassell.

Popper, K. (1959) *The Logic of Scientific Discovery*. New York: Basic Books.

Popper, K. (1962) *The Open Society and Its Enemies*. Princeton, NJ: Princeton University Press.

Pring, R. (1971) Bloom's taxonomy: a philosophical critique. *Cambridge Journal of Education*, 2: 83–91.

Pring, R. (1998) Debate: are universities turning out effective teachers? in J. Carvel, Woodhead under fire, *Guardian Education*, 15 December: 16–17.

Rasenen, M. (1997) *Building Bridges*. Helsinki: University of Art and Design.

Reynolds, D. (1992) What is competent beginning teaching? a review of the literature. *Review of Educational Research*, 62: 1–35.

Reynolds, D. (1998) Teacher effectiveness: better teachers, better schools. *Research Intelligence*, 66: 26–9.

Rich, R.W. (1933) *The Training of Teachers in England and Wales During the Nineteenth Century*. Cambridge: Cambridge University Press.

Rogers, C. (1983) *Freedom to Learn for the 80s*. Columbus, OH: Charles Merrill.

Ruddock, J. and Hopkins, D. (1985) *Research as a Basis for Teaching*. London: Heinemann.

Russell, T. (1988) From pre-service teacher education to first year of teaching: a study of theory and practice, in J. Calderhead (ed.) *Teachers' Professional Learning*. London: Falmer Press.

Rust, F.O. (1994) The first year of teaching: it's not what they expected. *Teaching and Teacher Education*, 10(2): 205–18.

Ryan, K. (ed.) (1970) *Don't Smile Until Christmas*. Chicago, IL: University of Chicago Press.

Ryan, K., Newman, K.K., Mager, G., Applegate, J.H., Lasley, T., Flora, U.R. and Johnston, J. (1980) *Biting the Apple: Accounts of First Year Teachers*. New York: Longman.

Salmon, P. (1988) *Psychology for Teachers: An Alternative Approach*. London: Hutchinson.

Salter, B. and Tapper, T. (1981) *Education, Politics and the State*. London: Grant McIntyre.

Sanger, J. and Tickle, L. (1987) Art for pupils' sakes: deprogramming student teachers, in L. Tickle (ed.) *The Arts in Education: Some Research Studies*. London: Croom Helm.

Schön, D. (1971) *Beyond the Stable State*. San Francisco, CA: Jossey-Bass.

Schön, D. (1983) *The Reflective Practitioner*. New York: Basic Books.

Schön, D. (1987) *Educating the Reflective Practitioner*. London: Jossey-Bass.

Schubert, W.H. and Ayers, W.C. (eds) (1992) *Teacher Lore: Learning from Our Own Experience*. New York: Longman.

Scott, D. and Usher, R. (eds) (1996) *Understanding Educational Research.* London: Routledge.

Sergiovanni, T. (1992) *Moral Leadership: Getting to the Heart of School Improvement.* San Francisco, CA: Jossey-Bass.

Sergiovanni, T. (1998) Leadership as pedagogy, capital development and school effectiveness. *Leadership in Education,* 1(1): 37–46.

Shulman, L.S. (1986a) Those who understand: knowledge growth in teaching. *Educational Researcher,* 15(4): 4–14.

Shulman, L.S. (1986b) Knowledge and teaching: foundations of the new reform, Mimeo, Stanford University, CA.

Sidgwick, S. (1996) Government policy and the induction of new teachers, in R. McBride (ed.) *Teacher Education Policy.* London: Falmer Press.

Simco, N. (1995) Professional profiling and development in the induction year. *British Journal of In-Service Education,* 21(3): 261–72.

Simco, N., Burdon, M., Cooper, H., Huggins, M., Prendiville, F. and Sixsmith, C. (1996) Key issues in the professional development of newly qualified teachers. Paper presented to the British Educational Research Association Conference, Lancaster, September.

Simon, B., Galton, M. and Croll, P. (1981) *Inside the Primary Classroom.* London: Routledge and Kegan Paul.

Simons, H. (1987) *Getting to Know Schools in a Democracy.* London: Falmer Press.

Smyth, J. and Shacklock, G. (1998) *Re-Making Teaching.* London: Routledge.

Snow, S. (1988) Concerns of the first year teacher, in P. Holborn, M. Wideen, and I. Andrews (eds) *Becoming a Teacher.* Toronto: Kagan and Wood.

Sockett, H. (1986) Teacher professionalism and curriculum research. Mimeo, University of East Anglia.

Sockett, H. (1987) Has Shulman got the strategy right? knowledge and teaching: foundations of the new reform: a critique. Mimeo, University of East Anglia School of Education.

Sockett, H. (1993) *The Moral Base for Teacher Professionalism.* New York: Teachers College Press.

Somekh, B. (1995) The contribution of action research to development in social endeavours: a position paper on action research methodology. *British Educational Research Journal,* 21(3): 339–55.

Sparkes, A.C. (1994) Self, silence and invisibility as a beginning teacher: a life history of lesbian experience. *British Journal of Sociology of Education,* 15(1): 93–118.

Stenhouse, L. (1975) *An Introduction to Curriculum Research and Development.* London: Heinemann.

Stenhouse, L. (1979) Research as a basis for teaching. Inaugural lecture, University of East Anglia, February.

Swanson, G.E. (1989) On the motives and motivation of selves, in D.D. Franks and E.D. McCarthy (eds) *The Sociology of Emotions.* Greenwich, CT: JAI Press.

Taba, H. (1962) *Curriculum Development: Theory and Practice.* New York: Harcourt, Brace and World.

Tabachnick, B.R. and Zeichner, K. (eds) (1991) *Issues and Practices in Inquiry-Oriented Teacher Education.* London: Falmer Press.

Taylor, J.K. and Dale, I.R. (1971) *A Survey of Teachers in Their First Year of Service.* University of Bristol School of Education.

Taylor, J.K. and Dale, I.R. (1973) The first year of teaching, in D. Lomax (ed.) *The Education of Teachers in Britain.* London: John Wiley.

Taylor, W. (1978) *Research and Reform in Teacher Education*. Slough: Council of Europe and National Foundation for Educational Research.

Taylor, W. (1991) Ideology, accountability and improvement in teacher education, in G. Grace and M. Lawn (eds) *Teacher Supply and Teacher Quality*. Clevedon; Multilingual Matters.

Teacher Training Agency (TTA) (1996) *Improving the Quality of Teaching*. London: TTA.

Teacher Training Agency (TTA) (1997) *Career Entry Profile for Newly Qualified Teachers: Standards for The Award of Qualified Teacher Status*. London: TTA.

Teacher Training Agency (TTA) (1998a) *Induction for Newly Qualified Teachers*. London: TTA.

Teacher Training Agency (TTA) (1998b) *Teaching as a Research Based Profession: The Teacher Research Grant Scheme*. London: TTA.

Teacher Training Agency (TTA) (1998c) *National Standards for Qualified Teacher Status*. London: TTA.

Teacher Training Agency (TTA) (1999a) *Career Entry Profile for Newly Qualified Teachers 1999*. London: TTA.

Teacher Training Agency (TTA) (1999b) *Teacher Induction Guidelines*. London: TTA.

Thompson, M. (1993) The weakest link: ATL's Proposals. *British Journal of In-service Education*, 19(1): 12–15.

Tickle, L. (1983) One spell of ten minutes or five spells of two . . . ? Teacher–pupil encounters in art and design education, in M. Hammersley and A. Hargreaves (eds) *Curriculum Practice: Some Sociological Case Studies*. London: Falmer Press.

Tickle, L. (1987a) *Learning Teaching, Teaching Teaching: A Study of Partnership in Teacher Education*. London: Falmer Press.

Tickle, L. (ed.) (1987b) *The Arts in Education: Some Research Studies*. London: Croom Helm.

Tickle, L. (1989a) New teachers and the development of professionalism, in M.L. Holly, and C.S. McLoughlin (eds) *Perspectives on Teacher Professional Development*. London: Falmer Press.

Tickle, L. (1989b) On probation: preparation for professionalism. *Cambridge Journal of Education*, 19(3): 277–85.

Tickle, L. (1991) New teachers and the emotions of learning teaching. *Cambridge Journal of Education*, 21(3): 319–29.

Tickle, L. (1992a) The assessment of professional skills in classroom teaching. *Cambridge Journal of Education*, 20(1): 91–103.

Tickle, L. (1992b) Capital T Teaching, in J. Elliott (ed.) *Reconstructing Teacher Education*. London: Falmer Press.

Tickle, L. (1992c) The first year of teaching as a learning experience, in D. Bridges and T. Kerry (eds) *Providing In-Service Teacher Education*. London: Routledge.

Tickle, L. (1992d) The wish of Odysseus: new teachers' receptiveness to mentoring, in D. McIntyre, H. Hagger and M. Wilkin (eds) *Issues in Mentoring*. London: Kogan Page.

Tickle, L. (1994) *The Induction of New Teachers: Reflective Professional Practice*. London: Cassell.

Tickle, L. (1995) Testing for quality in educational action research: a terrifying taxonomy? *International Journal of Educational Action Research*, 3(2): 235–8.

Tickle, L. (ed.) (1996a) *Understanding Art in Primary Schools: Cases from Teachers' Research*. London: Routledge.

Tickle, L. (1996b) Reflective practice: embrace or illusion, in R. McBride (ed.) *Teacher Education Policy*. London: Falmer Press.

Tickle, L. (1998) Teaching and teacher education: realities and dreams, England 1998. *Trends: The Yearbook of CONTACT*, 7: 9–28. Haifa, The Association of Teacher Educators for TEFL in Israel.

Tickle, L. (1999) Teacher self-appraisal and appraisal of self, in R.P. Lipka and T.M. Brinthaupt (eds) *The Role of Self in Teacher Development*. Albany, NY: State University of New York Press.

Tsui, A. (1999) Keynote address to the International Conference on New Professionalism in Teaching, Hong Kong, 15–17 January.

Tyler, R.W. (1949) *Basic Principles of Curriculum and Instruction*. Chicago, IL: University of Chicago Press.

Usher, R. (1998) The story of the self: education, experience and autobiography, in M. Erben (ed.) *Biography and Education*. London: Falmer Press.

Van Manen, M. (1977) Linking ways of knowing with ways of being practical. *Curriculum Inquiry*, 6(3): 205–28.

Veenman, S. (1984) Perceived problems of beginning teachers. *Review of Educational Research*, 54: 143–78.

Vonk, J.H.C. (1996) A knowledge base for mentors of beginning teachers: results of a Dutch experience, in R. McBride (ed.) *Teacher Education Policy*. London: Falmer Press.

Waller, W. (1932) *The Sociology of Teaching*. New York: Russell and Russell.

Warnke, G. (1987) *Gadamer: Hermeneutics, Tradition and Reason*. Cambridge: Polity Press.

Waterhouse, A. (1993) Mirror, mirror on the wall, what is the fairest scheme of all? – reflections on the induction needs of newly qualified teachers. *British Journal of In-service Education*, 19(1): 16–22.

Webb, R. (ed.) (1990b) *Practitioner Research in the Primary School*. London: Falmer Press.

Wilkin, M. (1996) *Initial Teacher Training: The Dialogue of Ideology and Culture*. London: Falmer Press.

Willis, P. (1977) *Learning to Labour: How Working Class Kids Get Working Class Jobs*. London: Routledge and Kegan Paul.

Wilson, S.M., Shulman, L.S. and Richert, A.E. (1987) 150 different ways of knowing: representations of knowledge in teaching, in J. Calderhead (ed.) *Exploring Teachers' Thinking*. London: Cassell.

Winter, R. (1987) *Action Research and the Nature of Social Enquiry*. Aldershot: Gower Publishing Co.

Winter, R. (1989) *Learning From Experience: Principles and Practice in Action Research*. London: Falmer Press.

Woodhead, C. (1998) Debate: are universities turning out effective teachers? in J. Carvel, Woodhead under fire, *Guardian Education*, 15 December: 16–17.

Wragg, E.C. (1982) *A Review of Research in Teacher Education*. Slough: NFER.

Wragg, E.C. (ed.) (1984) *Classroom Teaching Skills*. London: Croom Helm.

Young, M.F.D. (ed.) (1971) *Knowledge and Control*. London: Collier Macmillan.

Zehm, S.J. (1999) Deciding to teach: implications of a self-development perspective, in R.P. Lipka and T.M. Brinthaupt (eds) *The Role of Self in Teacher Development*. Albany, NY: State University of New York Press.

Zehm, S.J. and Kottler, J.A. (1993) *On Being a Teacher: The Human Dimension*. Newbury Park, CA: Corwin Press.

Zeichner, K.M. and Tabachnick, B.R. (1985) The development of teacher perspectives: social strategies and institutional control in the socialization of beginning teachers. *Journal of Education for Teaching*, 11(1): 1–25.

Zeichner, K.M. and Tabachnick, B.R. (1991) Reflections on reflective teaching, in B.R. Tabachnick and K.M. Zeichner (eds) *Issues and Practices in Inquiry-Oriented Teacher Education*. London: Falmer Press.

Zeichner, K.M., Tabachnick, B.R. and Densmore, K. (1987) Individual, institutional and cultural influences on the development of teachers' craft knowledge, in J. Calderhead (ed.) *Exploring Teachers' Thinking*. London: Cassell.

Zimpher, N.L. and Howey, K.R. (1987) Adapting supervisory practices to different orientations of teaching competence. *Journal of Curriculum and Supervision*, 2(2): 101–27.

Zimpher, N.L. and Howey, K.R. (1990) Scholarly inquiry into teacher education in the United States, in R.P. Tisher and M.F. Wideen (eds) *Research in Teacher Education: International Perspectives*. London: Falmer Press.

Index

UNDERSTANDING MENTORING
REFLECTIVE STRATEGIES FOR SCHOOL-BASED TEACHER PREPARATION

Peter Tomlinson

The current move to school-based mentoring offers the possibility of considerable improvement over traditional arrangements for initial teacher preparation. But this opportunity will only be realized if old assumptions about theory and practice are modified and new practices based on a better understanding of ways in which effective teaching may be acquired. Starting from the assumption that practising teachers already possess many resources relevant to mentoring, *Understanding Mentoring* offers practical strategies and programmes for mentoring in the context of recent work on intelligent skill development, professional thinking and learning, counselling and helping strategies, and the nature and assessment of teaching competence. It should therefore be a useful resource for teachers taking on a mentoring role, and for those engaged in training and academic courses on school-based teacher education.

> ... Peter Tomlinson's book is particularly welcome because while it deals with the 'how to' issues it does not duck the wider and deeper contextual and pedagogical issues that are implicit in the mentoring role ... this book will push its way to the front. Anyone wanting to think seriously about mentoring ought to read it.
>
> *Times Educational Supplement*

> This is a very useful book for teacher educators and teacher mentors, particularly for those who are following a formal course in mentoring as a module for a higher degree. It would also be a valuable resource in a staffroom library in a school committed to school-based teacher training.
>
> *Educational Studies*

> The book will be of great value for any mentor and mentor trainer embarking on the new route to Initial Teacher Training.
>
> *British Educational Research Journal*

> ... I found that the book has much to offer nurse teachers and nurse practitioners ... It should prove an excellent guide and reference source in helping nurse teachers provide effective supervision.
>
> *Nursing Times*

Contents
School-based teacher education: opportunity and challenge – Learning teaching: a framework for understanding mentoring – The reflective coach: functions and forms of mentoring – The effective facilitator: interpersonal aspects of mentoring – Classroom strategies and their pupil management potential – Teaching competence profiling for student assessment and development – Mentoring in practice: coaching tactics – Mentoring in practice: student programmes and organizational issues – Appendix – References – Name index – Subject index/glossary.

256pp   0 335 19306 4   (Paperback)

THE INTUITIVE PRACTITIONER
ON THE VALUE OF NOT ALWAYS KNOWING WHAT ONE IS DOING

Terry Atkinson and Guy Claxton (eds)

Much of the time, experienced professionals in both education and other fields cannot explain what they are doing, or tell you what they know; and students cannot articulate their learning. Yet professional development and practice are often discussed as if conscious understanding and deliberation are of the essence. *The Intuitive Practitioner* tackles this apparent paradox head on, and explores the dynamic relationship between reason and intuition in the context of professional practice. Focusing mainly on the professional world of the teacher, but with illustrative discussions of medical and business practice, the contributors delicately unpick the vexed and neglected nature of intuition, and demonstrate the vital role it plays in the development of professional judgement and expertise.

Contents
Part 1: Perspective on intuition in professional learning and practice – Introduction – Intuition and the crisis in teacher professionalism – The anatomy of intuition – Trusting your own judgement – Part 2: Intuition and initial teacher education – Learning to teach: intuitive skills and reasoned objectivity – Awareness and intuition: how student teachers read their own lessons – The role of intuition in mentoring and supporting beginning teachers – Elaborated intuition and task-based English language teacher education – Part 3: Intuition and continuing professional development – The development of professional intuition – The formal and the intuitive in science and medicine – Complex decision making in the classroom: the teacher as an intuitive practitioner – Developing intuition through management education – Part 4: Intuition and assessment – Assessment and intuition – Measurement, judgement, criteria and expertise: intuition in assessment from three different subject perspectives – Intuition and the development of academic literacy – Part 5: The intuition practitioner: a critical overview – Index.

c.192pp   0 335 20362 0   (Paperback)   0 335 20363 9   (Hardback)